# Leading with Integrity

*A lesson in leading with integrity, from migrating geese*

Have you ever watched geese migrating in formation? As each goose flaps its wings it creates an 'uplift' for the bird following. By flying in a V formation, the flock increases its flying range by over 70% in comparison to a bird flying solo. When the lead bird gets tired, it rotates back in the group and another goose flies in the point position.

Geese also honk in flight to motivate the group to keep flying at speed. If a goose cannot keep up, two geese drop out of the formation and flank them, providing encouragement and support.

Leadership based on strong, clearly communicated values builds an environment of trust and respect, creating a unique sense of shared purpose in following a common path to the successful achievement of the group's goal.

# Leading with Integrity: A Practical Guide to Business Ethics

Ros O'Shea

Published in 2016 by
Chartered Accountants Ireland
Chartered Accountants House
47–49 Pearse Street
Dublin 2
www.charteredaccountants.ie

ISBN 978-1-910374-65-8

Typeset by Datapage
Printed by Turner's Printing Company, Longford, Ireland

PEFC Certified

This product is from sustainably managed forests and controlled sources

PEFC

PEFC/17-33-007     www.pefc.org

*To my 'true north', Barry, our three wonderful girls, Kate, Lily and Jennifer, and to my mum and dad, to whom I owe everything*

# Contents

# Introduction

*"Where shall I begin, please your Majesty?" he asked.*
*"Begin at the beginning," the King said gravely, "and go on till you come*
*to the end: then stop."*
**Lewis Carroll, Alice's Adventures in Wonderland**

There is nothing unethical about making money – let's make that clear from the start. While we may not agree that "greed is good" (as argued charismatically by Gordon Gekko in *Wall Street*), the desire for wealth is a necessary catalyst for any successful enterprise. Ambition and the pursuit of profit motivate the efficient production of goods and services. This gives greater choice to consumers and opportunities to prospective employees; it yields returns to providers of capital and taxes to government. Overall, it promotes innovation, economic growth and a generally higher standard of living. In short, a little 'greed' helps make the world go around.

This book does not therefore prescribe eschewing the capitalist model in favour of an alternative, perhaps loftier, economic paradigm. It does not promote the pursuit of purely philanthropic endeavours at the expense of rewarding and lucrative career choices. Nor will it require you to throw away your laptop, swap your pinstripes for hemp cloth or begin knitting your own yoghurt!

Instead, it is based on the premise that ethics and profit can be compatible. They do not have to be mutually exclusive. Indeed, the integrity and reputation of an organisation *cannot* be compromised if shareholder value is to be sustained over the long term. Recent global financial crises highlight with devastating effect what happens when industry and its leadership, under pressure to 'make the numbers', unmoor from an ethical base. Stakeholders: employees, customers, suppliers, shareholders and debt providers, the community and government, are now demanding that business leaders restore integrity to its proper place at the heart of enterprises. *How* you do things is now as, or more, important as *what* you do. Strategy and culture must be aligned.

Achieving this alignment and equilibrium between values and purpose is a principal function of leadership. When a leader is appointed, he or she is given the organisation's most precious resource – its reputation – and charged with the ultimate responsibility of its safekeeping. Their job is to ensure that the core values of the organisation, upon which its reputation is staked, solidly underpin its long-term strategic objectives and deliver sustainable shareholder value. Furthermore, they must ensure that all employees fully understand the high standards expected of them and that they follow these values and guiding principles in their daily work. But more than that, it is the primary role of the leader to model these expected behaviours and serve as a beacon for integrity and ethical conduct for all of the organisation's stakeholders, both internal and external.

Typically, by the time someone has achieved a position of business leadership, they will have encountered many challenges, made multiple decisions, chalked up a few mistakes, hopefully achieved many more successes and built up a wealth of executive experience. En route they will have also undertaken numerous training courses, completed many personal development plans and received plenty of instruction and advice along the way. However, the main focus of such programmes has tended to be on the 'hard' tasks or mechanics of leadership: how to determine the appropriate strategy for the enterprise, set organisational goals, assess business opportunities, motivate and manage a team, and so on. Business ethics, if taught at all, is often treated as an arcane subject, with related instruction sometimes couched in theoretical, or even theological, terms; or worse, delivered as part of a 'tick-the-box' compliance exercise; in any case, too far removed from the day-to-day business of leading an organisation to have any compelling interest or lasting impact. As a result, leaders, in one of their most important duties, if not the most important duty – that of steering the enterprise in the right direction – leaders may find themselves largely on their own, bereft of practical guidelines, without any useful frameworks and perhaps even lacking the requisite basic tools and skills.

This book aims to address that gap. No abstract theories here – this is a *practical* guide. It does not assume a 'holier than thou' perspective but takes a pragmatic approach to navigating ethical roadblocks and successfully leading the enterprise to safe harbour. It will equip you with the understanding and tools to articulate an authentic governance style, to set the tone for your organisation and, with the right building-blocks in place, to embed a culture of integrity.

The book is therefore aimed at leaders in any sector and at all levels. While the focus may appear to be primarily on the corporate world, experience has shown that the central themes of this text also have resonance in the public and non-profit sectors. It is also equally applicable to those more advanced on their leadership journey and those just starting out or aspiring to leadership positions. Likewise, non-executive directors who, together with their executive management colleagues, are collectively responsible for setting the tone at the top for an organisation should find this book a useful read. Similarly, the text should be germane to those working in any supporting governance functions, including compliance, company secretarial, legal, internal audit, human resources, risk management, etc. and also may prove a helpful reference for regulators and business school lecturers alike. Finally, this book is for anyone with a general interest in either ethics or leadership and particularly where the two transect.

The text is divided into three principal parts, which can be summarised as follows:

**Part I**, "A Leader of Integrity", introduces the topic of ethical leadership and prescribes the groundwork for the practice of leading with integrity. Like the other parts of the book, Part I comprises three chapters.

**Chapter 1**, "The Case for Ethical Leadership", examines the legislative, stakeholder and governance context for an ethical approach. It also explores the more noble motivation of most intelligent, hard-working executives to pursue interesting and rewarding careers while preserving their own reputation and that of their organisations, and building a legacy of decency and respect. The chapter also outlines the principal benefits accruing to organisations with a strongly beating ethical heart.

Given the case for an ethical approach and the positives associated with 'doing the right thing', **Chapter 2** addresses why and how leaders can lose their way. With the help of some high-profile examples, we examine some common hazards that can divert anyone from the path of ethical business conduct. The chapter concludes with some leadership 'Dos and Don'ts' and proposes two principal antidotes to corporate malfeasance: a structural solution at the level of the organisation; and a behavioural shift on the part of its leadership.

**Chapter 3**, "The Groundwork for Leading with Integrity: It Starts with You", elaborates on these behavioural leadership pre-requisites in detail, prescribing the personal groundwork required to become a strong, ethical leader. After a brief review of the various schools of ethical thought, a short journey of self-awareness follows, including an articulation of core values, assessments of Moral DNA™ and emotional intelligence, and a discussion on how to develop authenticity. The chapter concludes with some reflections on ethical leadership strengths, style and desired legacy.

**Part II** of the book, "Building the Ethical Organisation", complements the ethical behavioural competencies identified in **Part I** by advocating the organisational building blocks necessary to provide the structural support for a culture of integrity to flourish. Again, this part has three chapters, with each chapter dealing with the respective components of an ethical framework and strategy.

**Chapter 4**, "Creating an Ethics and Compliance Framework", outlines the characteristics that define organisational culture and tackles the critical risk assessment and planning phases of implementing an agenda of cultural change. This includes putting in place the right team to drive implementation, drafting practical codes of conduct and policies to translate values and guiding principles into useful, instructive documents and designing effective training modules to convert 'pieces of paper' into the right set of behaviours.

Chapter 4 also emphasises the importance of continuous communication and the need for effective channels through which employees can report any issues that concern them. The alignment of strategic processes with core values is also examined, including recruitment, reward and disciplinary procedures as well as monitoring, evaluation and reporting tools.

**Chapter 5**, "Leading with Integrity, Everywhere", provides an international perspective for organisations with a more global footprint and addresses the challenges of doing the right thing *everywhere*, specifically in the areas of bribery, labour practices and human rights. We will examine how to mitigate associated risks by reviewing merger and acquisition due diligence procedures, considering ethical sourcing processes and highlighting the need for an aligned corporate social responsibility (CSR) agenda.

In **Chapter 6**, "Ethical Corporate Governance", the role of the board is examined as another pillar supporting an organisation's ethical framework. Having identified the expectations of the board and its various responsibilities in the areas of ethics, we will look at how best it can deliver on these requirements to set the 'tone from the top'. We will explore how boardroom dynamics impact on the board's effectiveness and review the critical role of non-executive directors (NEDs) and, in particular, the chairman. The chapter concludes with a summary list of the hallmarks of an effective boardroom.

**Part III**, "Mastering the Art of Leading with Integrity", brings it all together and discusses ethical leadership in practice, or 'how to make a difference that makes the difference'.

**Chapter 7**, "The Leading with Integrity Toolbox", leverages the groundwork in leadership behaviour from **Part I** with the structural foundations laid in **Part II** and provides the leader with a set of tools to merge these soft skills with the supporting frameworks. Topics covered include how to model and inspire appropriate behaviours, communicate clear expectations, identify and maximise 'moments that matter', create an open, honest culture and, by example, how to truly lead with integrity. We will also discuss the ethical leader abroad and how leadership styles may need to be adapted in order to reap the benefits of an international career, while retaining personal integrity. The chapter concludes with a crises survival guide, i.e. what to do when it all goes wrong, including how to go about rebuilding trust.

**Chapter 8**, "Ethical Dilemmas and the 'ETHIC' Framework", provides a robust ethical framework to employ when faced with a moral dilemma and includes a series of hypothetical scenarios from a variety of sectors and from different leadership perspectives. This provides you with an opportunity to exercise your newly calibrated 'moral compass' and hopefully put into practice some of the key lessons that you have learned over the course of the preceding chapters.

And finally, **Chapter 9** can be read as a masterclass in ethical leadership. I have been fortunate enough to interview some of Ireland's most inspiring chief executive officers across a range of sectors, as well as a highly successful international non-executive director. This chapter collates the notes from these insightful, entertaining and very candid discussions. There is a lot to be learned from these interviews, so the chapter, and the book, concludes with a helpful summary list of 'Ethical Leadership: Essential Dos and Don'ts'.

I very much hope you enjoy reading this book and that you find it useful. Please share any thoughts or comments with me at www.leadingwithintegrity.ie

# Acknowledgements

I would like to express my sincere gratitude to:

- the business leaders who were kind enough to be interviewed for this book, and whose candid, inspirational insights elevate the text, providing a masterclass in 'tone from the top';
- my publisher and editor, Michael Diviney, for his challenging yet warm, collegiate approach and the publishing team at Chartered Accountants Ireland for their professionalism and patience;
- Dr Jonathan Westrup, Nicola McCracken and Darren Byrne, who read and commented on an early draft making the final book eminently more readable; and
- my family, for their kind forbearance and endless cups of tea.

*Thank you*

# I

# A Leader of Integrity

1. The Case for Ethical Leadership

2. Obstacles to Ethical Leadership:
   *Why and How Leaders Lose their Way*

3. The Groundwork for Leading with Integrity:
   *It Starts with You*

# 1

# The Case for Ethical Leadership

*Your beliefs become your thoughts,*
*Your thoughts become your words,*
*Your words become your actions,*
*Your actions become your habits,*
*Your habits become your values,*
*Your values become your destiny.*

**Mahatma Gandhi**

- Introduction
- Reputation and Transparency
- Legislation and Enforcement
- Whistleblowing
- Stakeholder Demands
- Corporate Governance
- Personal Integrity and Legacy
- The Business Case for Ethical Leadership?

## Introduction

Why bother with ethical leadership? In this chapter we will address this question, and others like it, as well as some common misconceptions, including, for example:

- "Why all the fuss now with business ethics?"
- "Isn't it a lot of 'motherhood-and-apple-pie' mumbo jumbo?"
- "Won't this obsession with ethics and proper conduct all pass once we all start making serious money again?"
- "Does ethical leadership really matter or even make a difference?"
- "You can't learn this stuff – you're either a good guy or you're not."
- "Business is business – I'm not paid to be 'nice' as well."
- "Anyway, we never have a problem with any of our employees, so we're OK, right?"

We will start by examining 'the fuss', i.e. the pressing need for a much greater focus on the manner in which organisations conduct their business and the ethical standards of their leadership. The reasons are manifold but clear, and **Figure 1.1** below sets them out in overview.

FIGURE **1.1: T**HE **C**ASE FOR **E**THICAL **L**EADERSHIP

The primary reason for the renewed focus on ethical leadership is due to the collapse in society's trust in business leaders to do the right thing following a decade or more of case after case of corporate malfeasance.

Companies and their leadership have been called upon to earn that trust back by putting ethics at the heart of everything they do and safeguarding reputation alongside the pursuit of profit.

In 2015 the Irish Medical Council published the results of a survey it commissioned into the public's attitude to doctors' professionalism.[1] Wanting to find out if doctors were still the most trusted profession, the survey asked: "Can you please tell if you trust each of the professions listed to tell the truth or not?" The analysis, shown in **Figure 1.2** below, says it all.

FIGURE 1.2: IRISH PUBLIC'S TRUST IN BUSINESS LEADERS
AMONG OTHER PROFESSIONS

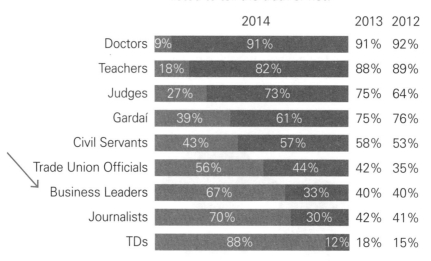

*Can you please tell if you trust each of the professions listed to tell the truth or not?*

|  | 2014 | | 2013 | 2012 |
|---|---|---|---|---|
| Doctors | 9% | 91% | 91% | 92% |
| Teachers | 18% | 82% | 88% | 89% |
| Judges | 27% | 73% | 75% | 64% |
| Gardaí | 39% | 61% | 75% | 76% |
| Civil Servants | 43% | 57% | 58% | 53% |
| Trade Union Officials | 56% | 44% | 42% | 35% |
| Business Leaders | 67% | 33% | 40% | 40% |
| Journalists | 70% | 30% | 42% | 41% |
| TDs | 88% | 12% | 18% | 15% |

■ Would not tell the truth ■ Would tell the truth

This is not just a local phenomenon. The 2016 Edelman Trust Barometer (an annual global study of public trust in business, government and NGOs) found that while trust had recovered somewhat since the financial crash, almost half of the general population still mistrust business and only 27% believe that leaders exhibit highly ethical behaviour (see 2016 Edelman Trust Barometer, www.edelman.com).

To paraphrase Professor Jeffrey Pfeffer of Stanford University, in his book *Leadership BS: Fixing Workplaces and Careers One Truth at a Time*,[2] bosses are not modest, leaders are bound to lie, authenticity is overrated and the gap between aspiration and reality is one reason that trust in leaders and leadership gurus has evaporated. This loss of faith in business leaders has been accompanied by an unprecedented increase in legislation requiring companies to establish protocols to help prevent such lapses. In tandem, there has been a dramatic step-up in enforcement, with record levels of prosecutions in western economies as well as in the developing world, which traditionally has had a benign and even acquiescent attitude to corruption. Furthermore, whistle-blowers are gaining newfound respect and protection, while powerful stakeholders – investment groups, rating agencies, NGOs and community groups – are also demanding a much bigger say in how things are done. This is all against the backdrop of corporate governance and compliance obligations that continue to develop apace.

In this chapter we will review all of these factors in detail, but will also acknowledge the desire of most intelligent, hard-working executives to pursue an interesting, rewarding career while building a legacy of decency and respect. Besides, strong values are good for business, so we will also outline the business case for business ethics. Finally, we will deconstruct some common misconceptions about the need for business ethics and conclude the chapter with a summary of the principal benefits accruing to organisations with a solid ethical backbone.

## Reputation and Transparency

> *"It takes 20 years to build a reputation and 5 minutes to lose it."*
> Warren Buffett

If Warren Buffett is right, then consider the impact on the reputation of the companies appearing on the following news front pages and home pages:

> *"Siemens to pay $1.34 Billion in Fines"*
> The Wall Street Journal

> *"Vast Mexico Bribery Case Hushed Up by Wal-Mart After Top-Level Struggle"*
> The New York Times

> *"EU imposes record 1.47 billion euro cartel fine on Phillips, 5 others"*
> Reuters

> *"GlaxoSmithKline fined $3bn after bribing doctors to increase drugs sales"*
> The Guardian

7

> *"Power giant Alstom to pay record $772 million to settle bribery charges"*
> The Washington Post

> *"British banks pay £12bn in penalties"*
> Financial Times

> *"FBI on Fifa arrests: 'This is the World Cup of fraud and today we are issuing Fifa a red card'"*
> BBC

> *"Dirty secrets*
> *A scandal in the motor industry"*
> The Economist

These are just a few examples of large corporations hitting the headlines for all the wrong reasons. If these seem a little remote, then consider the following snapshot of just a few months' headlines from the *Irish Times*, clearly closer to home.

> THE IRISH TIMES
> Three Anglo officials jailed for hiding
> accounts linked to Seán FitzPatrick
> Beacon Hospital employee resigns
> following procurement claims
> Four men charged following report on
> alleged Garda corruption in Donegal
> Price-fix inquiry on flooring contracts at
> Google HQ and other landmark buildings
> Banking Inquiry: Ex-regulator urges
> action over white-collar crime
> HSE investigates Lloyds pharmacy
> prescription payments
> IFA hopes governance review 'rebuilds
> trust' of farmers

Research by academics at Stanford University in the US has suggested that an accounting scandal typically takes a reputation-related toll equal to about 27% of a company's pre-scandal share price and it can

8

take several years for a full recovery.[3] For serious transgressions, fines are often in the billions rather than millions. These are usually only the headline numbers, which can often be doubled to arrive at a more accurate estimate of the total cost of defending a case, accounting for lawyers' fees, internal compliance clean-up costs, etc. This is all before putting a price on all the management time and energy invested in justifying negative past behaviour, rather than developing positive future strategies and ignoring the heavy toll that such exposures in the media have on employee morale and perception.

The first argument in the case for ethical leadership is therefore a pragmatic one – it pays to be nice.

This is especially so when you consider how quickly even the whiff of scandal can be tweeted, posted, shared, tagged, 'liked', texted or blogged in the new world of lightning-fast digital media. In his book, *Stranger than We Can Imagine,* John Higgs explores how the development of computer technology in the late 20th Century and, more latterly, the proliferation of horizontal social networks between individuals have deconstructed the more traditional vertical hierarchies and created a much more transparent society.[4] In particular, the idea of the corporate body as a distinct, private entity is no longer and the secrecy of its protected and orderly management structures and chains of command likewise have been opened up to public scrutiny. With the informality of Twitter, transparency of LinkedIn and ubiquity of Facebook, there is literally nowhere to hide. As David Tapscott irreverently observes in *The Naked Corporation*: "If you have to be naked, you had better be buff!"[5]

As a consequence, many companies are embracing values and ethics as a distinct element of their unique selling proposition or 'USP'. Consider Kenco and their recent "Coffee vs Gangs" marketing campaign; Innocent Drinks, who donate 10% of their profits to charity; and Rabobank's transparent approach to marketing banking products in unusually clear, jargon-free language. These explicit efforts to link principles with profits build reputational capital in the minds of consumers and stakeholders.

## Legislation and Enforcement

While social media can gleefully expose all manner of transgressions in milliseconds, one of the principal reasons for the increasing number of companies finding themselves in the spotlight is, as noted above, that regulators the world over have been getting serious about anti-corruption legislation and, critically, about enforcement. **Figure 1.3** on the following page shows how anti-corruption legislation has evolved globally over the last 40 years.

9

FIGURE 1.3: THE EVOLUTION OF ANTI-CORRUPTION LEGISLATION

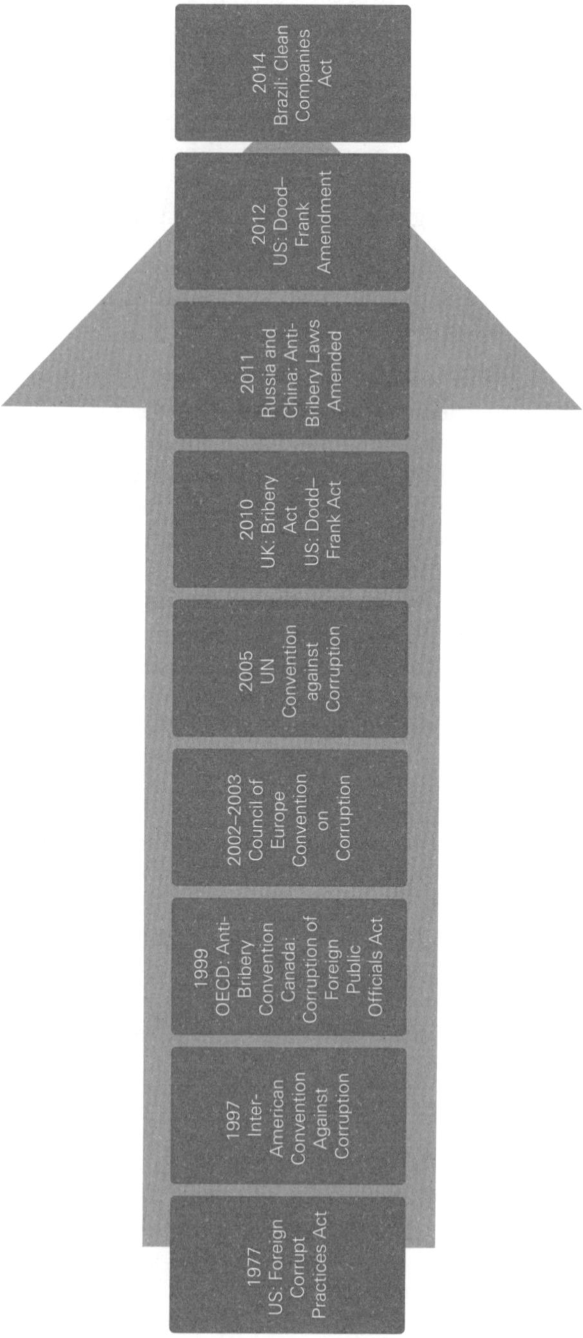

1977
US: Foreign
Corrupt
Practices Act

1997
Inter-
American
Convention
Against
Corruption

1999
OECD: Anti-
Bribery
Convention
Canada:
Corruption of
Foreign
Public
Officials Act

2002–2003
Council of
Europe
Convention
on
Corruption

2005
UN
Convention
against
Corruption

2010
UK: Bribery
Act
US: Dodd–
Frank Act

2011
Russia and
China: Anti-
Bribery Laws
Amended

2012
US: Dodd–
Frank
Amendment

2014
Brazil: Clean
Companies
Act

All was more or less quiet on the anti-corruption front prior to and then after the Foreign Corrupt Practices Act (FCPA) in the US in 1977, but from the early 2000s, and especially towards the end of the decade, a plethora of new laws and regulations were introduced worldwide. This included the UK, with its Bribery Act 2010, and also Russia, China and Brazil, historically not known for their diligence on corruption matters, but now also showing a keen appetite for reform through prosecution.

Indeed, since Xi Jinping's accession as President of the People's Republic of China in 2013, the country has witnessed another 'Red Revolution', this time against graft. He has already delivered on his electoral promise to crack down on "tigers and flies" (high-level officials and civil servants) involved in corruption by the "Four Winds of Decadence" (formalism, bureaucracy, hedonism and extravagance), with the campaign having already resulted in the imprisonment and/ or prosecution of over 100 high-ranking officials and some 100,000 other politicians and lower ranking officials indicted for corruption. The country's anti-corruption agency has even introduced a mobile 'App' with which the Chinese public can report cases of bribery directly from their smart phone, complete with photos and video footage.[6] Meanwhile, century-old traditions, such as the giving of a basket of 'mooncakes' for the Chinese mid-autumn holiday, which were often lined with a red envelope full of cash, are no more.[7]

In India, another country historically beleaguered by chronic levels of corruption, a groundswell of grassroots insurgency, borne of frustration with the status quo, is having an impact on levels of low-grade, everyday bribery. For example, the 'I Paid A Bribe.com' movement is gaining momentum, whereby victims of corruption are invited to anonymously share online their experiences of bribery, what it was for, where it took place and how much money was involved.[8] While the ultimate aim is to shame government departments into tackling corruption, a key benefit in the meantime is that it has evolved into a corruption prevention database, where people can get information and advice in different languages on how to avoid paying bribes.

In countries with more established anti-corruption frameworks and institutions, there has also been a clear increase in activity levels. For example, the US FCPA, referred to earlier, which "prohibits representatives of US corporations from offering or providing significant payments to foreign political parties, candidates or government officials for the purpose of inducing those recipients to misuse their positions of power to assist the company to obtain, maintain or retain business" was for many years referred to as "the sleeping giant". Someone clearly gave this sleeping giant a poke with a very big stick in recent years, with the growing trend in overseas enforcement contributing to the eye-watering total of over $7 billion in fines collected by the US authorities to date.[9] The same is true for other forms of white-collar crime. Authorities on both sides of the Atlantic have stepped up the enforcement of competition law, insider dealing rules, money-laundering legislation and fraud offences, with penalties for infringements at record highs.

Another recent and distinct trend is the prosecution of company directors and employees who are involved in corrupt acts, as well as the companies themselves, possibly reflecting a view that sometimes corporations 'build in' the cost of potential fines in a given jurisdiction as a levy for doing business there. For example, in September 2015, in a significant shift in the enforcement of the FCPA, the US Deputy Attorney General issued a memo ('the Yates memo') to all US attorneys announcing a policy to prioritise the prosecution of employees involved in corporate crime – not just their companies – and to pressure corporations to turn over evidence against culpable executives.[10]

Closer to home, the UK's Serious Fraud Office secured its first conviction under the 2010 Bribery Act in December 2014 in connection with a Ponzi fraud scheme, with combined sentences of 28 years handed down to the three men involved.[11] The extraterritorial reach of this draconian piece of legislation, both in terms of its scope and sanctions, should not be underestimated, especially given that the UK is Ireland's largest trading partner.

Soon, it will be the turn of Ireland's lawmakers. At the time of writing, the Criminal Justice (Corruption) Bill is waiting in the wings. If and when enacted, it will bring Ireland's anti-corruption legislation squarely in line with international best practice and set a new bar for countering bribery in both the public and private sectors. As well as requiring companies to "take all reasonable steps" and "exercise all due diligence" to prevent corrupt practices, it will shine a light on directors and managers who "wilfully neglect" the commission of an offence, imposing criminal liability with potential sanctions, including unlimited fines and up to 10 years in prison.

Nothing focuses the mind of a board or an executive management team quite like the possibility of personal fines, imprisonment, or both. This is especially true for companies with international operations, where the prospect of prolonged imprisonment in a foreign jail means these matters are becoming a staple board agenda item.

## Whistleblowing

Another trend contributing in no small way to the heightened focus on ethics and probity is the coming of age of the 'whistleblower'. Historically, it would seem that whistleblowing was perceived as a distasteful activity, more or less equated with corporate tale-telling and generally frowned upon. Whistleblowers were treated with suspicion at best or, at worst, vilified and the subjects of reprisal. Some well-known examples include the following:

- William Mark Felt, better known as 'Deep Throat', was the FBI agent who leaked information about the Watergate scandal to Woodward and Bernstein of the *Washington Post*. He denied his role in highlighting the matter for more than 30 years, until in 2005, at the age of 91, he revealed to *Vanity Fair* magazine: "I'm the guy they used to call Deep Throat."
- More recently, Michael Woodford, former CEO of Olympus, exposed corruption on a massive scale in the uppermost echelons of the Japanese corporation. He vividly recounts the story in his book *Exposure*, including episodes in which he genuinely feared for his life.[12]
- Sherron Watkins, former VP of Corporate Development at Enron, who exposed the financial irregularities at the company in 2001 and, though subject to criticism from some corners for not speaking up sooner, was nominated as a 'Person of the Year' by *Time* magazine for her "exceptional guts and sense".[13]
- Closer to home we have the example, in 2014, of Martin Callinan, who reported wrongdoing by senior Gardaí. He subsequently told the Dáil Public Accounts Committee that, in hindsight, he would not do it again as the disclosures had "destroyed him, his career and his family".[14]

Although we have more to do to move away from a culture of reprisal, the importance of having safe channels for people to report unethical conduct is becoming more generally accepted and, critically, those who 'blow the whistle', or more correctly, 'report in good faith', are being formally safeguarded and protected. In Ireland, the Protected Disclosures Act 2014 protects workers in both the public and private sectors against reprisal in circumstances where they disclose information relating to any wrongdoing that comes to their attention in the workplace. It also aims to make good faith reporting a key element of corporate risk management and to foster a culture that supports it.

While this is a step forward, the US has taken whistleblowing to a whole new level and, in some circles at least, it seems to be considered a national sport. This new zeal for speaking up owes its origins to a unique feature of the 2010 Dodd-Frank Wall Street Reform and Consumer Protection Act, which entitles whistleblowers who bring violations of securities law, commodities law or the FCPA to the attention of the relevant authorities up to 30% of any government recovery in excess of $1 million. This has motivated a number of individuals to come forward, with some interesting results, including Bradley Birkenfeld, the ex-UBS investment banker who helped the US authorities unleash an international crackdown on tax evasion. While one branch of the US Government awarded him "$104 million in what is believed to be the largest-ever whistleblower payout to an individual", another branch gave him a 40-month jail sentence for his part in the conspiracy.[15]

While this approach undoubtedly has 'teeth', there is a balance to be struck in these matters to avoid employees being perversely incentivised to sidestep internal reporting systems or to simply 'drum up' or exaggerate potentially spurious cases. Ireland is still ahead of some other countries, where the culture is such that reservations still linger with regard to any form of 'snitching', especially in jurisdictions with any history of informers in totalitarian or autocratic regimes. For example, the occupation of France during the Second World War has translated into an ongoing sensitivity towards any form of denunciation. Over time these misgivings should make way for understanding and support for the principle of protected disclosure, although there is no doubt that 'speaking up' will always take significant courage, wherever one happens to be in the world.

## Stakeholder Demands

The growing trend of 'voicing your values' is not confined to the whistleblower. Companies today must accommodate a whole range of, sometimes competing, stakeholders, all increasingly vocal about their requirements for the business to be run in a manner aligned with their needs and expectations. These are depicted in **Figure 1.4** below.

FIGURE **1.4**: STAKEHOLDER DEMANDS

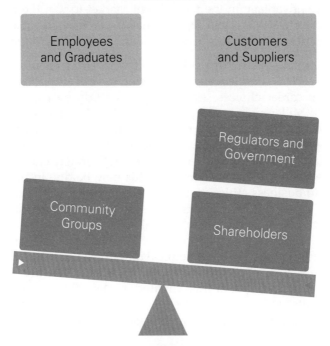

Let's consider each of these stakeholders and their respective demands.

## Employees and Graduates

People want to be proud of where they work. I recall being at a corporate governance conference during the banking crisis and in conversation asking a fellow attendee where he worked, to which he replied vaguely, "in town". I subsequently established that he was a senior executive with one of the major UK banks, but could not bring himself to admit that he worked in the financial sector, let alone at one of the banks that was in the news for the wrong reasons at the time.

The fact is that values bind employees to their companies at a fundamental and emotional level. This can often have a more powerful impact and influence on them than the size of the pay cheque on offer. This is overwhelmingly supported by hard evidence. A 2014 survey by *Corporate Responsibility Magazine* in the US examined the impact a company's reputation has on willingness to accept a job offer. Not surprisingly, it found that prospective candidates are very reluctant to join organisations that have a bad reputation and, that among those who may be willing to accept a job offer, a significant pay raise is required. Conversely, they can be tempted to move to a company with a good reputation for a significantly lower pay lift.[16]

Employers of good standing should, therefore, use their reputation as a competitive advantage in the recruitment market to win the best talent, whereas those with damaged reputational capital may find that they will need to dig deeper to attract the calibre of employees they require.

The 'Millennial Generation' is especially exercised about employers' social and ethical conscience and not afraid to vote with their feet when it comes to career choices. According to a study by Deloitte, almost nine in 10 'Millennials' surveyed believe that "the success of a business should be measured in terms of more than just its financial performance", while 80% believe their values are shared by the organisation they work for, a strong indicator that they deliberately choose employers whose values reflect their own.[17] This may be due in part to their exposure to business ethics as a mainstream subject in the curricula of the more forward-thinking business schools, sensitising students to their ethical responsibilities at a critical juncture in their development. It is also possibly their reaction to the inheritance of an almost toxic business culture with lacklustre ethical initiatives and a general paucity of values, and their commitment to doing things differently. The 'MBA Oath' is a good example of this. Created in May 2009 by a group of 20 MBA students at Harvard University, it was an attempt to articulate the values for which they felt their degree should stand:

## THE MBA OATH[18]

"As a business leader I recognize my role in society.
- My purpose is to lead people and manage resources to create value that no single individual can create alone.
- My decisions affect the well-being of individuals inside and outside my enterprise, today and tomorrow.

Therefore, I promise that:
- I will manage my enterprise with loyalty and care, and will not advance my personal interests at the expense of my enterprise or society.
- I will understand and uphold, in letter and spirit, the laws and contracts governing my conduct and that of my enterprise.
- I will refrain from corruption, unfair competition, or business practices harmful to society.
- I will protect the human rights and dignity of all people affected by my enterprise, and I will oppose discrimination and exploitation.
- I will protect the right of future generations to advance their standard of living and enjoy a healthy planet.

> • I will report the performance and risks of my enterprise accurately and honestly.
> • I will invest in developing myself and others, helping the management profession continue to advance and create sustainable and inclusive prosperity.
>
> In exercising my professional duties according to these principles, I recognize that my behavior must set an example of integrity, eliciting trust and esteem from those I serve. I will remain accountable to my peers and to society for my actions and for upholding these standards.
>
> **This oath I make freely, and upon my honor."**

The MBA Oath has since been adopted by over 300 institutions around the world and signed by over 6,000 students and graduates.

In some countries, the emphasis on ethics is starting even earlier in the education cycle. For example, in Ireland, as part of planned changes to the national primary school curriculum, a consultation paper has proposed that teaching time be set aside for new ethics classes, which will focus on making choices in a way that considers the effect on others and covers the importance of dignity and human rights and responsibilities in society.[19] This should ensure that future generations of employees will have a greater appreciation for positive values and set an even higher bar for their prospective employers.

## Customers, Suppliers and Community Groups

Naturally, employees and prospective employees have a strong basis for influencing a company's ethical orientation from the inside. The same is also true of external third-party relationships, i.e. with customers, suppliers and community groups alike. Such is their perceived importance that there is a growing appreciation of the commercial case for a company adopting an explicitly ethical profile. For example, with its 'Plan A', Marks & Spencer enjoys a reputational edge over its competitors, derived from its pledge and programmes to "help protect the planet – by sourcing responsibly, reducing waste and helping communities".[20] While price and quality are always likely to reign supreme, consumers are increasingly exercised about where and how products are sourced, providing impetus for initiatives such as the 'Fair Trade' movement.

Furthermore, international companies, keen to be part of a visibly ethical supply chain, are subscribing to the principles of the UN's Global Compact and/or writing their own ethical procurement codes to ensure their suppliers comply with minimum corporate social responsibility requirements.

17

We will discuss sustainable and responsible leadership in more detail in **Chapter 4**. Suffice to say, customers and suppliers are getting their point across – loudly.

## *Shareholders*

Activist shareholders and portfolio managers can also be distinctly powerful voices for a more ethical approach, specifically incorporating the sustainability agenda. In the past, the 'green' investor might have been dismissed as an oddity. However, 'sociably responsible invest-ment' (SRI), which embraces values-based investment, shareholder advocacy and community investment, was estimated to be worth some $21.4 trillion in 2014, or 30.2% of the professionally managed assets in the regions reviewed.[21] This suggests that investors are investing with their heads *and* their hearts. It is consistent with the growing popularity and reliance on indices of environmental, social and governance perfor-mance, including the two most well-known, the FTSE4Good Index and the DowJones Sustainability Index.

A dramatic example of how heavily investment funds can rely on these ethical standards was the decision in 2015 by the Government Pension Fund of Norway to sell its stakes in four Asian companies (including Daewoo) over environmental concerns.[22] The Fund, one of the world's largest, owning on average c. 1.3% of every stock traded globally, has now excluded more than 50 companies from its investment pool, including Boeing, British American Tobacco, Rio Tinto and Walmart. Conversely, companies with a strong record of ethical performance can use this to their advantage and credibly compete for investment dollars, or indeed Krone.

## *Regulators and Government*

Perhaps an organisation's most powerful and demanding stakeholder in an ethical governance context is government and its regulatory authori-ties. We have seen how active legislatures have been across the globe in introducing stronger safeguards, their energies matched by the zeal of enforcement agencies. Regulators too have been setting the bar high for ethical standards, in some sectors presiding over and contributing to the development of compliance programmes for their constituent mem-bers. Consider, for example, the Central Bank of Ireland, which is the ultimate arbiter of ethical conduct for the Irish financial sector, author of the governance code for the institutions it governs without whose endorsement these businesses have no licence to operate. Indeed, since the introduction of the 'Fitness and Probity' regime in 2011, the prior approval of the Central Bank is required before an individual can even be appointed to certain senior positions in the financial sector.

While higher standards and more rigorous enforcement of regulation are to be welcomed, it is also important to note that eventually, in a forest of regulation, one cannot see the 'wood for the trees'. For example, in the years immediately preceding the financial crises of 2007 and 2008, the Financial Services Authority in the UK increased its rulebook by almost a third. While regulation is clearly a driver for business ethics, it will only take us so far.

Fiona Muldoon, formerly of the Central Bank, captured a similar sentiment when addressing the 2013 MacGill Summer School:

> "I believe ... the financial sector will need to undergo a fundamental cultural shift whereby it will view regulation and the law as the outside parameter of acceptable behaviour rather than an obstacle to be overcome, something that can be worked around or whose boundaries are there to be tested."[23]

## Corporate Governance

While 'hard law', and its enforcement, has undoubtedly been a driver of governance standards, 'soft law', including primarily corporate governance codes, has also contributed to moving the dial. If you sit on a board, particularly of a PLC, you will no doubt be taken aback by just how much of the agenda is taken up with 'conformance' matters or ensuring the company complies with the myriad of applicable rules and regulations, often at the expense of strategy or performance issues. Corporate scandals from the late 1980s to early 2000s, including Maxwell, Polly Peck, Enron, WorldCom and Parmalat, led to a proliferation of corporate governance reports and codes for listed companies, with almost annual revisions imposing even more requirements. Patricia Barker summarises developments in corporate governance thus:

> "... started when Sir Adrian Cadbury recommended pieces of elastoplast to plug the wounds left by Maxwell. The Cadbury Code focussed attention on the board, separating the role of the Chief Executive Officer (CEO) and Chairman. Greenbury augmented the Code by responding to the 'fat cats' debate around directors' excessive remuneration. Hampel targeted pension fund trustees. Turnbull responded to the poor internal controls highlighted by the Nick Leeson scandal. Higgs responded to Enron by making recommendations about the proportion of non-executive directors, and Smith dealt with the role of the Audit Committee."[24]

19

These and subsequent developments have been helpful in highlighting the need for accountability around proper systems and structures of corporate oversight. However, corporate governance compliance, as with regulation, can only achieve so much. We will take a 'warts and all' look at corporate governance in **Chapter 6** and argue that the integrity of a board, the ethical standards of its members and the dynamics of how they work together will ultimately determine the efficacy or otherwise of their collective governance.

## Personal Integrity and Legacy

The last chapter in this book is a series of interviews with some inspirational business leaders. Though from different sectors, there are a number of striking similarities in what they have to say, particularly with regard to personal legacy. Without exception, each wants to be remembered for *how* they achieved success rather than their accomplishments *per se*. Of course, these confident, ambitious leaders want to grow the business, delight the customer, develop talent, but more so they want their legacy firmly underpinned by an acknowledgement of their qualities of decency, integrity, respect and fairness.

For every reason why we *should* do the right things, there is another reason why we would *want* to, and most business leaders *want* to do the right thing. This is not referring to extreme corporate philanthropists, such as Warren Buffett, Bill and Melinda Gates and, more recently, Mark Zuckerberg. While their actions are laudable, charitable largesse on that scale is beyond most of us. However, the desire to make a difference does drive many of us to approach our work in a certain way, to aim for a legacy of decency and respect, and to strive to make the right choices en route. James Dimon, CEO and Chairman of JPMorgan Chase captured this perfectly in his address to the MBA class of 2009 at his alma mater, the Harvard Business School:

> "There is a book in each of you. It's already being written. If I spoke to your teachers, your friends, your professionals, your parents, I would know whether you are trusted, how hard you work, whether you are ethical ... That book is already growing. Write it the way you want it to be written ... When you are caught in situations that are uncomfortable, you can always make the right decision ... At a lot of companies, you'll hear 'Don't worry about it, everyone does it that way'. No, they don't. It's your responsibility whether you accept to do something or not and it will be in that book written by you."[25]

## The Business Case for Ethical Leadership?

In considering the business case for an ethical approach to leadership and the possibility of a compliance cost–benefit analysis, it is useful to recall the old maxim: "not everything that can be counted counts, and not everything that counts can be counted" (William Bruce Cameron).

There have been many studies carried out on whether enterprises that behave responsibly do in fact make better returns for their shareholders than their more reprobate corporate cousins. Psychologist Fred Kiel, in researching for his book *Return on Character*,[26] found that values-driven CEOs can create up to five times more wealth for all their stakeholders than those that are 'self-focussed'.

However, to a large extent, this kind of research is superfluous. In any truly meaningful way, how can you assign a percentage to integrity, or report a decency statistic or accredit truth and fairness indices?

Instead, it is much more productive to focus on the *value* of an ethical programme rather than its cost. To think about the assets protected rather than the line item in the 'P&L'. Sharon Allen, Chair of Deloitte LLP, makes a compelling case for an alternative 'ROE' – not the traditional financial metric, return on equity, but a more enlightened measure of business performance: 'Return on Ethic'.[27] Her view is that stakeholders invest their trust long before they invest their dollars; that relationships account for far more than goodwill on a balance sheet; and that ethical behaviour can appreciate over time into lasting value. Similarly, Stephen Covey (of the 'Seven Habits' fame) refers to a "low trust tax" that doubles the cost of doing business and triples the time it takes to get things done, concluding that: "Nothing is as profitable as the economics of trust."[28]

## *Debunking Some Myths about the Ethical Approach to Business*

Convinced yet? Not quite? Despite the strong case for an ethical approach to business, misconceptions can still abound. Some of these are addressed below.

> • "Isn't ethics all a bit 'motherhood-and-apple-pie' mumbo-jumbo?"
>
> Far from being a 'touchy-feely' topic, business ethics is a management discipline requiring a systematic approach with the right tools and frameworks, best espoused by intelligent, authentic leaders, trained and equipped with the requisite skill set.

21

- "Isn't this just CSR, only with a fancier title?"

Corporate social responsibility (CSR) is an important aspect of a values-based approach to business, but ethical leadership embraces the concept of 'doing the right thing' in a much more holistic way. It includes the responsibility to society at large, but also extends to employees, customers, suppliers and all other stakeholders to whom the company owes a duty to conduct its business ethically.

---

- "This obsession with ethics is just a phase – it will pass once the economy picks up again."

Ethics has been in the news for at least 2,500 years, since the time of Plato and Aristotle. Legislation and governance requirements, increased transparency through digital media and societal demands mean it is not going away any time soon.

---

- "Business is business. We can't be nice also. It's impractical and costs too much."

Business ethics and profit need not be mutually exclusive but can co-exist compatibly. In the long term, return on equity and 'return on ethics' should follow the same trajectory. Compliance is not what it costs but what it is worth. In other words, you cannot afford *not* to be nice.

---

- "Anyway, you can't learn this stuff; you're either a good guy or a bad guy."

Ethics can be a complex and grey area and even employees of impeccable character need to be guided on how to navigate tricky dilemmas in the workplace. According to Trevino and Brown, "the ethical decision-making process involves multiple stages and contextual pressures. Individuals may not have the cognitive sophistication to make the right decision."[29] Character should be calibrated to be cultivated.

---

- "Fine, but then let's get consultants or 'philosophers' in to take care of this."

22

You can outsource lots of things, but your value system is not one of them. Management must lead the ethics programme and pay special attention to related communication and training initiatives. An external, rushed-through e-learning programme is not the solution. (Besides, the aim is not to convert employees or save their souls, but to communicate a clear message on expected standards of expected behaviour.)

• "Our employees all play by the rules, so we are OK."

I'm sure those nice people at Volkswagen head office believed the same.

## The Benefits of an Ethical Approach

In presenting the case for ethical leadership, we have discussed the reasons for a renewed focus on values in business, from a reputational, legislative, governance, stakeholder, personal legacy and business-case perspective. Hopefully, we have also exposed some common misconceptions relating to the profit vs. integrity debate. Let's finish with a summary of the 10 principal benefits accruing to the leaders and their companies who truly embrace a values-based approach.

**10 BENEFITS OF AN ETHICAL APPROACH TO LEADERSHIP**

1. Provides a behavioural roadmap for the organisation
2. Builds trust with customers and suppliers
3. Establishes credibility with stakeholders
4. Attracts (the right kind of) employees
5. Opens up new avenues of investment
6. Best defence against sanctions
7. Builds reputation capital for the tough times
8. It is good for business
9. Underwrites a valuable leadership legacy
10. It's the right thing to do.

## References to Chapter 1

[1] Irish Medical Council, *Survey of Public Attitudes to Doctors' Professionalism 2015*, available at www.medicalcouncil.ie. (Research carried out by Amárach Research. Sample of 1,000 adults aged 16+ aligned to the population in terms of gender, age, social class and region.)

[2] Pfeffer, Jeffrey, *Leadership BS: Fixing Workplaces and Careers One Truth at a Time* (HarperBusiness, 2015).

[3] Chakravarthy, Jivas, deHaan, Ed and Rajgopal, Shivaram, "Reputation Repair after a Serious Restatement" (2014) *The Accounting Review*, Vol. 89, No. 4, 1329–1363.

[4] Higgs, John, *Stranger than We Can Imagine: Making Sense of the Twentieth Century* (Signal, 2015).

[5] Tapscott, David, *The Naked Corporation: How the Age of Transparency will Revolutionize Business* (Free Press, 2012).

[6] Wan, Adrian, "China upgrades anti-graft app so whistleblowers can send images of officials caught red-handed", *South China Morning Post*, 19 June 2015. Available at http://www.scmp.com/tech/apps-gaming/article/1823789/china-upgrades-anti-graft-app-so-whistleblowers-can-send-images (accessed January 2016).

[7] Dexter, Roberts, "Mooncake Economy Is Hit in China's Corruption Crackdown", *Bloomberg Business*, 5 September 2014. Available at http://www.bloomberg.com/bw/articles/2014-09-05/chinas-corruption-crackdown-hits-mooncakes (accessed January 2016).

[8] Campion, Mukti Jain, "Bribery in India: A website for whistleblowers", BBC.com, 6 June 2011. Available at http://www.bbc.com/news/world-south-asia-13616123 (accessed January 2016). See also www.ipaidabribe.com.

[9] See http://fcpamap.com

[10] See Greaves, Catherine, "DOJ Stresses Individual Accountability in New 'Yates Memo'", (2015–16) *ABA Journal*, Vol. 12, No. 2. Available at http://www.americanbar.org/publications/aba_health_esource/2015-2016/october/yatesmemo.html (accessed February 2016).

[11] See Cohn, Carolyn and Ridley, Kirstin, "SFO nails its first convictions under new bribery laws", *Reuters*, 8 December 2014. Available at http://uk.reuters.com/article/uk-courts-britain-bribery-idUKKBN-0JM22M20141208 (accessed February 2016).

[12] Woodford, Michael, *Exposure: Inside the Olympus Scandal: How I Went from CEO to Whistleblower* (Portfolio, 2012).

[13] Lacayo, Richard and Ripley, Amanda, "Persons of The Year 2002: The Whistle-blowers", *Time*, 30 December 2002. Available at http://content.time.com/time/magazine/article/0,9171,1003998,00.html.

[14] Press Association, "Garda Whistleblower Destroyed", *Irish Independent*, 23 January 2014. Available at http://www.independent.ie/irish-news/garda-whistleblower-destroyed-29944120.html (accessed January 2016).

[15] Saunders, Laura and Sidel, Robin, "Whistleblower Gets $104 Million: Now a Felon, Former Banker Told U.S. About Tax-Evasion Tactics by UBS and Its Wealthy Clients", *Wall Street Journal*, 11 September 2012.

Available at http://www.wsj.com/articles/SB100008723963904440175
04577645412614237708 (accessed January 2016).

[16] *The Cost of a Bad Reputation: The impacts of corporate reputation on talent acquisition* (October 2014). Available at http://www.commitforum.com/wp-content/uploads/2014/10/Cost-of-a-Bad-Reputation-2014.pdf (accessed February 2016).

[17] Deloitte, *The 2016 Deloitte Millennial Survey: Winning over the next generation of leaders"*. See: https://www2.deloitte.com/content/dam/Deloitte/global/Documents/About-Deloitte/gx-millenial-survey-2016-exec-summary.pdf (accessed March 2016).

[18] See http://mbaoath.org/take-the-oath/ (accessed January 2016).

[19] National Council for Curriculum and Assessment, *Education about Religions and Beliefs (ERB) and Ethics in the Primary School: Consultation Paper* (November 2015).

[20] See M&S, *Plan A Report 2015*, available at http://planareport.marksandspencer.com/M&S_PlanAReport2015.pdf (accessed January 2016).

[21] The Global Sustainable Investment Alliance, *Global Sustainable Investment Review 2014* (February 2015). Available at http://www.gsi-alliance.org/wp-content/uploads/2015/02/GSIA_Review_download.pdf

[22] Milne, Richard, "Norway fund excludes four Asian groups over palm oil links", *Financial Times*, 17 August 2015. Available at http://www.ft.com/cms/s/0/b8305bbe-44c7-11e5-b3b2-1672f710807b.html#axzz3xoQtUOPK (accessed January 2016).

[23] Address by Director of Credit Institutions and Insurance Supervision Fiona Muldoon, FCA, to the MacGill Summer School. See https://www.centralbank.ie/press-area/speeches/Pages/AddressbyDirectorofCreditInstitutionsandInsuranceSupervisionFionaMuldoontothe-MacGillSummerSchool.aspx (accessed March 2016).

[24] Barker, Patricia, "An Integrity Model of Ethics" in *The Business Compass: Perspectives on Business Ethics* (Chartered Accountants Ireland, 2012).

[25] See James Dimon's address to the Harvard Business School MBA class of 2009. Available at https://www.youtube.com/watch?v=9T9Kp4NE5l4

[26] Kiel, Fred, *Return on Character: The Real Reason Leaders and Their Companies Win* (Harvard Business Review Press, 2015).

[27] Allen, Sharon, "The New ROE: Return on Ethics", *Forbes*, 21 July 2009.

[28] Covey, Stephen, *The Speed of Trust: The One Thing that Changes Everything* (Free Press, 2006).

[29] Trevino, Linda K. and Brown, Michael E., "Managing to be Ethical: Debunking five business ethics myths", (2004) *Academy of Management Executive* Vol. 18, No. 2, 69–81.

# 2

## Obstacles to Ethical Leadership:
## *Why and How Leaders Lose their Way*

*"Ethics is knowing the difference between what
you have a right to do and what is right to do."*

**Potter Stewart, US Supreme Court**

- Introduction
- The Dark Side of Leadership
- To Err is Human
- Ethical Failings
- The Requisite Response

## Introduction

We have looked at the case for ethical leadership and the variety of compelling reasons why integrity should be restored to its rightful place at the heart of the enterprise. But why did it become dislodged in the first place? How can we explain a decade or more of wrongdoing at the highest levels in some of world's most esteemed enterprises? Why is this renewed focus on ethical leadership necessary at all?

At first review, the cases of misconduct appear to be so different as to deny the prospect of establishing a shared root cause. How can one compare a team of rogue Volkswagen engineers installing software aimed at doctoring emissions results with top FIFA officials conspiring to receive bribes in exchange for football TV rights, or with a former City trader who deliberately manipulated Libor rates "for as little as a Mars bar"?[1] When you dig a little deeper, however, you find that there is a common denominator underlying each of these, sometimes complex, moral transgressions. Without exception, each case involved a significant lapse of human judgement. This begs the question: what makes normally trustworthy, intelligent, considerate executives and managers abandon their basic moral code and commit dishonest, thoughtless, callous acts? Why and how *do* leaders lose their way?

In this chapter we will attempt to answer this question, beginning with some perspectives on the 'dark side' of leadership (including the remote yet real possibility that some businesses are directed and managed by functioning psychopaths). Then, with the aid of several high-profile examples, we will explore in detail the more conventional moral hurdles that, under pressure or in a moment of weakness, can potentially trip up anyone at some stage on their leadership journey. Finally, we will conclude with a practical checklist of behavioural dos and don'ts, as an aide-mémoire to help.

## The Dark Side of Leadership

### Egomaniacs and Bullies

In an article in the *Harvard Business Review,* former CEO of Medtronic, Bill George, addresses the idea that leadership can have a 'dark side'.[2] He describes how some get to the top simply by destroying the people in their way, focussing on external gratification instead of inner satisfaction, and, when they start to lose their grounding, often "reject the honest critic who speaks truth to power". On they go, imposing their will on others and masking their own shortcomings until their capacity for constructive challenge diminishes and, eventually, they are incapable of even honest exchanges. He writes of the "leadership trap": young executives starting out value fair compensation for their hard work, but over time the rewards, including bonuses, share options, power, perks and press coverage, begin to fuel a desire for more. George quotes former Novartis Chairman Daniel Vasella, who once told *Fortune* magazine:

"... for many of us the idea of being a successful manager – leading the company from peak to peak, delivering the goods quarter by quarter – is an intoxicating one. It is a pattern of celebration leading to belief, leading to distortion. When you achieve good results ... you are typically celebrated and you begin to believe that the figure at the centre of all that champagne-toasting is yourself."[3]

In other words, you start to believe your own press, thereby sowing the seeds for the development of an unshakeable, inflated belief in one's personal ability, privilege and infallibility, all combined with a desire for continuous ego-stroking and flattery.

George refers to this constant need for external gratification as often being rooted in a need to salve the emotional scars of a tormented childhood. For example, someone who was bullied as a youngster may surround himself with a comfort blanket in the form of a team of sycophants upon whom he can impose his will and, in effect, bully in turn, while scapegoating any dissenters for his own failings.

## A Bully in Action – Caught on Tape

A prime example of this bullying, autocratic style in action can be heard in a leaked recording of Tim Armstrong, CEO of AOL, who, during a conference in 2013 call with over 1,000 employees to announce the closure of one-third of the web channels for their local news network, Patch, and in a wholly unsuccessful attempt to rally the troops:

(a) tells people more than once that they can just leave if they don't agree with him; then

(b) without missing a beat or even changing the tone of his voice, fires a colleague (Abel Lenz) who had the temerity to take a photo of the event during the call.[4]

Afterwards, Armstrong admitted he hadn't been entirely fair on a "human level" – as opposed to, what, a CEO level?

30

## The Psychopath

The C-suite,* it seems, can be a magnet for those with fragile egos in need of constant shoring up. According to Kevin Dutton in *The Wisdom of Psychopaths* it can also be a good breeding ground for psychopaths.[5] "Psychopaths appear, through some Darwinian practical joke, to possess the very personality traits that many of us would die for", he asserts, listing exceptional persuasiveness, captivating charm and razor-sharp focus under immense pressure as among those innate to the personality type – characteristics commonly attributed to successful CEOs, surgeons, lawyers and even presidents. Paraphrasing the physician Hervey Cleckley from his seminal study on psychopathy, Dutton describes the psychopath as:

> "an intelligent person, characterised by a poverty of emotions, the absence of shame, egocentricity, superficial charm, lack of guilt, lack of anxiety, immunity to punishment, unpredictability, irresponsibility, manipulativeness and a transient interpersonal lifestyle."

Ever worked with someone like this? To be fully sure, you could use the 'Hare Psychopathy Checklist' to assess how many of the 21 psychopathic characteristics your colleague typically displays. Developed by renowned psychologist Robert Hare and further expounded in the foundational book on the subject *Snakes in Suits*,[6] it includes the following principal indicators of a psychopathic nature:

| | |
|---|---|
| Grandiose assessment of self | Poor behavioural controls |
| Superficial charm | Impulsivity |
| Shallow emotional response | Callousness and lack of empathy |
| Pathological lying | Need for stimulation |
| Lack of remorse or guilt | Unrealistic long-term goals |
| Cunning and manipulativeness | Early behavioural problems |

Reading through this list, it is understandable how someone possessed of these traits might do rather well in business, where a degree of ruthlessness combined with just the right amount of charisma can often help to accelerate career progression. It can be difficult to distinguish drive, confidence and professional polish from naked ambition, narcissism and phony, manipulative charm, making true psychopathic tendencies hard to spot.

---

\* The 'C-Suite' is a widely used term used to refer collectively to a corporation's most senior executives. It gets its name because the titles of these executives tend to start with the letter 'C': **Chief** Executive Officer, **Chief** Operating officer, **Chief** Financial Officer, etc.

Furthermore, corporate life necessarily involves some unpleasant tasks from time to time, such as shutting down operations, letting staff go and slashing costs. Most executives would rather avoid these assignments if possible, given the associated emotional trauma. The psychopathic manager, however, will accept such jobs without compunction, taking the human suffering in their stride. Ultimately, they may be well-rewarded for 'getting the job done'. Remuneration and performance systems are often structurally biased to reward this type of results-oriented, macho behaviour, creating magnetic conditions for the ambitious, highly-qualified psychopath, which may explain why research has found that psychopaths represent 3% to 4% of corporate executives, more than three times their representation in the general population.[7]

## The Careerist

The extreme emotional detachment so symptomatic of the psychopathic personality type is also indicative of another alarming executive affliction which, in a classic and still disturbing book entitled *The Gamesman*, psychoanalyst Michael Macoby calls "careerism". He defines it thus:

> "Obsessed with winning, the gamesman views all of his actions in terms of whether they will help him succeed in his career. The individual's sense of identity, integrity and self-determination is lost as he treats himself as an object whose worth is determined by its fluctuating market value. Careerism demands [emotional] detachment."[8]

Macoby argues that careerism ultimately leads to a state of emotional atrophy that corrodes personal integrity by knocking out of balance traits of "the head" (initiative, flexibility, composure, etc.) and traits of "the heart" (honesty, compassion, generosity, etc.). Management need the latter in equal, if not greater, measure if morality is not to be anaesthesized in the work environment. He concludes that without a developed sense of empathy and sensitivity, the executive lacks the necessary qualities to manage creative people and complex tasks, while, at the opposite extreme, a creative person with an underdeveloped emotional core does not possess the inner strength to make tough decisions. Macoby also has some strong things to say about the nature of modern corporations and the role that their structures and systems have in reinforcing careerism by selecting and promoting those who display particular mastery of it.

## *Over-confidence*

Perhaps a less manic but much more prevalent failing derives simply from over-confidence. While all major bookstores have whole self-help sections lined with books dedicated to the idea of boosting confidence as the route to unlocking leadership potential (the 'fake it 'til you make it' approach), Professor of Business Psychology Tomas Chamorro-Premuzic is much more sanguine about what he refers to as "manifestations of hubris" and the very big difference between confidence and competence, which are often equated but seldom matched.[9]

His conjecture is that people are generally over-confident, typically displaying all the signs of the 'Dunning Kruger effect' (where less competent people rate their abilities higher than they actually are, while a minority humbly rate their abilities as below average). These over-estimators are also blind to the associated toxic effects of their inflated self-belief, including reckless risk-taking, and a tendency to arrogance, laziness and complacency. Perhaps rather harshly, in another article Chamorro-Premuzic singles out "Millennials–Generation Y" as being "more narcissistic and entitled than any other generation".[10] In support of his argument he shares the startling statistic that some 85% of the photographs ever taken have been taken in the previous year and that at least 50% of those were 'selfies', a much-loved Millennial–Generation Y practice. Back to leadership, his view is that humility or modesty is the key ingredient and he concludes that "until we stop making decisions on the basis of confidence rather than competence, we will keep having arrogant, impulsive, narcissistic people in charge, and … we will keep making it hard for women, who are usually both more humble and competent than men in these domains, from rising to the top". It is a concern shared by Nobel prize-winner, and author of bestselling book *Thinking Fast and Slow*, Daniel Kahneman, who warns against over-confidence, or 'the illusion of skill', which he says is merely a feeling and does not necessarily match with reality.[11]

## To Err is Human

So, whether deriving from a fragile, needy ego, an excessively robust sense of self or a manic career focus, there appears to be a 'dark side' to corporate leadership. Such innate wickedness may account for some of the worst cases of unethical conduct that have destroyed the companies over which these dysfunctional executives have presided and wreaked havoc with the lives of their colleagues.

However, let's not be fixated on this nasty but rather narrow slice of organisational dystopia. For every corporate bully, megalomaniac manager and psychopathic executive there are many more well-intentioned and highly motivated leaders trying to do their best but who, from time to time, fall short. Perhaps we can blame Adam for the fact that we are all programmed to be fallible, to succumb to temptation and to make mistakes. Or we can return to Bill George, who captures it nicely in his HBR article:

> "Leaders who lose their way are not necessarily bad people; rather, they lose their moral bearings, often yielding to seductions in their paths. Very few people go into leadership roles to cheat or do evil, yet we all have the capacity for actions we deeply regret unless we stay grounded."[12]

George goes on to outline the importance for every leader of devoting time to cultivate their moral compass, or 'true north', through self-awareness, reflection and reliable mentoring from those who are not vested and will give them honest feedback, advice and direction. We will discuss these topics in more detail in the next chapter, but first let's look at some of these 'seductions' and the more common reasons why good people do bad things, i.e. some regular, garden-variety examples of ethical failings.

## Ethical Failings

While every transgression is slightly different in terms of motivation, execution and impact, the causes of ethical failure in a business context can generally be categorised into one or more of the six types shown in **Figure 2.1** and examined in more detail below.

FIGURE 2.1: STANDARD CAUSES OF ETHICAL FAILURE

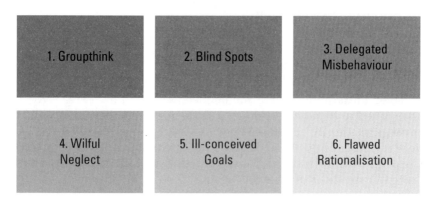

| 1. Groupthink | 2. Blind Spots | 3. Delegated Misbehaviour |
| 4. Wilful Neglect | 5. Ill-conceived Goals | 6. Flawed Rationalisation |

# 1. Groupthink

Have you ever thought about speaking up at a meeting and then, though convinced your point is valid, decided against it because you did not want to seem contrary, difficult or unsupportive of the team's efforts? 'Groupthink', a term first coined by social psychologist Irving Janis in the 1970s, occurs when the desire for harmony or conformity in a group of people results in irrational or dysfunctional decision-making because group pressures lead to a deterioration of "mental efficiency, reality testing, and moral judgement".[13]

Janis suggests that groupthink happens when there is:
- a strong, persuasive group leader;
- a high level of group cohesion; and
- intense pressure from the outside to make a good decision.

A group is also especially vulnerable to the phenomenon of groupthink when:
- its members are similar in background;
- the group is insulated from outside opinions; and
- there are no clear rules for decision-making.

The principal symptoms of groupthink, as identified by Janis, are outlined below, together with some examples of how these might manifest themselves in real situations[14]:

## SYMPTOMS OF GROUPTHINK

1. **Illusion of Invulnerability and Collective Rationalisation** Members of the group ignore obvious danger, take extreme risk, and are overly optimistic, discrediting and explaining away warnings contrary to group thinking.

   Example: "Our track record speaks for itself. We are unstoppable!"

2. **Illusion of Morality** Members believe their decisions are morally correct, ignoring the ethical consequences of their decisions.

   Example: "We know the difference between right and wrong, and this is definitely right."

3. **Excessive Stereotyping** The group constructs negative stereotypes of rivals outside the group.

   Example: "Lawyers will find any excuse to argue, even when the facts are clearly against them."

4. **Pressure for Conformity** Pressure is put on any in the group who express arguments against the group's stereotypes, illusions or commitments, viewing such opposition as disloyal.

Example: "Well, if you really feel that we're making a mistake, you can always leave the team."

5. **Self-Censorship** Members withhold their dissenting views and counter-arguments.

Example: "If everyone else agrees, then my thoughts to the contrary must be wrong."

6. **Illusion of Unanimity** The false perception that everyone agrees with the group's decision; silence is seen as consent.

Example: "I see we all agree, so it's decided then."

7. **Mindguards** Some members appoint themselves to the role of protecting the group from adverse information that might threaten group complacency.

Example: "Those other people don't agree with us because they haven't researched the problem as extensively as we have."

Research into the psychology of conformity originated in the 1950s when social psychologist Solomon Asch conducted a series of experiments to investigate the extent to which social pressure from a majority group could influence a person to conform. This included the 'elevator experiment', originally conducted as part of a 1962 Candid Camera episode entitled "Face the Rear".[15] The video shows a young man (the test subject) entering an elevator at a particular floor and joining four others (actors) who are on their way to a higher level. As the elevator door closes, all of the actors turn to face the rear of the lift. Slowly but surely the young man joins them. Then they turn to the right and again he follows suit, and once again, until the group has completed a full 360 degree rotation, for no apparent reason! The desire to fit in and not be the only contrarian facing 'the wrong way' is enough to make the young man bend to the group dynamic.

An equally engaging but altogether more sinister take on the psychology of the group and how people will readily conform to the social roles they are expected to play within set cliques is the infamous 'Stanford prison experiment' of 1971.[16] Over 40 years later, a Stanford alumnus and Deputy Editor of *Bloomberg Businessweek*, Romesh Ratnesar, included the following reflections on the case study in the *Stanford Alumni* magazine.[17]

"It began with an ad in the classifieds:

**Male college students needed for psychological study of prison life. $15 per day for 1–2 weeks.**

More than 70 people volunteered to take part in the study, to be conducted in a fake prison housed inside Jordan Hall, on Stanford's Main Quad. The leader of the study was 38-year-old psychology professor Philip Zimbardo. He and his fellow researchers selected 24 applicants and randomly assigned each to be a prisoner or a guard. Zimbardo encouraged the guards to think of themselves as actual guards in a real prison. He made clear that prisoners could not be physically harmed, but said the guards should try to create an atmosphere in which the prisoners felt "powerless." The study began on Sunday, August 17, 1971. But no one knew what, exactly, they were getting into.

Forty years later, the Stanford Prison Experiment remains among the most notable—and notorious—research projects ever carried out at the University. For six days, half the study's participants endured cruel and dehumanising abuse at the hands of their peers. At various times, they were taunted, stripped naked, deprived of sleep and forced to use plastic buckets as toilets. Some of them rebelled violently; others became hysterical or withdrew into despair. As the situation descended into chaos, the researchers stood by and watched—until one of their colleagues finally spoke out."

While the Stanford prison experiment was an extreme case, with manufactured conditions and contrived circumstances, history is replete with examples of situations when the pressure to conform and meet the expectations of the given role compromised independent judgement with disastrous effects. Consider:
- the Bay of Pigs affair of 1961, when a presidential advisory group almost led Kennedy into invading Cuba and potential nuclear war. As it was no secret in his administration that Kennedy wanted to overthrow Castro, under pressure, the team jumped to conclusions, ignored many false assumptions and came up with a plan to please the President, rather than one that made any strategic sense. Kennedy's direct involvement in the analysis and decision-making process only added to the group's self-censorship. Arthur Schlesinger, who took part in that decision process, later wrote that "our meetings were taking place in a curious atmosphere of assumed consensus, [and] not one spoke against it"[18];

37

- the Space Shuttle *Challenger* disaster in 1986, largely caused by NASA officials who were aware of engineers' concerns but, with the eyes of the world on Cape Canaveral, assumed a collective 'we are go' mode and decided to launch the shuttle regardless; and
- more recently, the banking crisis in Ireland, about which the Nyberg Report scathingly concluded that throughout the 'Celtic Tiger' boom a chronic all-pervasive groupthink afflicted the Irish banking system, government and society at large.[19]

In organisations, and particularly in the boardroom, conditions are often ripe for groupthink to thrive and prosper. When groupthink, as a cause of ethical malfunction, is further facilitated by a general failure of governance, the results can be truly catastrophic. Anglo Irish Bank was a particularly egregious example, displaying all the hallmarks of the phenomenon as outlined by Janis above, i.e:
- a strong, charismatic chairman;
- a close, inter-connected board;
- intense internal and external pressure to keep making the numbers and propel the share price on its continued upward trajectory.

Simon Carswell described the bank as "the one-trick pony in a frenetic landgrab, leading a poorly regulated and highly competitive race for market share and profit".[20]

Anglo's failure is widely seen as the most costly in Irish corporate history. Could it have been avoided if there had been a little less consensus and a lot more challenge in the boardroom? It is a salutary lesson in the need for courage, independence and diversity of perspective at the highest levels of governance in order to maximise the opportunity for robust challenge and debate, and to minimise the potential for collective hubris and groupthink. In *The Corporate Board: Confronting the Paradoxes*, Ada Demb and F.-Friedrich Neubauer describe the requirement for this "healthy tension" thus:

> "It is the collective strength of the directors that gives the board its capability for judgement – the capability that translates into a distinct additive role. The challenge of this paradox is to forge a set of relationships among a group of strong individuals that will permit information to be shared, recommendations challenged and actions evaluated, while at the same time avoiding the trap of becoming a group so trusting, familiar and comfortable with itself that judgement is undermined by cosy self-satisfaction."[21]

We will examine the role of the board in relation to ethics in **Chapter 6**. For now it is sufficient to note that the average board can contain agar plate conditions for groupthink to flourish unless there is a healthy balance of trust and challenge among its members. Directors and executives could learn a lot from "Man in crowd" in *Monty Python's Life of Brian*[22]:

| | |
|---|---|
| **Brian:** | Please, please, please listen! I've got one or two things to say. |
| **The Crowd:** | Tell us! Tell us both of them! |
| **Brian:** | Look, you've got it all wrong! You don't NEED to follow ME. You don't NEED to follow ANYBODY! You've got to think for your selves! You're ALL individuals! |
| **The Crowd:** | Yes! We're all individuals! |
| **Brian:** | You're all different! |
| **The Crowd:** | Yes, we ARE all different! |
| **Man in crowd:** | I'm not... |

As a cause of ethical failure, groupthink is, by definition, one that requires the company of others. The remaining causes of moral dereliction need no such companionship and can easily lead a lone executive astray, sometimes even unwittingly. The first of these is the universal problem of natural bias: 'blind spots'.

## 2. Blind Spots

Take a look at the following image:

What do you see: an old woman, a young lady or a moustachioed man?

39

And in this image, which are more apparent to you: black bats or white angels?

The point is that we often do not see the full picture, at least not initially or until someone else reveals it to us. We all have 'blind spots'. These can blur the obvious, meaning that we miss additional or alternative information that is contradictory to our expectations. We can become so attached to certain perspectives, people, places and even projects that our thought processes may be confined, our judgement clouded and our decisions compromised.

Inherent biases become very obvious when they involve choices with an ethical dimension. Max Bazerman and Ann Tenbrunsel in their work on "ethical breakdowns" in companies note that this is especially the case with conflicts of interest when "motivated blindness" can be particularly pernicious.[23] The 2008 financial collapse again proves a rich vein of examples of ethical failure; Bazerman and Tenbrunsel point to the "'independent' credit rating agencies [Standard & Poor's, Moody's, Fitch, etc.] that famously gave AAA ratings to collateralised mortgage securities of demonstrably low quality, which helped build a house of cards that ultimately came crashing down, driving a wave of foreclosures that pushed thousands of people out of their homes. Why did the agencies vouch for those risky securities?"

They attribute this behaviour to the "powerful conflicts of interest that helped blind the rating agencies to their own unethical behaviour and that of the companies they rated." While the agencies' purpose is to provide stakeholders with an objective determination of the creditworthiness of financial institutions and their respective debt instruments, "they are paid by the companies they rate". Their profits, therefore, are more dependent on their good relationships with these companies than the accuracy of their assessments.

As Matt Taibi writing in *Rolling Stone* described it: "Given a choice between money and integrity, they took the money, which wouldn't be quite so bad if they weren't in the integrity business."[24] This inherent dishonesty is played out to dramatic effect in the film adaptation of Michael Lewis's book, *The Big Short.*[25] Together with the explosion of sub-prime debt, further exacerbated by the unfettered sale of Collateralised Debt Obligations (CDOs), the US banking sector was destined for implosion, leading to hedge-fund manager Mark Baum, played by Steve Carrell in the film, to observe: "We live in an era of fraud in America ... What bothers me isn't that fraud is not nice. Or that fraud is mean ... fraud and short-sighted thinking have never, ever worked. Not once. Eventually you get caught, things go south. When the hell did we forget all that? I thought we were better than this, I really did." He concludes: "I have a feeling in a few years people are going to be doing what they always do when the economy tanks. They will be blaming immigrants and poor people."

In a similar analysis on ethical dilemmas at work, John Boatright suggests that in situations where minor lapses are accepted, incremental transgressions are also likely to be tolerated, until the organisation is on 'the slippery slope'. Then, seemingly all of a sudden, blatant disregard for ethical protocols has become the norm and 'the way things have always been done'.[26] In such cases, executives do not think in ethical terms anymore when evaluating business decisions but apply pure economic reasoning in isolation, analysing hard data only, without regard to context or consequence. The Ford Pinto story, although dating back to the 1970s, illustrates the point with alarming clarity. I have relied below on Bazerman and Tenbrunsel's succinct and insightful analysis of the case.

## THE FORD PINTO[27]

"The Ford Pinto, a compact car produced during the 1970s became notorious for its tendency in rear-end collisions to leak fuel and burst into flames." Twenty-seven people were killed or injured before the company issued a recall (although other estimates put the death toll from burns related to Pinto crashes as high as 500[28]). Scrutiny of the decision process behind the launch revealed that under intense competition from rival marques, Ford had rushed the Pinto into production and although problems with the fuel tanks were noted by engineers in pre-production testing, the assembly line was ready to go and the decision was taken to proceed.

Far from seeing the decision as having any moral dimension, the management had conducted a formal cost–benefit analysis, putting dollar amounts on a re-design, potential lawsuits and even lives, and determined that it would be cheaper to pay off legal cases than make the repair.

What about Lee Iacocca, the VP most closely involved with the launch? Did no-one think to tell him? Seemingly not, sources in the company have said, stating that safety wasn't a popular subject in Ford at the time and apparently with Lee it was taboo. Whenever a problem was highlighted that had the potential to delay the launch, apparently Lee would look out the window and say, 'Read the product objectives and get back to work'.

Innate psychological biases, 'blind spots', when allowed to go unchecked or, worse, when contradictory evidence or an opposing view is deliberately supressed, have led to some of the most grave ethical failures, of which the Ford Pinto story is just one.

If blind spots are one reason why our '20:20' ethical vision may be obscured, another cause of corrupt behaviour is the potential to deflect any association with an unethical action by simply delegating the task to someone else.

## 3. Delegated Misbehaviour

For most executives the idea of intentionally engaging in corrupt acts is unconscionable. However, sometimes a job has to get done 'one way or the other', so in theory at least delegating it might be a highly convenient option. It enables the manager and the company to maintain a veneer of respectability while outsourcing the more unsavoury elements of a business transaction to a third party. The Mexico bribery scandal at Walmart, which first broke in April 2012 and is still under investigation by the US Department of Justice, is a good example of this particular flavour of malfeasance. The case is summarised below.[29]

### WALMART: THE MEXICO BRIBERY SCANDAL

In April 2012 the *New York Times* published a report alleging that key executives in Walmart HQ in Arkansas were aware of and had covered up bribery on a vast scale in its Mexican subsidiary.

The essence of the story was that the Walmart country manager in Mexico and his general counsel entered into arrangements with third-party agents to pay substantial bribes to Mexican government planning officials in order to secure the expeditious grant of permits to open new stores across the country. To make matters worse, when a Walmart lawyer in Mexico blew the whistle on the practice, his senior officers in both Mexico and head office tried to bury the issue and thwarted any attempt to investigate the matter further.

These press accusations have since drawn a host of investor lawsuits in addition to a US government investigation into Walmart's global operations, centred on whether the company violated the Foreign Corrupt Practices Act (FCPA). Although the investigation is still underway, it is notable that those senior officers at the time, including the CEO, General Counsel, Country Manager, the General Counsel in Mexico and the Head of Walmart International, have since either left Walmart or retired from their positions.

Since then the company has also overhauled its compliance and governance framework, increasing its compliance staff to some 2,000 people, establishing a 'pay for performance with integrity' incentive system and introducing a number of initiatives aimed at combatting the cover-up culture that allowed the Mexican scandal to happen.

As at November 2015, Walmart had retained three different law firms and spent in excess of $700 million[30] on an internal investigation of the allegations and related compliance improvements, as well as paying numerous other lawyers to represent the 30 Walmart executives who have been questioned in the probe. Meanwhile, the scope of the investigation has been broadened to include possible improprieties in Brazil, China and India.

Delegating misbehaviour to third parties, apart from being prima facie wrong, is especially cavalier given that most international and domestic anti-corruption legislation specifically outlaws illicit business partner relationships entered into for these purposes. The practice of 'turning a blind eye' where misconduct is deemed necessary can also happen inside an organisation, with equally damaging consequences. In this context, we will refer to it as 'wilful neglect'.

## 4. Wilful Neglect

In the same way that senior executives do not generally engage in explicit, unethical business practices, rarely do they ask their subordinates to blatantly break the law, for example, directly ordering them to pay a bribe. However, as the late professor and management consultant Saul Gellerman put it in his seminal article for the *Harvard Business Review*, "Why Good Managers Make Bad Ethical Decisions":

> "Company leaders sometimes leave things unsaid or give the impression that there are things they don't want to know about .... Often they lure ambitious lower level managers by implying that rich rewards await those who can produce certain results – and that the methods for achieving them will not be examined too closely."[31]

At worst, this constitutes implicit approval of unethical behaviour; at best, a wilful neglect on the part of the executive to ensure that employees follow proper protocol; yet it is nonetheless incredibly common practice. In his book *Ethics in Finance*, John Boatright, cites the results from interviews with 30 graduates of Harvard Business School, many of whom said that that had "received explicit instructions from their middle manager bosses or felt strong organisation pressures to do things that they believed were sleazy, unethical or sometimes illegal". He also reports that a study of more than 1,000 Colombia Business School graduates found that:

- 40% had been rewarded for taking some action they considered to be "ethically troubling"; and
- 31% of those who refused to act in ways they considered to be unethical believed they were penalised for their choice.[32]

These studies reveal how pervasive, insidious and sometimes even blatant can be the expectation of managers that their subordinates will comply, without question, with an unethical mandate.

The case of the accounting irregularities that came to light at Tesco in 2014 illustrates how the unrealistic and unforgiving demands of managers to 'make the numbers' at all costs can pressure employees to overstep the line. It also highlights the perils of being a publicly quoted company, chasing short-term results required by a myopic stock market, instead of pursuing the long-term success of the company in the interests of all its stakeholders.

## THE TESCO ACCOUNTING SCANDAL[33]

Tesco, which once enjoyed a dominant position in the UK grocery sector, came under serious threat in recent years from rivals, including discount supermarket chains from Germany. Industry observers have noted, however, that rather than addressing market realities and fixing the problem, instead Tesco engaged in a 'window dressing' exercise and pushed up the numbers to make the profit & loss account appear healthier than it actually was.

Reports also suggest that the principal form of 'creative accounting' employed by Tesco was the early booking of supplier contributions that were conditional on hitting sales targets that the company was never going to reach. It is understood that a few employees, realising these sales targets were wholly unrealistic, struck deals with suppliers to nonetheless make these payments by offering benefits in the next financial period. These benefits were kept secret and in the worst-case scenario involved Tesco actually paying money back to some of these suppliers during the following financial cycle. A whistleblower eventually tipped off the new CEO, Dave Lewis, who just three weeks into the job initiated an investigation that eventually found profits had been overstated by over £325 million.

Seven senior executives have since left Tesco and many more have been called in for interview by the UK Serious Fraud Office, which expects to resolve the case in 2016. In the meantime, the senior management team has been overhauled with a new chairman, CEO (as above) and finance director. Relationships with suppliers have also been radically restructured and PwC UK, auditors to the company for over 30 years, have been replaced, having been excluded from the tender process "by mutual agreement" with the retailer.[34]

While 'every little helps', it cannot be at all costs.

Nothing, however, can trump the Siemens bribery scandal for the extent and nature of the corruption involved; the scale of the fines levied; the catastrophic damage suffered by the company; and the cost and effort expended in rebuilding its reputation. It is also a lesson in the pitfalls

of operating a global business and acquiescing in local customs without heeding the requirements of international governance standards.
We will come back to this in **Chapter 5**.

## SIEMENS: CORRUPTION ON A GRAND SCALE[35]

Headquartered in Munich, Germany, Siemens AG employed
some 475,000 people in 190 countries and reported sales of $110
billion in the year to end December 2006.

On 15 November of that year, German prosecutors raided the offices
and the homes of Siemens staff on a tip-off that the company was
engaged in some level of bribery. The subsequent investigations
covered businesses representing 60% of Siemens's revenues and
spanned operations in Asia, Africa, Europe, the Middle East and the
Americas. They uncovered evidence of a litany of bribes and kickbacks paid by Siemens executives to foreign officials to secure government contracts for projects like a national identity card project in
Argentina, mass transit work in Venezuela, a nationwide cellphone
network in Bangladesh and a UN oil-for-food program in Iraq.

After two years of investigations, legal proceedings were concluded
in both Germany and the US and resulted in the company paying
$1.6 billion in fines to the respective authorities, as well as $850 million
to cover the internal investigations, which involved over 200 outside
lawyers. As a result of the investigation, Siemens dismissed more
than 500 employees who were implicated in the corruption and sued
nine former members of its managing board for breaching their
duties. The CEO resigned and was replaced with an external candidate, Peter Loscher, the first time this position was filled from outside
the company since its establishment in 1847. Within months of
Loscher taking over, about 80% of top-level of executives had been
replaced, 70% of the next level down and 40% of the level below that.
As Loscher himself has written:

> "... never miss the opportunities that come from a good
> crisis—we certainly didn't miss ours. The scandal created
> a sense of urgency without which change would have
> been much more difficult to achieve. ... Siemens is a very
> proud company with a history of innovation and success.
> In the absence of a catalyst like this, people would have
> asked themselves, 'Why alter anything?'"[36]

Indeed, Siemens has made a present virtue of past vice and, under the banner 'only clean business is Siemens business', has since been lauded for its unequivocal tone at the top, exemplary compliance programme and sustainable business practices.

In the immediate aftermath of the Siemens bribery scandal, when the company's newly appointed chief compliance officer reviewed the compliance programmes, he found a full suite of professional policies and procedures. It all looked good in theory, but in practice was simply not supported. Instead, the leadership's rallying call of 'Bring me the business' drove middle management to extreme lengths in terms of the complexity and extent of corrupt contracts secured.

## 5. Ill-conceived Goals

The performance management system in an organisation is one of the primary drivers of culture and conduct. When goal-setting and concomitant rewards are fundamentally ill-conceived, in that they fail to properly consider how they will drive behaviours in practice, all manner of weird and not so wonderful things can often follow.

Culture and ill-conceived goals had a part to play in the downfall of the Irish banking sector. By 2007, the international bond borrowings of the six main Irish banks had grown to over half of Ireland's GDP, fuelled principally by their enormous increase in lending to the Irish property market. The collapse of Lehman Brothers and the stalled liquidity of the world's interbank market in 2007–2008 presented the Irish banks with a collective domestic liquidity and solvency problem. This in turn exposed the fragile cash flows of developers and stratospheric property valuation, ultimately requiring a sectoral recapitalisation to the tune of 40% of GDP and heralding an austerity programme that had a devastating impact on Ireland's social and economic development.

Although the impact of the Irish banking disaster was multifaceted and far-reaching, it was also a clear and straightforward demonstration of our fifth reason for ethical failure: ill-conceived goals, or how poorly designed metrics can drive behaviour in disastrous directions. Loan officers across all the major banks were primarily rewarded on the value of the loan cheques drawn down, with often scant regard for the borrower's ability to repay. Traditional financial analysis and lending protocols were gradually less observed, no longer deemed relevant in a world of rising property prices and endless credit, while managers with a firmer stand on risk management and credit worthiness were replaced or demoted. The rest, as outlined above, is a history we will be paying off well into the future.

Sometimes even well-intentioned goals can unwittingly promote dysfunctional behaviour, as demonstrated by the example below, which was shared on a Chatham House Rules basis by an attendee at a meeting of international compliance professionals. The company involved was in the heavy industry sector and, with large-scale machinery and complex engineering processes, had prioritised the safety of its workforce as a key focus area.

## THE RIGHT PRIORITY, WRONGFULLY EXECUTED

Safety was at the top of the agenda of every manager meeting; facility managers and employees were fully trained to understand safety risk analysis and accident prevention principles; and best practices were developed by a central safety executive and shared extensively across the organisation. Furthermore, the safety performance of operating units was routinely and rigorously assessed, and safety was a significant part of the appraisal and reward process for each business unit's management team.

In his role as Chief Compliance Officer, the meeting attendee oversaw the 'hotline', a channel through which employees could report any unsafe, unethical or illegal behaviour, and was privy to the transcripts of all such calls. He spoke about one in particular that stood out. It came from a warehouse employee, 'Dave', whose colleague 'Ken' had injured his arm while clearing an area to make way for more stock. The injury, although not life-threatening, was sufficiently serious to require medical attention. Ken duly asked the warehouse manager to be excused to go to the doctor. The warehouse manager asked him not to seek medical advice on company time and not to report it as a workplace incident, saying that the company could not afford that hit to their safety statistics for the month. To add insult to injury, Dave reported that the next day he saw the MD of the company give Ken a voucher as a thank you for not reporting the incident.

Both the MD and the warehouse manager in this case were subsequently dismissed, following a swift and comprehensive investigation. However, it shows how easily targets and goals, even with the best intentions, can encourage the most unexpected and unwelcome of behavioural responses and how important it is to fully think through, from every possible angle, how specific metrics may drive specific behaviours and promote certain practices.

## 6. Flawed Rationalisation

*"...a ruler ... should do what is right if he can; but he must be prepared to do wrong if necessary."*

Niccolò Machiavelli, *The Prince*

Many forms of bad behaviour can be justified when one's focus is exclusively on outcomes rather than the means of achieving them. This is especially so when those outcomes are seen as being desirable, worthwhile, even noble. For example, the practice of waterboarding terrorist suspects at Guantanamo Bay detention camp seems to have been deemed acceptable by CIA operatives because the 'end', i.e. protecting US citizens from further terrorist attacks, justified the means. As a cause of ethical failure, such 'flawed rationalisation' can be also be characteristic of and overlap with some of the factors discussed above.

In *Meeting the Ethical Challenges of Leadership*, Craig Johnson outlines different rationalisation techniques in what he refers to as a "deactivation of moral standards".[37] The principal techniques are outlined below, with some statements that may typically accompany the enactment of these Machiavellian perspectives together with some examples, both illustrative and real.

### RATIONALISATION TECHNIQUES

* **Devaluing the victims of the wrongdoing**
Sometimes people can feel less badly about their own actions when they are able to transfer the blame to its victims, especially when they can dehumanise those victims in the process. The Ford Pinto case above had echoes of this where the potential crash fatalities were reduced by the company's finance analysts to base statistics or a cost to be written off. In other cases, often involving workplace bullying or harassment, bad behaviour is justified by claiming that its victim somehow deserved it. This may be expressed thus: "He got what was coming to him – I had to put manners on him."

49

- **Diffusion of responsibility**
Linked to groupthink (see above), diffusion of responsibility involves someone avoiding being personally accountable for an action (or inaction) when there is a larger group to whom collective blame can be assigned. This explains crowd behaviour such as looting and rioting and, in the corporate world, may be used to justify corrupt practices and couched in terms such as: "Everybody does it – you have to if you want to survive in this game".

- **Euphemistic language**
This rationalisation technique uses neutral language to frame unethical situations or behaviour while avoiding more negative terms that may trigger a more ethical response. Innocent victims killed in drone attacks are referred to as "collateral damage". Or consider when, according to President Clinton's former national security advisor, his administration refused to use the word 'genocide' for six weeks after the killing of some 800,000 Tutsi people by Hutu rebels in Rwanda in 1994, because it would have demanded commensurate action.[38]

- **Advantageous comparisons**
Sometimes people downplay their own misconduct by comparing it to the even more reprehensible behaviour of others. This is common in fraud cases, for example: "Sure, I kept a few percent for myself – small beer compared to what my boss skimmed off."

- **Justifying the cause**
This is common in the case of competition law violations, and happens when executives claim that their unethical behaviour was necessary and in the best interest of the company or the industry. For example, in the case of collusion: "Sure, we agreed to let them concentrate on the commercial market – we make more money on the residential side."

- **Belief in the improbability of being discovered**
Self-explanatory really, i.e. "I may as well – what are the chances of getting caught?"

Rationalisation due to individual financial pressure could also be included, i.e. when executives keep doing things that they know are not right or tacitly acquiesce in a general corporate malaise because they find themselves in a 'gilded cage', which they believe they cannot afford to leave, even at the expense of their principles. As the late American TV critic, humourist and author Marvin Kitman once remarked: "A coward is a hero with a wife, kids and a mortgage."

It is a fact that any high-pressure situation is more likely to lead to a failure in ethical reasoning, whether due to financial issues, pressing deadlines, the possibility of humiliation, loss of face, etc. In an article for the *Washington Post*, entitled "You're not as virtuous as you think", Nitin Nohria, Dean of the Harvard Business School, refers to the related concept of 'moral overconfidence', or the gap between how people believe they would behave and how they actually behave, providing the following representative examples from the world of politics, business and sport:

> "There are political candidates who say they won't use attack ads until, late in the race, they are behind in the polls and under from pressure from donors and advisers, their ads become increasingly negative. There are chief executives who come in promising to build a business for the long term but then condone questionable accounting gimmickry to satisfy short-term market demands. There are baseball players who shun the use of steroids until they age past their peak performance and then start to look for something to slow the decline. These people may be condemned as hypocrites. But they aren't necessarily bad actors. Often they've overstated their inherent morality and the influence of situational factors."[39]

Many years earlier, Bowen H. McCoy, a former managing director of Morgan Stanley in a poignant autobiographical reflection entitled "The Parable of the Sadhu" had anticipated Nohria's conjecture, in extremis.[40] In the article, he described a climbing expedition in the Himalayas when, at 15,000 feet, the group of which he was part came across an Indian holy man, a "Sadhu", who was lost and at risk of dying of hypothermia. The group had to decide whether to abandon the climb and bring the man to safety or to proceed to the summit. They decided on the latter course. McCoy recalls:

> "I felt and continue to feel guilt about the Sadhu. I had literally walked through a classic moral dilemma without fully thinking through the consequences. My excuses for my actions include a high-adrenaline flow, a superordinate goal and a once-in-a-lifetime opportunity – factors in the usual corporate situation, especially when one is under stress."

Applying the parable to executives as well as to corporations, McCoy went on to articulate the following:

"Organisations that do not have a heritage of mutually accepted, shared values tend to become unhinged during stress, with each individual bailing out for himself. Because corporations and their members are interdependent, for the corporation to be strong the members need to share a preconceived notion of what is correct behaviour, a 'business ethic', and think of it as a positive force, not a constraint."

We could probably fill another book with examples of toxic executive decisions that were solely and wholly due to fundamentally flawed rationalisation processes. The Libor-rigging scandal would surely feature, the GlaxoSmithKline case involving the bribery of doctors in China would warrant a chapter,[41] as would the collapse of Enron and the story behind the biggest ever anti-trust violation involving the rigging of the cathode ray tube market by Phillips and Samsung, along with many more. However, for now, we will conclude this catalogue of corruption by looking at just two examples: the demise of Arthur Andersen and the ongoing emissions scandal at Volkswagen.

### THE DEMISE OF ARTHUR ANDERSEN[42]

In 1913 Arthur Andersen founded the accounting firm bearing his name; he was still in his twenties. As CEO, his mantra 'Think straight – talk straight' went to the core of the organisation where "integrity mattered more than fees". A favourite story among alumni was the one in which Andersen confronted a railway executive who insisted that the firm approve his books, with the line: "There's not enough money in the city of Chicago to induce me to change that report". Andersen lost the business, which subsequently went bankrupt, while the firm became known as one people could trust to be honest and do the right thing.

Andersen died in 1974, but was succeeded by leaders with similar beliefs and the firm's strong cultural identity was upheld for decades. By the mid-1990s, the firm still provided formal ethical instruction; it even established a separate consulting group, led by Barbara Toffler, to help other businesses manage their own ethics programmes. However, Toffler quickly became concerned about the changing culture and ethical practices of her own employer, which she has since chronicled in her book, *Final Accounting: Ambition, Greed and the Fall of Arthur Andersen.*[43] She attributes much of the change to the fact "that the firm's profits increasingly came from management consulting rather than auditing... the cultural standards that worked so well in auditing were inconsistent with the needs of the consulting business" and "rather than standing for principles of honesty and integrity, consultants were encouraged to keep clients happy and to concentrate on getting return business, because now only fees mattered. They were even expected to pad prices or create work to increase profits."

Training for new recruits, once considered so integral to their learning 'the Andersen way', was no longer mandatory; instead they were advised to stay home and concentrate on lucrative client work. Toffler refers to the ethical standards being filed in a big maroon binder, but adds: "When I brought up the subject of internal ethics, I was looked at as if I had been teleported in from another world."

In 2002, Andersen was convicted of obstruction of justice for shredding documents associated with its role as Enron's auditing firm and quickly went out of business.

And finally, to 'the people's car', or Volkswagen, and the emissions scandal that hit the headlines in the autumn of 2015 and is likely to cloud the carmaker's future for many years to come.

## THE VOLKSWAGEN EMISSIONS SCANDAL

Though various investigations on both sides of the Atlantic were still underway at the time of writing and the total cost to the company is as yet unknown, in terms of fines, vehicle recalls, civil claims and, moreover, damage to its reputation and future prospects, things are looking especially *'furchtbar'* (awful) for Volkswagen.

As at January 2016, the status, as reported in the *New York Times*, was as follows[44]:
- the company posted its first quarterly loss in 15 years (Q3 2015);
- it had halted sales of affected cars in the US;
- the share price had plummeted;
- Volkswagen's CEO had stepped down;
- several high-ranking executives had been suspended by the company;
- regulators across the globe had initiated investigation as had attorneys general in all 50 states in the US;
- the US Justice Department had recently filed a civil lawsuit against the company over the deception;
- the company also faced lawsuits from owners seeking compensation for the decreased resale value of their cars;
- the carmaker had announced that it would set aside c. $7.3 billion to cover the cost of bringing vehicles with illegal software into compliance;
- it had also admitted it had understated the output of carbon dioxide, which could mean an additional $2.2 billion in costs and penalties.

While the investigations will be thorough and the fines exacting, 10 questions that may remain elusive and unanswered include:
1. Did the board and/or the CEO know?
2. Why did no-one speak up?
3. Is this a case of 'wilful neglect'?
4. Was governance incompetent, dysfunctional, overly complex, or all of the above?
5. Did the pursuit of turnover topple the preservation of values?
6. Did those responsible think they could get away with it?
7. Was cheating systematic?
8. Why were an impartial external CEO and chairman not appointed?
9. Can the company ever fully recover?
10. Volkswagen has had scandals in 1993, 2005 and 2015. Will there be another one?

## The Requisite Response

What, if anything, can we learn from all of these examples of corporate ethical failure and their contributory factors? Is there something about the pursuit of profit that inevitably drives certain people to cross the line? Is there a cure for the epidemic of enterprise-wide moral flabbiness?

Business ethicists have yet to develop a vaccine, spin doctors do their best to mask the effects, but in the meantime well-intentioned leaders genuinely struggle to balance their conformance or compliance responsibilities with the performance or profit-driven aspects of their role. The requisite response is two-fold and involves a combination of:
1. embedded structural 'antidotes' in the organisation; **and**
2. behavioural accountability on the part of its leadership.

In other words: an ethical organisation, guided by an ethical leader.

We will explore the structural, organisational 'antidotes', or those building blocks necessary to support a corporate culture of integrity, in **Part II**, while the next chapter, **Chapter 3**, prescribes the personal groundwork necessary to truly lead with integrity. Before delving into the detailed steps on this individual ethical expedition, it is useful to reflect on the principal lessons we have learned about why and how leaders can lose their way. The 'Behavioural Dos and Don'ts' listed below should help ensure this is a more straightforward journey, with clear signposts for when the terrain becomes more challenging.

## LEADING WITH INTEGRITY: DOS AND DON'TS

| Do | Don't |
|---|---|
| Become more self-aware and cultivate your moral compass (see **Chapter 3**) | Believe your own hype! Seek honest, balanced feedback from reliable sources. |
| Embrace diversity in all its forms, refresh your team when appropriate and actively seek the contrarian view and independent perspective | Get too caught up with power, money or career – no one on their death bed ever said "I wish I spent more time at the office". |
| Recognise the potential for inherent bias in every situation and employ safeguards to regulate potential conflicts of interest | Overlook seemingly trivial ethical lapses; avoid the 'slippery slope' |
| Assess what bad behaviours your reward systems could encourage – think "what would the devil do?" | Dehumanise a situation. Think through the real impact of your decision on people affected by it |
| Look closely at how results are obtained. Reward good decision processes, not just good outcomes | Delegate corruption. Take ownership of the ethical impact of all work carried out on your behalf |
| Celebrate the right choices when the wrong one was promoted or would have been easier to take | Wilfuly neglect, tacitly acquiesce or silently condone bad behaviour |
| Become a 'first class noticer'[45] by following your instincts, analysing past mistakes and asking the right quesions at the right time of the right people | Rationalise, blame or excuse unethical conduct – follow your instincts |
| Seek counsel when in doubt and consider broader perspectives to seemingly insurmountable problems | Bury the issue or obfuscate – come clean, quickly. 'Fess up' fast if you find something |
| Exercise humility and don't forget who you really are and where you came from | Be afraid to vote with your feet if all else fails – stay true to your principles. Things will work out. |

# References to Chapter 2

1 Vaughan, Liam and Finch, Gavin, "Hayes Said Traders Would Help Rig Libor for a Mars Bar", *Bloomberg Business*, 8 July 2015. Available at http://www.bloomberg.com/news/articles/2015-07-08/hayes-said-traders-would-help-rig-libor-for-a-mars-bar- (accessed January 2016).

2 George, William W., "Why Leaders Lose Their Way", *Harvard Business Review*, 6 June 2011. Available at: https://hbr.org/2011/06/why-leaders-lose-their-way.html (accessed February 2016).

3 *Ibid.*

4 Adams, Susan, "AOL's Chief Demonstrates The Worst Way To Fire Someone", *Forbes*, 14 August 2013.

5 Dutton, Kevin, *The Wisdom of Psychopaths: Lessons in Life from Saints, Spies and Serial Killers* (Scientific American/Farrar, Straus and Giroux, 2013).

6 Babiak, Paul and Hare, Robert, *Snakes in Suits: When Psychopaths Go to Work* (HarperBusiness, 2007).

7 See Babiak, Paul and Hare, Robert, *op. cit.* above, n.6, citing their own research published in "Corporate Psychopathy: Talking the Walk" (2010) *Behavioural Sciences and the Law*, Vol. 28, No. 2, 174–193.

8 Marcoby, Michael, *The Gamesman: The New Corporate Leaders* (Simon & Schuster, 1977).

9 Chamorro-Premuzic, Tomas, "Why Do So Many Incompetent Men Become Leaders?", *Harvard Business Review*, 22 August 2013. Available at https://hbr.org/2013/08/why-do-so-many-incompetent-men (accessed March 2016).

10 Chamorro-Premuzic, Tomas, "The Dangers of Confidence", *Harvard Business Review*, IdeaCast, July 2014. Available at https://hbr .org/2014/07/the-dangers-of-confidence/ (accessed March 2016).

11 Kahneman, Daniel, *Thinking Fast and Slow* (Farrar, Straus & Giroux, 2013).

12 George, William W. (2011), *op. cit.* above, n.2.

13 Janis, Irving L., *Victims of Groupthink: A psychological study of foreign-policy decisions and fiascoes* (New York: Houghton Mifflin, 1972).

14 For the examples I have relied on the excellent Mindtools website and "Avoiding Groupthink: Avoiding Fatal Flaws in Group Decision Making". Available at https://www.mindtools.com/pages/article/newLDR_82.htm (accessed February 2016).

15 Versions of the experiment are viewable on YouTube, e.g. https://www.youtube.com/watch?v=BgRoiTWkBHU

16 A film about the original "Stanford Prison Experiment" can be seen at https://www.youtube.com/watch?v=760lwYmpXbc

[17] Romesh, R., "The Menace Within", *Stanford Alumni* July/August. Available at https://alumni.stanford.edu/get/page/magazine/article/?article_id=40741 (accessed January 2016).

[18] Hansen, Morten T., "How John F. Kennedy Changed Decision Making for Us All", *Harvard Business Review*, 22 November 2013. Available at https://hbr.org/2013/11/how-john-f-kennedy-changed-decision-making (accessed February 2016).

[19] *Misjudging Risk: Causes of the Systemic Banking Crisis in Ireland* (Report of the Commission of Investigation into the Banking Sector in Ireland, March 2011) (the 'Nyberg Report').

[20] Kelly, Fiach, "Simon Carswell of 'Irish Times' appears at Banking Inquiry", *Irish Times*, 10 March 2015.

[21] Demb, A. and Neubauer, F., *The Corporate Board: Confronting the Paradoxes* (Oxford University Press, 1992).

[22] Directed by Terry Jones, 1979.

[23] Bazerman, Max H. and Tenbrunsel, Ann E., "Ethical Breakdowns: Good People often let bad things happen. Why?", (2011) *Harvard Business Review* Vol. 89, No. 4, 58–65.

[24] Taibi, Matt, "The Last Mystery of the Financial Crisis", *Rolling Stone*, 19 June 2013.

[25] *The Big Short*, directed by Adam McKay (2015).

[26] Boatright, John R., "Confronting Ethical Dilemmas at Work: Why Do Good People Do Bad Things", CFA Institute, 21 October 2013. Available at https://blogs.cfainstitute.org/investor/2013/10/21/confronting-ethical-dilemmas-at-work-why-do-good-people-do-bad-things/(accessed February 2016).

[27] See Bazerman, Max H. and Tenbrunsel, Ann E., *op. cit.* above, n.23.

[28] See Dowie, Mark "Pinto Madness", *Mother Jones*, September/October 1977.

[29] See Heineman Jr, Ben W., "Who's Responsible for the Walmart Mexico Scandal?" *Harvard Business Review*, 15 May 2014.

[30] See Viswanatha, Aruna and Nassauer, Sarah, "U.S. Probes Possible Wal-Mart Misconduct in Brazil", *Wall Street Journal*, 24 November 2015.

[31] Gellerman, Saul W., "Why "Good" Managers Make Bad Ethical Choices" (1986) *Harvard Business Review* July–August 85–90.

[32] Boatright, John, *Ethics in Finance* (Wiley-Blackwell, 2014).

[33] See, for example, Miller, Alex, "The Tesco Scandal: The perils of aggressive accounting", ACCA Global, 11 August 2015.

[34] See McCabe, Sarah "Tesco drops auditor PwC for Deloitte after accounting scandal", *Irish Independent*, 17 May 2015. Available at http://www.independent.ie/business/tesco-drops-auditor-pwc-for-deloitte-after-accounting-scandal-31228555.html (accessed January 2016).

[35] See Healy, Paul M. and Petkoski, Djordjija,"Fighting Corruption at Siemens: A Multimedia Case Study", *Harvard Business Review*, 28 March 2012 (available to purchase from www.HBR.org).

[36] Loscher, Peter, "The CEO of Siemens on Using a Scandal to Drive Change" (2012) *Harvard Business Review*, November. Available at https://hbr.org/2012/11/the-ceo-of-siemens-on-using-a-scandal-to-drive-change (accessed January 2016). In an interesting footnote to Peter Loscher's 2012 piece in the HBR, the editors explain that "[u]ntil 1999, paying bribes abroad was legal in Germany. In fact, German corporations could deduct bribes from taxable income." While German law changed, under pressure from the US, it seems that the mindset and culture at Siemens did not; that they found "it hard to break the habit". Critically, the company also failed to recognise the need to consider the risks of non-compliance with the Foreign Corrupt Practices Act when its shares were listed on the New York Stock Exchange for the first time in 2001, proving Peter Drucker's point that "Culture eats strategy for breakfast".

[37] Johnson, Craig E., *Meeting the Ethical Challenges of Leadership: Casting Light or Shadow* (Sage Publications, 2011).

[38] Darnton, John, "Revisiting Rwanda's Horrors with an Ex-Security Adviser", *New York Times*, 20 December 2004. Available at http://www.nytimes.com/2004/12/20/movies/revisiting-rwandas-horrors-with-an-exnational-security-adviser.html (accessed January 2016).

[39] Nohria, Nitin, "You're not as virtuous as you think", *Washington Post*, 15 October 2015. Available at https://www.washingtonpost.com/opinions/youre-not-as-virtuous-as-you-think/2015/10/15/fec227c4-66b4-11e5-9ef3-fde182507eac_story.html (accessed January 2016).

[40] McCoy, Bowen H., "The Parable of the Sadhu" (1983) *Harvard Business Review*, September/October 1983.

[41] See Plumridge, Hester and Burkitt, Laurie, "GlaxoSmithKline Found Guilty of Bribery in China", *Wall Street Journal*, 19 September 2014. Available at: http://www.wsj.com/articles/glaxosmithkline-found-guilty-of-bribery-in-china-1411114817 (accessed February 2016).

[42] In briefly telling the Anderson story, I am grateful to the account provided in Trevino, Linda K. and Nelson, Katherine A., in *Managing Business Ethics: Straight Talk About How To Do It Right* (Wiley, 2011).

[43] Toffler, Barbara Ley, *Final Accounting: Ambition, Greed and the Fall of Arthur Andersen* (Broadway Books, 2003).

[44] Russell, Karl, Guilbert, Gate, Keller, Josh and Watkins, Derek, "How Volkswagen Got Away with Diesel Deception", *New York Times*, 5 January, 2016.

[45] Bazerman, Max H., "Becoming a First-class Noticer", (2014) *Harvard Business Review* 116–119.

# 3

# The Groundwork for Leading with Integrity:
## *It Starts with You*

> *"This above all: to thine own self be true.*
> *And it must follow, as the night the day,*
> *thou canst not then be false to any man."*

**Polonius in *Hamlet* [Act I, Scene iii, 78–82]**

- Introduction
- Ethical Theories and Frameworks
- The Core Competencies of Ethical Leadership:
  1. Core Values ('What Drives Me?')
  2. Emotional Intelligence ('How Do I Relate to Others?')
  3. Authenticity ('What Makes me Unique?')
- Why Should Anyone be Led by You?

## Introduction

In the last chapter we looked at how easily and understandably many of us struggle to always make the right decision when presented with ethical issues in the workplace. We saw examples of how normally good, decent people sometimes fail spectacularly in these situations. Yet, for every executive who falls down in the face of moral adversity, there are more who will remain surefooted in their approach, instinctively knowing the right thing to do and, more importantly, able to motivate others to do likewise. In this chapter we will examine the qualities that account for this difference, in other words, the competencies of ethical leadership. These include strong core values, emotional intelligence and authenticity, and we will set out the personal groundwork required for you to master these competencies. This will entail self-awareness exercises to facilitate a full understanding of your ethical perspectives, values and vision.

However, before we can fully appreciate our own guiding principles and decision-making processes, it is necessary to consider the principal schools of ethical thought and how these have developed over time. The application of ethical principles is more effective and systematic when informed by an understanding of leading moral philosophies. Once we have, albeit briefly, distilled some of the highlights of several millennia of thinking, we will be better equipped to articulate our own values-based approach to leadership.

## Ethical Theories and Frameworks

### The Principal Schools of Ethics

'Ethics' is a philosophical term which derives from the Greek word '*ethos*', meaning habit or custom. For the purposes of this book:
* 'morality' is concerned with the norms, values and beliefs embedded in social processes which define right and wrong for an individual or a community;
* 'ethics' is the study of morality and the application of reason to elucidate specific rules and principles that determine right and wrong for any given situation;
* these rules and principles are called 'ethical theories'.

As represented in **Figure 3.1** below, in *Management Ethics: Integrity at Work*, Joseph Petrick and John Quinn provide a useful map of the principal schools of ethics. It plots the various ethical theories and some of

63

the great thinkers behind them on two axes. Those on the left employ a principles-based approach to determining what is right from wrong, regardless of consequences, whereas those on the right measure the correctness of a decision based on whether the choice brings us closer to a desired end result. The vertical dimension contrasts a focus on the individual responsibility to develop judgement and self-awareness with the need for a more institutional framework to govern ethical issues.

FIGURE 3.1: A MAP OF THE PRINCIPAL SCHOOLS OF ETHICS[1]

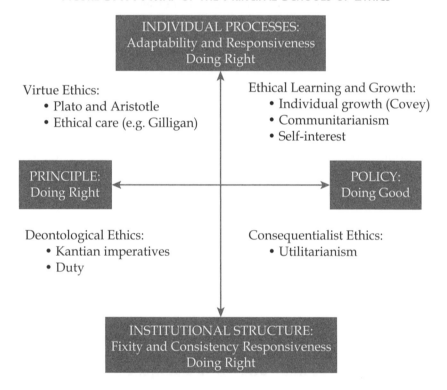

**Virtue Ethics**  In the western world at least, written records of a formal, systematic debate about what is right and what is wrong, i.e. moral philosophy or ethics, began with Plato in the third century BCE and the exposition of his ideas on '**virtue ethics**'. He identified four principal virtues: wisdom, courage, self-control and justice. Plato's student, Aristotle, developed this philosophy further, elevating justice as the primary virtue and focussing on the individual in society

64

and the role of character or personal virtues in shaping ethical behaviours and creating "a good life".

In addressing an ethical dilemma, a person influenced by the teachings of Plato and Aristotle would ask: "What would the virtuous person do?" or, more specifically, "How does my decision balance justice and the other virtues of courage, wisdom, etc. and impact on maintaining a good life?" Because in ancient Greece respect of one's peers was also critical to one's own assessment of self-worth, a follow-on question would most likely invoke the so-called 'light of day' test, i.e. "Would I be happy if others knew of my decision?"[2]

Many have since taken exception to Aristotle's presumption that justice is the primary virtue, arguing that it must be tempered by wisdom or similarly valid qualities. For example, Carol Gilligan contends that the ethic of care should rank *pari passu* with justice when an individual is evaluating a given moral maelstrom, suggesting that women, in particular, tend to naturally default to this position.[3]

**Consequentialism** The school of 'consequentialist ethics', as the name suggests, considers a decision or action right or acceptable if it accomplishes a desired result, such as pleasure, knowledge, career growth, the realisation of self-interest or utility. The more common consequentialist theory is *'utilitarianism'*, which approaches moral reasoning by identifying all of the stakeholders that are affected by the issue, assessing alternative courses of action and their consequences, and choosing on the basis of the best overall outcome for all concerned; in other words, seeking the greatest good for the greatest number of people.

**Deontological Ethics** In contrast, deontology, or ethical formalism, is the strand of ethics that emphasises duty as the main driver of ethical behaviour. In this school of thought it is the intent that matters, rather than the consequence. The motivation behind behaviour is what is critical in deciding whether it is good or not. Ethical formalists regard certain behaviours as inherently right, and their determination of rightness focuses on the individual actor, rather than on society. This philosophy has been greatly influenced by the work of Immanuel Kant, in particular his 'categorical imperative': "Act as if the maxim of your action were to become by your will a universal law of nature." Put another way, this position would lead you to pose the following practical question: "What kind of world would this be if everyone behaved in this way or made this kind of decision in this type of situation?"

## Other Ethical Theories and Contributions

A number of other philosophers and management theorists have put forward alternative contributions or variations on the principal ethical schools of thought. Their focus is largely back on the individual, their development as an ethical person and contribution to an ethical society. It includes modern work, such as that of Steven Covey, who recommended self-reflection and awareness as a critical step in developing character.[4]

Another approach, the *'communitarianism'* perspective, is of the view that people can become more ethical collectively, or as part of a community that shares and promotes a common values system.

'Rational egoism' is a third, which suggests that everyone should act in their own self-interest and use their own rational, independent and objective judgement as their guide in making ethical decisions. It includes the rather extreme stance known as *'objectivism'*, as propounded in the novels of Ayn Rand in the US in the mid-20th Century, which rejects any form of government or institutional intervention in favour of individual choice as the only ethical influence in shaping economic and social development. She described man as "a heroic being, with his own happiness as the moral purpose of his life, with productive achievement as his noblest activity, and reason as his only attribute".[5]

## The Application of Ethical Theory

What does this all mean in practice for ethical business leadership? This is perhaps best answered by way of an example. In their book *Business Values and Ethics: Individual, Corporate and International Perspectives*, Colin Fisher and Alan Lovell present a practical and quite typical ethical dilemma:

> "Would you pay a large commission to an intermediary to obtain his influence to secure a large overseas deal?"[6]

They then provide an instructive framework with which to apply the main ethical theories, and the core questions and tests they pose (see **Figure 3.2**). Using these approaches to the problem, please answer Yes or No to each question and then rank each question in order of its importance to you. This is designed to bring clarity to how you prioritise your guiding ethical principles.

## Figure 3.2: An Ethical Evaluation Framework

| School of Ethics | Principal Question/Test | Answer | Rank |
|---|---|---|---|
| Virtue | **Light-of-day Test**<br>Would I feel good or bad if others (friends, family and colleagues) learned of my action? | | |
| | **Virtuous Means Test**<br>Does my decision add to, or detract from, the creation of 'a good life' by finding a balance between justice, care and other virtues? | | |
| Consequentialist | **Consequential Test**<br>Are the anticipated consequences of my decision positive or negative? | | |
| | **Utilitarian Test**<br>Is my decision likely to have the best outcome for the greatest number of stakeholders? | | |
| Deontological | **Golden Rule**<br>If I took the place of the person affected by my decision, would I be happy with it? | | |
| | **Universality Test**<br>Would it be a good or bad thing if my decision were to become a universal principle applicable to all in similar situations? | | |
| Other Theories and Tests | **Communitarian Test**<br>Would my action help or hinder individuals and communities to develop ethically? | | |
| | **Self-interest Test**<br>Does the decision meet or defeat my own best interest and values? | | |

Some of these ethical theories, when explained in terms of the main issue they seek to address, will no doubt resonate with you more strongly than others. However, to a large extent, regardless of which ethical theory you subscribe to, the answer to the question as to whether you would pay the bribe is likely to be the same. Ethical theories provide a road map for the decision-making process, but none is wrong or right, or better or worse. Once you take the time to properly consider the consequences of a given decision, irrespective of the specific tests applied, you are much more likely to make a better, more ethical choice.

What is also interesting is that your moral reasoning process may change over time. This is confirmed by the work of developmental psychologist Laurence Kohlberg, who researched the development of children's capacity for ethical reasoning and subsequently applied that research to adults and organisations. In this context, his 'theory of cognitive development' holds that moral reasoning as the basis for ethical behaviour has six phases, which develop (or not) as we mature.[7] In other words, our sense of ethical values should evolve alongside our intellectual development. These stages, which are summarised nicely by Patricia Barker in her essay "An Integrity Model of Ethics", are reproduced in **Figure 3.3** below.

### FIGURE 3.3: KOHLBERG'S SIX STAGES OF COGNITIVE DEVELOPMENT[8]

| Stage | Description | In deciding whether some action is right or wrong, someone at this stage might say: |
|---|---|---|
| 1 | Obedience and punishment | I will do that because I won't be caught and punished |
| 2 | Self-interest | I will do that because there is something in it for me |
| 3 | Accord and conformity | I will do that because my gang would like it – I want to be liked and accepted |
| 4 | Maintenance of social order | I will do that because it is required by the law/rules, even though it would not necessarily be good for me |
| 5 | Social contract orientation | I will do that because even though the law says I should not/need not do it, I can achieve the greater good for the greater number by doing it |
| 6 | Universal ethical principles | I will do that because even though the law says I should not and the greater number may not benefit, it is simply just |

As part of his research, Kohlberg assessed the responses of his subject sample to a number of ethical dilemmas over the course of their development, from young boys to teenagers and into adulthood. The most famous of these dilemmas is the story of 'Heinz'[9]:

## THE DILEMMA OF HEINZ

Heinz's wife was dying from a particular type of cancer. Doctors said a new drug might save her. The drug had been discovered by a local pharmacist and Heinz tried desperately to buy some, but the pharmacist was charging 10 times the money it cost to make the drug and this was much more than Heinz could afford. Heinz could only raise half the money, even after help from family and friends. He explained to the pharmacist that his wife was dying and asked if he could have the drug cheaper or pay the rest of the money later. The pharmacist refused, saying that he had discovered the drug and was going to make money from it. The husband was desperate to save his wife, so later that night he broke into the chemist and stole the drug.

In assessing the respondents' answers, Kohlberg was less interested in whether they thought Heinz was right or wrong, than in the reasons they gave for the decision. He found that these changed over time, that people tended to pass through the stages of cognitive development in the sequence listed above, with each later stage replacing the reasoning of the stage preceding it. Curiously, he also noted that not everyone reached the final stage.

What is your own view? Should Heinz have broken into the lab to steal the drug for his wife? Reflect on the reasoning behind your decision and see if you can match your answer with the relevant stage in **Figure 3.3**. Now add this to your assessment of the ethical theory or theories to which you would gravitate for guidance, based on your ranking of their related tests in **Figure 3.2**. This provides an initial overview of your overall ethical philosophy, your form of moral reasoning and how you might go about applying these theories in practice.

From here, we can dig deeper, from the universal and general to the personal and specific, to excavate your own 'ethical garden' in order to sow the seeds for the development of the core competencies of ethical leadership.

## The Core Competencies of Ethical Leadership

As with the general topic of ethics, we will not attempt to cover all aspects of leadership. Rather, we are concerned with where business ethics and leadership meet, how ethical leadership can be developed and the degree to which it is innate.

The issue of whether a leader is born or can be 'made' has long been debated. Some argue that leadership is an inherent quality to those naturally possessing a combination of social intelligence and charisma that motivates others to work together. Others believe that leaders are made by developing their skills with practice, experience and mentoring. It seems that the latter group are more correct than the former. Research has found that leaders come by their talents partly through genetics but mostly acquire them through hard work. One study on 'heritability' (i.e. the innate skills you bring to the table) and human development (what you learn along the way) estimated that leadership is 24% genetic and 76% learned.[10] Whether inherent or acquired, the universal skills and attributes of an effective leader are outlined in **Figure 3.4** below:

FIGURE **3.4**: EFFECTIVE LEADERSHIP: THE FOUR QUADRANTS[11]

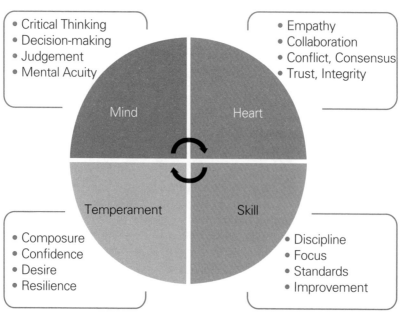

70

To make the right decisions, leaders must have good judgement, which involves marrying intellect with emotion, and possess the skills and disposition to motivate others to execute these choices. Therefore, it requires the combination of all four aspects of leadership: mind, heart, temperament and skill.

Leadership capacity evolves through developing particular 'learnable' mental abilities, such as critical thinking, decision-making and problem-solving. Skills such as discipline and focus can similarly be enhanced through practice and training. However, it is now also generally recognised that the softer, more elusive characteristics in the upper right-hand quadrant, if not naturally present in abundance, can also at least be enhanced. "Even elusive elements, such as empathy and the ability to collaborate, can be deepened though experience and self-awareness." We will be mainly concerned with these facets of leadership, and especially the heart, because from an ethics and governance perspective, the 'heart' is the source of our core values; it represents the emotional side of leadership, ruling how we relate to others; is the basis for our integrity and frames the quality that truly makes us unique and defines our genuine leadership style. The three competencies that are therefore at the 'heart' of leading with integrity are:
1. core values ('what drives me?');
2. emotional intelligence ('how do I relate to others?'); and
3. authenticity ('what makes me unique?').

We will examine each of these in turn and attempt to answer the questions posed above.

## 1. Core Values ('What Drives Me?')

*"He who knows the universe and does not know himself knows nothing."*
Jean de La Fontaine (17th-Century fabulist and poet)

Taking the time to think about and articulate your core values is a critical exercise in self-awareness and the first step on the journey to leading with integrity. Core values are the beliefs that you hold dear and the principles that guide your daily behaviours, forming the backbone for your choices. Understanding your values, beliefs, motivations and behavioural norms – being self-aware – is a prerequisite for being able to truly inspire, direct and manage others. Your core values are therefore the ignition to your ethical leadership.

*Why Should Anyone Be Led By YOU?* is the title of a well-known book on leadership by Rob Goffee and Gareth Jones.[12] It is a good question with which to start thinking about your leadership abilities (and, in the authors' experience, an effective question to ask if you want to

71

silence a room full of executives!). Answering it may require further soul-searching questions, such as:

- How would others describe your strengths and weaknesses?
- How would you describe your leadership style?
- What is your vision and legacy?

Or to distil the question further:

- What is your unique set of core values that inspires others to follow your vision?

Articulating your core values by writing them down is a powerful way to understand your principles and priorities. **Figure 3.5** below identifies some values that may resonate with you, with some blanks for additional values if your preferred choices are not represented. Choose the four or five values that are most important to you, including any you may have added.

## FIGURE 3.5: MY CORE VALUES

For each of your chosen values, think about what it means to you in real terms and consider some of your specific behaviours that exemplify this value in practice. This may take a little time, but it will help you to translate abstract, motivational ideals into a more meaningful, aspirational statement of personal conduct. As Chris Edmonds puts it in his book *The Culture Engine*:

"In the absence of clear [value] definitions, your head, heart and hands will work harder to figure out the right principles to model each day. With clear definitions, you move forward with clarity and confidence."[13]

Or, as Sir Adrian Cadbury has warned:

"This does not mean drawing up a list of virtuous notions, which will probably end up as a version of the Scriptures without their literary merit."[14]

In other words, while it may be relatively easy to identify lofty ideals to which you aspire, it requires a little more application and is much more productive to deliberately enunciate the behaviours required to ground those aspirations in reality, i.e. to translate words into actions.

You may find it helpful to use the 'SMART' system to make these behavioural goals more impactful, to see if you can describe them (although don't force it) in a way that is:

- S   specific

- M   measurable

- A   achievable

- R   realistic

- T   timely.[15]

The following is an example of how someone might choose a core value, in this case respect, how they might define what this value means for them and then outline four specific activities that will express the application of that value, as defined, in practice.

| Value | Definition | Action/Behaviour |
|-------|-----------|------------------|
| Respect | To have consideration for the feelings or wishes of others and be courteous in all dealings | 1. I treat **everyone** with dignity and sincerity<br>2. I genuinely acknowledge others' success<br>3. I follow through on my commitments<br>4. I am polite and appropriate, never rude or crude |

Now over to you. For each of the values you have identified as core to you in **Figure 3.5** above, provide a definition that best explains what that value means to you and then describe some explicit actions that you can or will undertake to demonstrate that principle in action in the workplace.

| Value | Definition | Action/Behaviour |
|-------|-----------|------------------|
| 1. | | |
| 2. | | |
| 3. | | |
| 4. | | |

You have taken the first step in articulating your own, personal code of conduct, which is an important step in the journey to integrity-based leadership as it sets out the principles that will guide your decisions and the behaviours you aspire to as an ethical leader.

**'MoralDNA™'\*** Testing your MoralDNA™ will also help facilitate an understanding of your overall moral make-up and the motivations in how you approach ethical issues. MoralDNA™ is a personality test that was co-designed by Professor Roger Steare of the Cass Business School and psychologist Pavlos Stamboulides. (It can be accessed using the following link: http://moraldna.org.)

---

\* MoralDNA™ is a trademark of Roger Steare Consulting Limited. Copyright © 2012 Roger Steare Consulting Limited. 'ETHICABILITY' is a UK Registered Trade Mark of Roger Steare Consulting Limited.

The profile it creates is designed "to help you understand your moral values, how you prefer to make good decisions and 'do the right thing'." With echoes of Kohlberg's work, it recognises that everyone may be at different stages of moral reasoning and may be 'wired' differently in terms of how they make decisions from an ethical standpoint. It describes three principal perspectives (which are further developed in Steare's book, *Ethicability*[16]):

• the ethic of obedience ('law');
• the ethic of care ('love'); and
• the ethic of reason ('reason').

People who are governed by the **ethic of obedience** make moral decisions by obeying or disobeying instructions and predicting likely consequences in terms of discovery, reward or punishment, i.e. it is a simplistic, almost childlike approach to following the rules (akin to Stage 1 in Kohlberg's moral development). Others may be guided more by the **ethic of care**, based on their experience that well-being for the individual and the group will result from decisions based on empathy, which is a more considered, nurturing approach. Finally, the **ethic of reason** applies to those individuals whose decisions are based on critical reasoning following moral principles that lead them to make the right choice because it is the wise, fair or moderate thing to do, rather than because it may have been legislated so.

The drivers of these ethical preferences, according to Steare, are the 10 values listed in **Figure 3.6** below (some of which you may have included in your core values).

### FIGURE 3.6: STEARE'S 10 VALUES

| | |
|---|---|
| **Wisdom** | I think through my decisions carefully |
| Fairness | I treat others fairly and with respect |
| **Courage** | I stand up for my beliefs and do what's right |
| Self-control | I am patient and self-disciplined |
| **Trust** | I encourage others to be positive |
| Hope | I treat others fairly and with respect |
| **Humility** | I am less important than the team |
| Love | I am empathetic and care about other people |
| **Honesty** | I speak the truth and encourage others to be open |
| Excellence | I try to do my best in everything I do |

The MoralDNA™ survey and profiling tool determines your preferred perspective (obedience, care or reason) when making ethical decisions and what values you consider when making those decisions and then determines which 'character' type you are, from the six types presented and briefly described in **Figure 3.7** below.

## FIGURE 3.7: MORALDNA™ CHARACTER TYPES

| Philosophers | Teachers |
|---|---|
| • good at solving complex dilemmas but will break the rules if they believe a higher principle is at stake, though may lack empathy<br>• they ask: "What would be the honest or courageous thing to do?" | • also caring people on whom you can rely to do what is right in the interests of humanity<br>• but may fail to consider moral principles and break the rules if they think they know best |

| Judges | Enforcers |
|---|---|
| • are also good at making those tough calls, though may lack empathy in taking those decisions<br>• they ask: "What would be the fair thing to do?" | • remind everyone about their duty to obey the law<br>• sometimes they can lack empathy and forget the principle or spirit behind the rule |

| Angels | Guardians |
|---|---|
| • are lovely people and great to have as friends, caring deeply about other people<br>• they ask: "What would build trust and respect?" | • protect us and tell us off for our own sake, believing we should all do as we are told<br>• they can also fail to consider principles such as freedom and trust and may lack empathy |

By taking the test you will be able to better understand how you make decisions through an ethical lens and the potential biases that may influence those decisions. Holding this mirror up to your ethical leadership style, you will also be able to appreciate some of the strengths or the challenges your character type may present in leading others in an ethical direction. You can document these conclusions below.

| | |
|---|---|
| **My MoralDNA™ character profile is:** (Philosopher, Judge, Angel, Teacher, Enforcer or Guardian) | |
| **I make decisions based on the ethic of (obedience, care or reason):** | |
| **How does this impact my leadership style for the better?** | |
| **What challenges does it present?** | |

Steare's own recommendations for leaders, having reviewed over 100,000 such profiles, include the following[17]:

| | |
|---|---|
| **Care more** | Understand how you make decisions and your ethical preferences. Do you listen to others? |
| **Stand up for your beliefs** | Be authentic. Speak up when you don't like what you see |
| **Be a leader** | Provide values-based leadership. People will follow you because of your character, not your job title |
| **Be inclusive** | Be open to challenge, dissent and diversity of thought |

Overall, the MoralDNA™ profiling tool and related research highlights the need for leaders to be more in tune with their own moral compass before they can expect to lead others on a path of shared objectives based on trust and integrity.

## 2. Emotional Intelligence ('How do I Relate to Others?')

Have you ever wondered why two people with more or less the same education and college scores (as a crude measure of IQ) can go on to have such different levels of success in their careers? Is there another set of factors at play, beyond pure luck? The concept of Emotional Intelligence (or 'EQ') was developed by Peter Salovey and John Mayer, who defined it as:

> "Emotional intelligence involves the ability to perceive accurately, appraise and express emotion; the ability to access and/or generate feelings when they facilitate thought; the ability to understand emotion and emotional knowledge and the ability to regulate emotions to promote emotional and intellectual growth."[18]

In his acclaimed book on the subject, Daniel Goleman defines EQ "as an array of skills and characteristics that drive leadership performance".[19] In a subsequent publication, he indicates that EQ accounts for 67% of the abilities deemed necessary for superior performance in leaders and matters twice as much as technical expertise, or IQ.[20] The five components behind EQ at work can be modelled as follows (from Goleman):

## FIGURE 3.8: PRINCIPAL COMPONENTS OF EMOTIONAL INTELLIGENCE

| | Definition | Hallmarks |
|---|---|---|
| **Self-Awareness** | The ability to recognise and understand your moods, emotions and drives, as well as their effect on others | • Self-confidence<br>• Realistic self-assessment<br>• Self-deprecating sense of humour |
| **Self-Regulation** | The ability to control or redirect disruptive impulses and moods<br><br>The propensity to suspend judgement – to think before acting | • Trustworthiness and integrity<br>• Comfort with ambiguity<br>• Openness to change |
| **Motivation** | A passion to work for reasons that go beyond money or status<br><br>A propensity to pursue goals with energy and persistence | • Strong drive to achieve<br>• Optimism, even in the face of adversity<br>• Organisational commitment |
| **Empathy** | The ability to understand the emotional make-up of other people<br><br>Skill in treating people according to their emotional reactions | • Expertise in building and retaining talent<br>• Cross-cultural sensitivity<br>• Service to clients/customers |
| **Social Skill** | Proficiency in managing relationships and building networks<br><br>An ability to find common ground and build rapport | • Effectiveness in leading change<br>• Persuasiveness<br>• Expertise in building and leading teams |

Developing EQ all starts with self-awareness and then goes further in practising the management of one's emotions. Once we are more aware of our thoughts and feelings and have acquired a degree of self-control, we can progress to developing an awareness of the emotions of and empathy for the feelings of others. The final step is to adapt our behaviours accordingly. Underlying all of this is the motivation to achieve, with a natural optimism and a commitment to the success of the organisation. The goal of developing EQ is a dramatic improvement in relationships and interpersonal effectiveness.

Daire Coffey and Deirdre Murray, authors of *EQ: A Leadership Imperative*, outline the 'TACT' approach, which provides four easy steps to mastering EQ, as follows:

FIGURE 3.9: THE 'TACT' APPROACH TO DEVELOPING EMOTIONAL INTELLIGENCE[21]

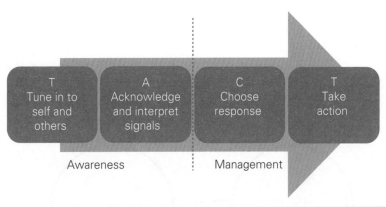

| Step 1 | Become an observer. What subtle information are you picking up about yourself and others, i.e. feelings, moods or body language? |
|--------|--------|
| Step 2 | Having interpreted those signals, choose when and how to respond appropriately. |
| Step 3 | What are these signals telling you? Is there a significant message behind them? |
| Step 4 | Follow through at the right time in the right way or, as Goleman puts it, "Choose the right club for each shot." |

In terms of leadership capabilities, EQ is now widely acknowledged as one of the key factors separating great leaders from those of middling ability. It is perhaps an even greater predictor of true *ethical* leadership ability. James Kouzes and Barry Posner, in their book *The Leadership*

*Challenge*,[22] point to five practices that great leaders demonstrate in "achieving extraordinary things through ordinary people". These are as shown in **Figure 3.10**:

**FIGURE 3.10: THE FIVE PRACTICES OF AN EMOTIONALLY INTELLIGENT LEADER**

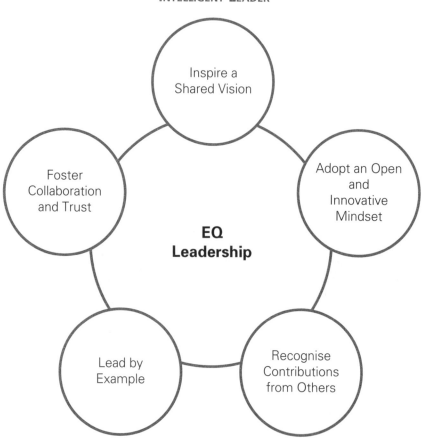

You can see just how critical these practices are in the context of setting tone at the top. Indeed, according to a worldwide survey conducted by the consulting group Gallup, the number one reason why people stay in an organisation is because of their immediate boss.[23] Unfortunately, it is also the number one reason why they leave. In other words: 'People join organisations but leave managers.'

It begs the question: would anyone would leave your organisation because of you, or the corollary, do they stay because of you? We said earlier that we would examine two tools to help our understanding of our ethical leadership make-up. We have already explored our MoralDNA™. Now let's take a more forensic look at our EQ score using the Emotional Capital Report™ designed by Martin Newman[24] and adapted in the following table, with definitions for each competence provided below. For each EQ competence, as defined, place your mark as honestly as you can on a range from a 'Development Opportunity', where you know you have work to do, to the other end of the spectrum, 'Signature Strength', where you are comfortable that you possess the competence in abundance.

| EQ Competence | Development Opportunity | Reasonable Competency | Strength to Build On | Signature Strength |
|---|---|---|---|---|
| Self-awareness | | | | |
| Self-confidence | | | | |
| Self-reliance | | | | |
| Self-actualisation | | | | |
| Straight-forwardness | | | | |
| Relationships | | | | |
| Empathy | | | | |
| Self-control | | | | |
| Adaptability | | | | |
| Optimism | | | | |

81

| Self-awareness | Being in tune with your feelings and emotions and how they impact your opinions and actions |
|---|---|
| Self-confidence | Accepting and respecting yourself and being confident in your abilities |
| Self-reliance | Being independent and taking responsibility for your choices and actions |
| Self-actualisation | Being challenged and committed to achieving your full potential |
| Straight-forwardness | Comfortable giving clear messages and challenging the views of others |
| Relationships | Able to establish and maintain mutually satisfying relationships |
| Empathy | Understanding and taking account of other people's emotions |
| Self-control | Managing emotions well and staying calm in stressful situations |
| Adaptability | Being open and responsive to changing circumstances |
| Optimism | Sensing opportunities even in the face of adversity |

Please note that this exercise can only provide a high-level overview of an ECR™, which is generally undertaken together with a coach or occupational psychologist and is much more comprehensive in terms of input and feedback. Nonetheless, hopefully this overview has given you a basic insight into your EQ.

The 'Johari Window' is another lens through which you can develop your self-awareness and is a tool that you may find particularly useful in the area of interpersonal skills. Developed by Joseph Luft and Harry Ingham in 1955,[25] this classic communications model is often used to help leaders in team situations to:
(a) build trust by becoming more comfortable disclosing personal information about themselves to others; and
(b) with the help of feedback from those others, learn more about themselves and adapt their communication style, if necessary.

As shown in **Figure 3.11** below, the Johari Window is a four-quadrant grid:

FIGURE **3.11**: THE JOHARI WINDOW[26]

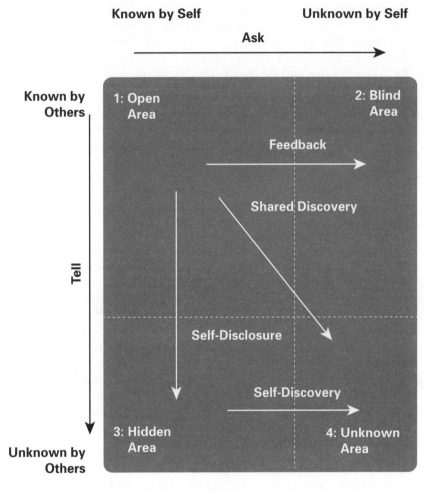

The quadrants can be described as follows:

- **Quadrant 1: Open Area** This represents what you know about your-self and what is also known to others, e.g. your behaviour, competencies, skills and 'public' history.
- **Quadrant 2: Blind Area** This is what others know about you, but of which you are unaware. It can include, for example, some deep-routed or buried insecurities which may be difficult to face but which are often apparent to others, or may simply represent self-ignorance or self-delusion, i.e. classic personal 'blind spots'.

- **Quadrant 3: Hidden Area** This is the opposite, i.e. what you know about yourself but keep hidden from others. It may include, for example, some sensitivities, personal fears, ambitions or secrets, which are kept personal and not picked up by others.
- **Quadrant 4: Unknown Area** The things that nobody knows about you, including yourself, and may include, for example, abilities or aptitudes that are underestimated or untried through lack of opportunity, confidence or encouragement, repressed or subconscious behaviours often carried over from childhood, and so on.

The overall goal for the leader is to maximise the Open Area and minimise the space in the other three quadrants by means of a two-way process involving appropriate self-disclosure and self-discovery, and by being more open to feedback. A fully occupied Open Area is deemed the healthiest state, occupied by those who are open, easy to talk to and who listen well. It is particularly conducive to good team dynamics where generally the more people know about each other, the more they will trust one another and therefore work together more collaboratively and effectively.

Take a moment to consider how, without over-sharing, you could be a little more open with your team, in terms of your thoughts, feelings and experiences and how, in turn, without seeming nosy, you might elicit similar information from them and so create a reciprocal dialogue based on trust and transparency. You might also consider why you don't share certain aspects of yourself with others, and if the reasons are due to, for example, low self-esteem or other such negative insecurities, think about how you could overcome these insecurities. Finally, the fun part involves entering into the unknown Quadrant 4 and uncovering hidden talents, which is about taking the opportunity to try new things without putting yourself under any great pressure to succeed.

## 3. Authenticity ('What Makes me Unique?')

*"Authentic leaders know the true north of their moral compass and are prepared to stay the course despite challenges and disappointments."*

Bill George[27]

The natural follow-on from self-awareness and a developed emotional intelligence, and our third and final core competency for ethical leadership, is the quality of authenticity. Dr Gareth Jones, co-author *Why Should Anyone Be Led by YOU?* (see above), together with Robert Goffee, both leading writers on authentic leadership, identifies four characteristics of inspirational, authentic leaders, which are outlined below.[28]

FIGURE 3.12: THE FOUR CHARACTERISTICS OF AUTHENTIC LEADERS

Let's explore these characteristics by way of examples.

**Rely on Your Intuition** For a lesson in intuition and, specifically, how to and how not to gauge the appropriate response in a given situation, compare the reactions of two high-profile CEOs following crises of tsunami-like proportions at each of their corporations.

(Former) CEO of BP, Tony Hayward, in the immediate aftermath of the Deepwater Horizon oil spill in 2010, the largest in US history, which claimed the lives of 11 crew members and released

5 million barrels of oil into the Gulf of Mexico, coating hundreds of miles of shoreline with oil, told a reporter: "There is no one that wants this thing over more than I do. I'd like my life back."

He later watched his yacht race off the Isle of Wight while gushing oil destroyed the livelihoods of Gulf residents and wildlife on the Florida coastline.[29] (In late 2015, the company agreed a final settlement with the US authorities for $20.8 billion and is potentially facing another huge compensation bill following the filing of a class action suit in Mexico for the damage caused by the catastrophe).[30]

Mary Barra, CEO of General Motors, on the recall in 2014 of millions of GM cars due to a faulty ignition switch issue that was linked to nearly 400 injuries and deaths: "I am deeply sorry."[31]

As published on GM's website, Barra has also stated at a "Global Town Hall Meeting":

> "I want everyone to know that I am guided by two clear principles: First, that we do the right thing for those who were harmed; and, second, that we accept responsibility for our mistakes and commit to doing everything within our power to prevent this problem from ever happening again."[32]

She then went on to meet families of the deceased, ensured claims were settled quickly and went about thoroughly overhauling the culture and management practices at GM.

Credible leaders must be able to rely on their instincts to gauge how to appropriately react to situations, whether of crisis proportions or in the normal round of daily interactions. In fairness to Tony Hayward, he may have been at his most authentic when uttering those infamous words, which shows that he was simply in the wrong job in the first place.

Show Your Humanity and Humility  As well as being able to intuitively read a situation correctly, we expect our leaders to have a clear vision, strong convictions and an ability to articulate strategy in a compelling way. We look to them as a source of power and authority. Yet, as demonstrated by Barra's genuine apology above, is there anything more powerful than a leader who is unafraid to show a little humility and vulnerability? In her TedTalk on "The power of vulnerability", author Brené Brown talks about the importance of this very human characteristic and concludes that it can be your biggest strength, facilitating coalitions at a very basic and profoundly emotional level.[33] This degree of connection often eludes the leaders of organisations, who may be either bound by more traditional communication hierarchies and/or feel entirely uncomfortable in revealing a chink in their armour to expose an element of human frailty.

The idea of what might be perceived as weakness being in reality a core strength is also developed by leadership guru Jim Collins in his *Harvard Business Review* article "Level 5 Leadership",[34] in which he describes a hierarchy of leadership skills from 1 to 5, with the Level 5 leader being at the very pinnacle and characterised by "the paradoxical combination of deep personal humility with intense professional will".

Henna Inam, in *Wired for Authenticity*,[35] gives the example of Indra Nooyi, CEO of PepsiCo, who, on receiving the news of her appointment to the top job, immediately got on a plane to visit her main competitor for the role and convince him to stay with the company, telling him that she needed him and that the company would be better with him on board. In so doing, she was effectively admitting that she did not have all the answers and needed his talent and support, setting aside her personal pride and appealing to him to do likewise in the interests of a shared ambition. Such humility requires courage and strength of character.

Practice Tough Empathy Humility and vulnerability in leaders are only effective when they are necessary and genuine. Overdoing it is unbecoming, while 'faking it' is easy to spot and does more damage than good. Show people that you care, but in a way that is natural to you and appropriate to the situation, and be as firm as circumstances require. Referring to this as 'tough empathy', or 'giving people what they need, not what they want', Jones and Goffee say:

> "Real leaders don't need a training programme to convince their employees that they care. Real leaders empathise fiercely with the people they lead ... and care intensely about the work [they] do ... Tough empathy balances respect for the individual with the task at hand."[36]

It is about being compassionate yet challenging, supportive yet strict, and approachable yet ambitious. It is not about apologising for expecting the best or sugar-coating messages but caring deeply, albeit from a little distance, to maintain some necessary detachment for when tough decisions need to be made. Another way of looking at it is being pleasant with the person, but tough on the task.

**Celebrate Diversity** Leaders who are brave enough to show a little humility and are naturally empathetic are usually also welcoming of the honest opinions of others and amenable to a diversity of views. In their article "Great Leaders who Make the Mix Work", Boris Groysberg and Katherine Connolly acknowledge that the source of a leader's commitment to diversity is often their own personal experience.[37] They provide the example of former CEO of Avon, Andrea Jung, who in describing her career, comments:

> "I was often the only woman or Asian sitting around a table of senior executives. I experienced plenty of meetings outside my organization with large groups of executives where people assumed that I couldn't be the boss."

Mastercard's CEO, Ajay Banga – a Sikh from India – shared a similar story:

> "My passion for diversity comes from the fact that I myself am diverse. There have been a hundred times when I have felt different from other people in the room or in the business. I have a turban and a full beard, and I run a global company—that's not common."

However, you do not have to be 'different' to either appreciate difference or value uniqueness. Based on their research, Bill George *et al.* give the following pointers in "Discovering Your Authentic Leadership"[38]:

- The journey begins with leaders understanding their life stories. They make time to examine their experiences and to reflect on them, and in doing so grow as individuals and as leaders.
- Authentic leaders also work hard at developing self-awareness through persistent and often courageous self-exploration. Denial can be the greatest hurdle in becoming self-aware, but authentic leaders ask for, and listen to, honest feedback.
- They also use formal and informal support networks to help them stay grounded and lead integrated lives.

The authors also provide a series of questions to stimulate reflection on one's leadership journey to date and the path to follow in order to become a more authentic leader. These questions are set out below.

| |
|---|
| 1. Which people and experiences in your early life had the greatest impact on you? |
| 2. What tools do you use to become self-aware? What is your authentic self? What are the moments when you say to yourself, this is the real me? |
| 3. What are your most deeply held values? Where did they come from? How have your values changed significantly since your childhood? How do your values inform your actions? |
| 4. What motivates you extrinsically? What are your intrinsic motivations? How do you balance extrinsic and intrinsic motivation in your life? |
| 5. What kind of support team do you have? How can your support team make you a more authentic leader? How should you diversify your team to broaden your perspective? |
| 6. Is your life integrated? Are you able to be the same person in all aspects of your life – personal, work, family and community? If not, what is holding you back? |
| 7. What does being authentic mean in your life? Are you more effective as a leader when you behave authentically? Have you ever paid a price for your authenticity as a leader? Was it worth it? |
| 8. What steps can you take today, tomorrow and over the next year to develop your authentic leadership? |

By taking some time to think about these questions and writing down your answers, you can begin building a framework for identifying your authentic self.

Let's now round out this analysis and bring together some of the common strands of self-awareness and authenticity.

## Why Should Anyone be Led by You?

In analysing ethical leadership competencies, such as self-awareness and authenticity, our focus in this chapter has been primarily on *you* and what *you* think of you; but what about '*them*' – what do *they* think of you? For a more complete view, ask others for some warts-and-all perspectives. You might like to include your family (who are likely to be the most honest), your peers, your boss and any mentors, who should also give you some direct feedback, and your team, who may be more circumspect. You can complete the chart below based on their feedback.

### HOW WOULD OTHERS DESCRIBE YOUR STRENGTHS AND WEAKNESSES?

| Strengths | Weaknesses |
|---|---|
|  |  |
|  |  |
|  |  |
|  |  |
|  |  |
|  |  |
|  |  |

Reflect on all the approaches and tools we have discussed in this chapter: your preferred approach to ethics; Kohlberg's cognitive development score; your core values and related behaviours; your MoralDNA™ profile and ethical decision-making process; your general level of EQ; communication preferences; and degree of authenticity. Now describe your leadership style:

## MY LEADERSHIP STYLE

Finally, what is your vision? How you would like to be remembered by those who came on the journey with you – what is your desired legacy? You might like to make the distinction here between what David Brooks, author of *The Road to Character* refers to as your 'resumé virtues' and your 'eulogy virtues', the former being those you bring to the job market and contribute to extrinsic success, the latter going much deeper, to the core of who you are, and that will be discussed at your funeral – "whether you are kind, brave, honest or faithful; what kind of relationships you formed".[39]

## MY VISION AND DESIRED LEGACY

## References to Chapter 3

[1] Adapted from Petrick, Joseph A. and Quinn, John F., *Management Ethics: Integrity at Work* (Sage Publications, 1997).

[2] See Fisher, Colin and Lovell, Alan, *Business Values and Ethics: Individual, Corporate and International Perspectives* (FT Prentice Hall, 2006).

[3] Gilligan, Carol, *In a Different Voice: Psychological Theory and Women's Development* (Harvard University Press, 1982).

[4] Covey, Stephen R., *The Seven Habits of Highly Effective People: Powerful Lessons in Personal Change* (DC Books, 2005).

[5] See https://www.aynrand.org (accessed February 2016).

[6] Adapted from Fisher, Colin and Lovell, Alan, *Business Values and Ethics: Individual, Corporate and International Perspectives* (FT Prentice Hall, 2006).

[7] Kohlberg, Lawrence T., "Moral Stages and Moralization: The Cognitive-development Approach" in Lickona, T. (ed.), *Moral Development and Behaviour: Theory, Research and Social Issues* (Holt, NY: Rinehart and Winston, 1976).

[8] Barker, Patricia, "An Integrity Model of Ethics" in *The Business Compass: Perspectives on Business Ethics* (Chartered Accountants Ireland, 2012), p. 39.

[9] See http://www.simplypsychology.org/kohlberg.html

[10] De Neve, Jan-Emmanuel, Mikhaylov, Slava, Dawes, Christopher T., Christakis, Nicholas A. and Fowler, James H., "Born to lead? A twin design and genetic association study of leadership role occupancy" (2013) *The Leadership Quarterly*, Vol. 24, Issue 1, 44–60.

[11] From Duff, Dermot, *Managing Professionals and Other Smart People* (Chartered Accountants Ireland, 2014).

[12] Goffee, Rob and Jones, Gareth, *Why Should Anyone Be Led by YOU?* (Harvard Business Review Press, 2006).

[13] Edmonds, Chris, *The Culture Engine: A Framework for Driving Results, Inspiring Your Employees, and Transforming Your Workplace* (Wiley, 2012), p. 49.

[14] Cadbury, Sir Adrian, "Ethical Managers Make Their Own Rules", an essay included in Andrews, Kenneth R. (ed.), *Ethics in Practice: Managing the Moral Corporation* (Harvard Business School Press, 1989).

[15] Doran, G.T., "There's a S.M.A.R.T. way to write management's goals and objectives" (1981) *Management Review* (AMA FORUM) Vol. 70, No. 11: 35–36.

[16] Steare, Roger, *Ethicability* (Roger Steare Consulting Ltd, 2013).

[17] Steare, Roger, *Managers and their MoralDNA: Better Values, Better Business* (Chartered Management Institute, 2014).

18  Mayer, John and Salovey, Peter, "What is Emotional Intelligence?" in Salovey, Peter and Sluyter, David (eds.), *Emotional Development and Emotional Intelligence: Educational Implications* (Basic Books, 1997) pp. 10–11.

19  Goleman, Daniel, *Emotional Intelligence* (Bantam Books, 1995).

20  Goleman, Daniel, *Working with Emotional Intelligence* (Bantam Books, 1998).

21  Coffey, Daire and Murray, Deirdre, *Emotional Intelligence (EQ) A Leadership Imperative* (Management Briefs, 2010).

22  Kouzes, James and Posner, Barry, *The Leadership Challenge* (Jossey-Bass, 2007).

23  Buckingham, Marcus and Coffman, Curt, *First, Break All The Rules: What the World's Greatest Managers Do Differently* (Gallup Press, 2000).

24  Newman, Martin, *Emotional Capitalists: the New Leaders* (Wiley, 2007).

25  Luft, J. and Ingham, H., "The Johari window, a graphic model of interpersonal awareness", *Proceedings of the western training laboratory in group development* (University of California, Los Angeles, 1955).

26  "The Johari Window: Using Self-discovery and Communication to Build Trust", Mindtools.com. Available at https://www.mindtools.com/CommSkll/JohariWindow.htm (accessed March 2016).

27  George, Bill, *Authentic Leadership: Rediscovering the Secrets to Creating Lasting Value* (Jossey-Bass, San Francisco, 2003).

28  Goffee, Robert and Jones, Gareth, "Why Should Anyone be Led by You?", an essay included in *HBR's 10 Must Reads: On Leadership* (Harvard Business Review Press, 2011).

29  Robbins, Liz, "BP Chief Draws Outrage for Attending Yacht Race", *New York Times*, 19 June 2010. Available at http://www.nytimes.com/2010/06/20/us/20spill.html?_r=0 (accessed January 2016).

30  Lakhani, Nina, "BP faces Mexican class action law suit over Deepwater Horizon oil spill", *The Guardian*, 11 December 2015.

31  Dye, Jessica, "General Motors to face trial over recalled ignition switch", www.reuters.com, 11 January 2016. Available at http://www.reuters.com/article/us-gm-recall-trial-preview-idUSKCN0UP0G620160111; Isadore, Chris and Lobosco, Katie, "GM CEO De Barra: I am Deeply Sorry", *CNN Money*, 1 April 2014. Available at http://money.cnn.com/2014/04/01/news/companies/barra-congress-testimony/ (accessed January 2016).

32  "GM CEO Mary Barra's Remarks to Employees on Valukas Report Findings". Available at http://media.gm.com/media/us/en/gm/news.detail.html/content/Pages/news/us/en/2014/Jun/060514-mary-remarks.html (accessed January 2016).

[33] Brown, Brené, "The power of vulnerability", TedTalks, filmed June 2010. Available at https://www.ted.com/talks/brene_brown_on_vulnerability?language=en (accessed January 2016, at which point it had over 23 million views).

[34] Collins, Jim, "Level 5 Leadership: The Triumph of Humility and Fierce Resolve" in *HBR's 10 Must Reads: On Leadership* (Harvard Business Review Press, 2011).

[35] Inam, Henna, *Wired for Authenticity: Seven Practices to Inspire, Adapt & Lead* (iUniverse, 2015).

[36] Goffee, Robert and Jones, Gareth, "Why Should Anyone be Led by You?" in *HBR's 10 Must Reads: On Leadership* (Harvard Business Review Press, 2011).

[37] Groysberg, Boris and Connolly, Katherine, "Great Leaders Who Make the Mix Work" (2013 September) *Harvard Business Review*.

[38] George, Bill, Sims, Peter, McLean, Andrew N. and Mayer, Diana, "Discovering Your Authentic Leadership" in *HBR's 10 Must Reads: On Leadership* (Harvard Business Review Press, 2011).

[39] Brooks, David, *The Road to Character* (Random House, 2015).

# II
# Building the Ethical Organisation

# 4

# Creating an Ethics and Compliance Framework

*"The loftier the building, the deeper must the foundation be laid."*

**Thomas à Kempis**

- Introduction
- Understanding and Changing Culture
- Building the Framework:
  1. Assess Risk
  2. Plan
  3. Act
  4. Monitor
  5. Evaluate

## Introduction

In the previous chapter we explored how authentic, emotionally intelligent leadership is essential if a culture of integrity is to flourish in an organisation.

Essential, but not enough.

In addition to a genuinely ethical 'tone at the top', an enterprise needs policies, procedures and programmes to facilitate the expression of primary core values into established patterns of behaviour and to support ethical decision-making at all levels. This chapter describes these systematic elements of organisational culture and prescribes the strategic building blocks necessary for establishing that ethical framework. The objective is not to create bureaucracy, but to provide principles-based references, resources and tools to help forge compliance with core values and steer the enterprise 'due north'. As always, the emphasis is on the practical, so you should be able to adapt this framework, in whole or in part, and apply it directly as your circumstances or those of your organisation require.

## Understanding and Changing Culture

As a concept, organisational culture is one to which 'the elephant test' readily applies, being something that is hard to describe yet immediately recognisable. Organisational culture was probably best captured by management consultants McKinsey & Company with their phrase "it's the way we do things around here". Culture is not, therefore, something that can be entirely encapsulated in a code of conduct or an employee handbook as it represents those subtle patterns and behavioural norms peculiar to every organisation. The South Sea islanders have a word, *'mokita'*, which translates as "a truth everyone knows but nobody speaks". So it is with culture. It is a subtle but powerful set of informal rules of behaviour, absorbed over time by employees, taking their cue from the actions and words of their leaders and informed by the in-built power and control structures of the organisation.

To build our understanding of this elusive concept, we will look at three different models of cultural analysis, their similarities, their differences and their practicality when trying to effect cultural change.

Edgar Schein defines culture as the product of three distinct levels of an organisation's development[1]:
1. the visible "artefacts" or characteristics of the organisation, including dress code, work climate and organisational structures;
2. its stated values, standards and rules of conduct; and
3. the underlying assumptions and values of staff based on their perceptions of and experiences of working within the organisation.

Schein suggests that to really understand an organisation's culture, you need to 'get under the bonnet' and assess its history, its values and the impact of the daily interplay of informal and formal organisational systems.

Geert Hofstede, another renowned thinker in this field, builds on the idea of organisational culture as the culmination of layers of experience and shared assumptions. His 'onion' model of culture is presented in **Figure 4.1** below.

### FIGURE 4.1: HOFSTEDE'S ONION MODEL OF ORGANISATIONAL CULTURE[2]

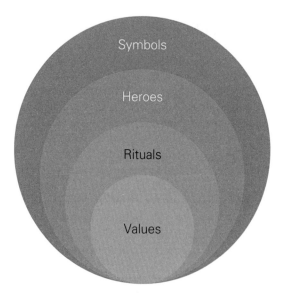

An organisation's 'values' are at the core of the 'onion' as they represent how people believe things 'should be' according to the beliefs they hold dear; 'rituals' are those collective activities that are deemed socially important (e.g. eating lunch together or not, whether birthdays are celebrated); 'heroes' are the role models in the organisation who possess characteristics that are highly prized and therefore tend to do well (although perhaps not in every organisation); and an organisation's 'symbols' are the most overt element of its culture and include the gestures, words or actions that are part of the group's 'vernacular', e.g. the dress code, preferred marques of company car, the manner of greeting (formal or informal), and so forth.

If you imagine the whole onion as a company's culture, by peeling away each layer the organisation reveals the distinct features that influence the 'way things are done around here'. The more you peel away and the closer you get to the centre of the onion, the more ingrained those elements become. Hofstede placed values at the very core because he believed these may be so deeply held by members of the organisation as to be close to impossible to change.

Johnson and Scholes's 'cultural web' is another interesting and instructive perspective and is reproduced below in **Figure 4.2**.

#### FIGURE 4.2: JOHNSON & SCHOLES'S CULTURAL WEB[3]

'The paradigm' in this model is the pattern of work behaviour in an organisation, its 'culture'. The interrelated elements around it can be summarised as follows:
- **Routines:** the unwritten ground rules as to how things are done.
- **Stories:** anecdotes and stories about the organisation, its history and people who reinforce the traditions, models and beliefs.

- **Symbols:** logos, language, etc., representing particular elements of the culture.
- **Power structures:** formal or informal power and influence, operating through resources, position, history, knowledge.
- **Organisational structure:** formal and informal roles, responsibilities and relationships.
- **Controls:** organisational measures and rewards that reinforce certain activities and behaviours.

These elements are not so different from those in the Schein and Hofstede models. The real power with this tool is in its application to align culture with strategy by following the steps outlined below and as demonstrated by the example that follows.

1. Assess the current culture by analysing each element in the 'cultural web' and articulating their dominant factors, i.e. draw the 'as is' diagram.
2. Define the ideal culture you want to see, i.e. the 'will be' diagram.
3. Map the differences between the two.
4. Prioritise required changes and develop a strategy to address the differences.

The following example of culture web analysis in practice is based on Gerry Johnson's "Mapping and Re-Mapping Organisational Culture: A Local Government Example".[4] It describes a facilitated cultural web mapping exercise carried out by the surveying department of a local government, based on the management team's perception of existing and ideal culture. In effect, **Figures 4.3** and **4.4** below are 'before' and 'after' shots.

## FIGURE 4.3: CULTURAL WEB ANALYSIS:
## LOCAL GOVERNMENT SURVEYING DEPARTMENT – EXISTING CULTURE

## FIGURE 4.4: CULTURAL WEB ANALYSIS:
## LOCAL GOVERNMENT SURVEYING DEPARTMENT – IDEAL CULTURE

The mapping exercise involved in cultural web analysis is particularly powerful when the management team required to transform the organisation from the 'as is' to the 'ideal' is included in the process. Such leaders can contribute to the vision for change, recognise potential barriers to that transformation and, critically, identify the subtle levers and mechanisms to make it happen for the benefit of all involved.

Further developing the theme of interconnectivity and culture, McKinsey's '7-S' model provides a helpful framework for mapping the interrelated factors that must all work in harmony in order to effect organisational change and address cultural alignment.[5]

## FIGURE 4.5: THE MCKINSEY '7-S' MODEL

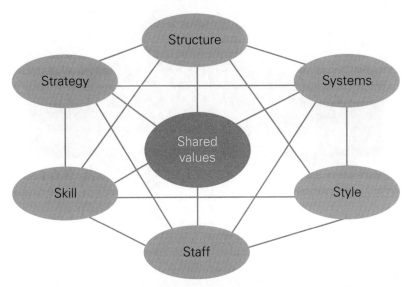

Again, the model places 'shared values' firmly at its nucleus, emphasising how central values are to the development of all the other elements and demonstrating that any change to these values will impact on all of the other inter-dependent elements, including 'harder' elements such as structure, systems and strategy. It is based on the theory that organisations work optimally when these seven elements are fully aligned and mutually reinforcing and is useful in identifying what needs to be changed, maintained or realigned in order to improve performance. Its principal value is in highlighting the interrelatedness of these organisational influences and in ensuring that the assessment of any change is broad and appreciation of its impact complete.

Summarising the above, we can say that culture is a powerful force in organisations, impacting widely on everyday operations. Its potency must be fully appreciated when considering change, particularly when a fundamental shift in culture is needed in order to raise the bar of ethical standards and a new compliance framework is contemplated. This requires careful planning, design and execution. We will now focus on the fundamental building blocks of an 'Ethics and Compliance Framework'.

## Building the Framework

### FIGURE 4.6: BUILDING BLOCKS OF AN ETHICS AND COMPLIANCE FRAMEWORK

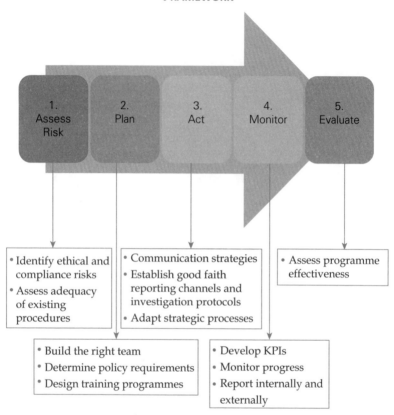

Let's examine each of these individual building blocks in more detail.

## 1. Assess Risk

> *"It's impossible that the improbable will never happen."*
> Emil Gumbel (in *Statistics of Extremes,* 1958)

The first step in building a coherent ethics and compliance framework is to identify the compliance risks to which the organisation is exposed. These may be defined as the threat posed to an organisation's financial or reputational standing resulting from a violation of laws, regulations, codes of conduct or organisational standards of practice.

In order to properly understand potential exposure to such threats and then mitigate against them, a comprehensive risk assessment should

106

be undertaken, reflecting a 'letter and spirit' approach. At minimum, all laws and regulations with which the organisation must comply are identified and reviewed, but additionally, codes of conduct and policies and, more importantly, core values and guiding principles should also be evaluated to assess the organisation's overall ethical and reputational well-being and any credible threats thereto.

As reproduced in **Figure 4.7** below, Deloitte in the US has developed a useful framework to outline the categories of risks to which an organisation may be exposed, as well as key elements of mitigation and management strategies to deal with those risks.

FIGURE **4.7**: ENTERPRISE ETHICS AND COMPLIANCE PROGRAMME AND RISK EXPOSURE FRAMEWORK – AN ILLUSTRATIVE EXAMPLE[6]

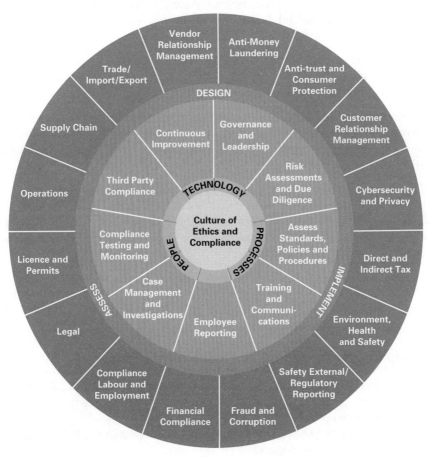

The outer ring represents the full range of compliance risks to which a business is potentially exposed, with the inner rings highlighting the principal aspects of the organisation's strategy to address these risks, including the various tools and resources it can employ to help ensure compliance and foster a culture of integrity.

Accurate initial identification of this risk landscape requires input from a wide constituency across the business and should not be confined to those within the ethics and compliance function or to the senior management team. A broad, inclusive approach is required to capture the full spectrum of potential threats to the organisation's reputation, including possible ethical and legal breaches. Therefore, front-line employees and business managers at all levels, as well as those in more functional areas such as finance, marketing, HR, etc., should all be canvassed. This can be done via questionnaire or interview, or more effectively through workshops with selected groups of employees where risks can be identified and their impact debated and assessed.

Existing data should also be leveraged. Prior-year audit reports, internal control findings, industry or sector analysis, country reports, economic data, etc., should all be mined for evidence of potential risk items or trends.

Bringing in outside expertise can also help to inform the process, particularly for more complex issues, where there may not be sufficient knowledge in-house or in areas where a breach would be costly in terms of litigation and/or sanction, e.g. competition law, data privacy, cyber security, etc.

The risk assessment process must be a dynamic one, carried out regularly and repeated for new risks. So, for example, if the company decides to enter a new market or launch a new service, if regulation changes or more stringent product safety standards are introduced, it's time to reassess the relevant risks.

Finally, the process should be clearly documented and kept as simple as possible, using accessible, jargon-free language so that it is clearly understood and resonates with all who will ultimately be involved in managing the risks identified.

## Evaluate the Adequacy of Existing Procedures

Once the compliance and ethical threats have been classified, it is then necessary to review the adequacy or otherwise of the existing policies and procedures to:
- mitigate against the risk of such events occurring in the first place;
- detect them if they do; and
- then respond appropriately to any breach.

Although widely perceived as a draconian piece of legislation, the UK's Bribery Act 2010 was accompanied by a very user-friendly 'how to' guide to help companies to understand the new rules and apply them in a manner commensurate with the nature of the business, its scale and complexity. Although concerned with the prevention of *corruption*, the approach is equally relevant in the wider context of assessing an organisation's general ethical health. The guidance prescribes a number of principles that can inform any preventative framework, which are summarised in **Figure 4.8** below:

### FIGURE 4.8: FIVE PRINCIPLES TO HELP PREVENT BRIBERY

| | |
|---|---|
| **Top-level Commitment** | Top-level management (be it the board of directors, the owners or any other equivalent body or person) are committed to preventing bribery by persons associated with it. They foster a culture within the organisation in which bribery is never acceptable. |
| **Risk Assessment** | The organisation assesses the nature and extent of its exposure to potential external and internal risks of bribery on its behalf by persons associated with it. The assessment is periodic, informed and documented. |
| **Due Diligence** | The organisation applies due diligence procedures, taking a proportionate and risk-based approach in respect of persons who perform services for or on behalf of the organisation in order to mitigate identified bribery risks. |
| **Communication (including training)** | The organisation seeks to ensure that its bribery prevention policies and procedures are embedded and understood throughout the organisation through internal and external communication, including training that is proportionate to the risks it faces. |
| **Monitoring and Review** | The organisation monitors and reviews procedures designed to prevent bribery by persons associated with it and makes improvements where necessary. |

For each risk identified, i.e. in the outer ring of the wheel in **Figure 4.7**, the adequacy or otherwise of the existing procedures to counter the specific nature of the threats posed should be assessed. This gap analysis will then inform the work that needs to be planned and executed to remediate, address and monitor any deficiencies. A 'risk heatmap', outlined below in **Figure 4.9**, is a helpful way to categorise these risks and their related tasks as high, medium or low priority:

### FIGURE 4.9: A RISK HEATMAP

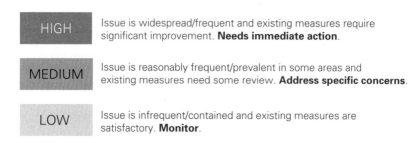

| HIGH | Issue is widespread/frequent and existing measures require significant improvement. **Needs immediate action**. |
| MEDIUM | Issue is reasonably frequent/prevalent in some areas and existing measures need some review. **Address specific concerns**. |
| LOW | Issue is infrequent/contained and existing measures are satisfactory. **Monitor**. |

An example of a heatmap framework for assessing risks across the specific compliance risk categories of bribery & corruption and competition law is set out in **Figure 4.10**.

## FIGURE 4.10: DIVISIONAL RISK ASSESSMENT: BRIBERY & CORRUPTION AND COMPETITION LAW

| Category | Risk Indicator | Division A | Division B |
|---|---|---|---|
| Bribery & Corruption | Country risk | (Low) | (High) |
| | Business norms | | |
| | Gifts & hospitality culture | | |
| | Use of agents/sub-contractors/JVs | (Medium) | |
| | Government interactions | | |
| | Sponsorships/donations | | |
| | Prior breaches | | |
| | Internal control procedures | | |
| | Etc., etc. | | |
| Competition Law | Dominant market share | | |
| | Interaction with competitors | | |
| | Trade association relationships | | |
| | Resale price maintenance | | |
| | Competition authority activity | | |
| | Past investigations | | |
| | Etc., etc. | | |

In this example the company has two divisions, A and B. The constituent businesses of Division A are large, with leading market positions in relatively stable economies with low levels of corruption and acceptable business practices. Internal controls are solid and there is little interaction with competitors. Risk factors from a bribery perspective include the fact that the division is reliant on several third-party relationships to conclude business on its behalf, including agents, subcontractors and joint ventures, and also that there is a high level of government interaction. Related protocols, therefore, will need to be reviewed. In terms of competition law risk, while there seems to be generally high levels of awareness and compliance with competition law policy, and no issues around resale price maintenance, the competition authorities are active and there have been some prior breaches. Also, as the division has dominant market positions, this is a high-priority focus area from a compliance risk perspective.

Division B includes a very different set of businesses, located in jurisdictions with a high risk of corruption and challenging business norms, including generally unacceptable gifts & hospitality practices. However, internal control procedures are good and there are no significant third-party relationships (agents/sub-contractors/JVs, etc.). The focus here should be to develop a robust anti-bribery policy and related controls, including clear guidelines on acceptable gifts & hospitality, with regular training for staff. From a competition law perspective, Division B is also different from Division A in that there are no issues around market share; rather the risk is due to the relatively high level of interaction with competitors, particularly through trade association involvement, and the competition authorities being active. Strong policies, training and communications, and monitoring will also be part of the compliance programme to mitigate these issues.

This framework can be developed for all ethical or compliance risk categories until a full programme of work has been developed to address, mitigate and monitor the issues arising.

## 2. Plan

### Build the Right Team

With ethical and compliance risks identified and a related work programme designed, the next step is to determine the right person/team to carry out the work programme and address the risks identified and assign **responsibility** and **accountability**.

The particular structure chosen for managing ethics and compliance responsibilities will depend on the nature and scale of the organisation. In larger organisations, the 'Three Lines of Defence' model is often used:
1. Line management in individual business units is the first line of defence and responsible for assessing and controlling their own compliance risks
2. The second line is the organisation's compliance, legal and risk functions, which ensure that those risks are identified and managed.
3. Internal audit, the third line of defence, independently assesses the effectiveness of the first and second lines.

While this level of resource will not be available to smaller enterprises, this need not compromise the effectiveness of introducing a framework for managing compliance with ethical standards as long as:

- one person (an 'Ethics Manager') is ultimately accountable for overseeing the process – this may be a dedicated role or, as would be the norm in smaller enterprises, this responsibility would be part of his or her function;
- he or she has clear access to the CEO (or equivalent) as well as a direct reporting line to an independent director on the board, e.g. typically the audit committee chair or equivalent or, again in the case of a smaller enterprise, is a person who is seen as being independent of the MD, such as the finance director, HR manager or a large shareholder;
- he or she has sufficient authority and is adequately resourced and supported; and
- he or she incorporates most, if not all, of the following competencies and characteristics:
  - sound judgement
  - strong character
  - understands the business
  - effective leader
  - charismatic
  - interpersonal influencing skills
  - integrity beyond doubt
  - gravitas
  - great collaborator
  - excellent communicator
  - pragmatic.

Once these are present, in terms of specific background, it is probably more about the will than the skill. While a legal or financial background would be helpful, and the risk/internal audit function may prove a useful resource tool, any experienced executive who understands the business, has the respect of his or her peers and has necessary support from related areas, such as legal and HR, is well placed to lead the ethics programme. At aerospace and technology company Lockheed Martin, ethics is taken so seriously that an assignment in the ethics department is part of the grooming process for high-potential executives.[7]

The role profile for this ethics manager could incorporate the following specific duties:

- ongoing design, leadership and delivery of the ethics programme;
- establishing and communicating standards, policies and procedures commensurate with the scale, risks, culture and ambition of the organisation;

113

- acting as trusted advisor to the governing body and executive management on all aspects of the organisation's reputation;
- ensuring the effective integration of the ethics and compliance function into daily operations;
- designing and implementing a continuous training and communication programme to foster a culture of integrity;
- establishing a good faith reporting ('whistleblowing') channel and investigation protocols;
- measuring, monitoring and reporting on the programme and improving its effectiveness;
- recommending remedial actions to respond to breaches or ethical issues arising and improvements to the programme.

Again, depending on scale and structure, the (lead) ethics manager may require representatives, or 'ethics co-ordinators', in different parts of the organisation to direct programme delivery at business unit, national or divisional level. They in turn need to be similarly plugged into their respective management teams to ensure the ethics programme gets the necessary focus and traction at local level. **Figure 4.11** below is a representative organisation chart for a large corporate showing how the ethics team would typically be structured, including reporting lines and their relationship with related functions and management teams.

**FIGURE 4.11: SAMPLE ETHICS ORGANISATION FOR A LARGE CORPORATE**

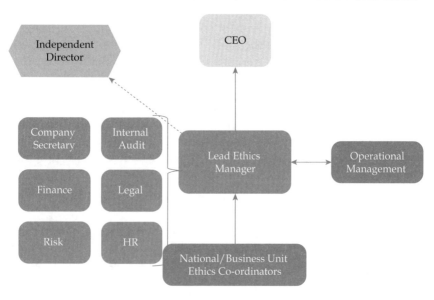

It may also be helpful to establish a 'Compliance & Ethics Advisory Group', comprised of a small group of senior executives from across the business, whose function is to help steer the compliance and ethics strategy and, in particular, to review from a practical, commercial perspective any ethics and compliance policy, training material or proposed system change prior to issue. This involvement can be both welcome and necessary in organisations where the greeting "Hi, I'm from Head Office" does not necessarily guarantee instant friendship or unquestioned authority.

Thus far 'Ethics Manager' or 'Lead Ethics Manager' has been used as a working title for this role. Job titles do need some thought and should fit the organisation. Some organisations might opt for something like 'Chief Compliance Officer', which has impact but denotes a policing role, befitting a stick-based approach. There is something to be said for not having 'compliance' in the title at all, it being up there with 'diet' and 'exercise' in most people's minds. It is hard to get it right without risking being a little contrived. Some other suggestions include:

- Corporate Ethics Manager
- Director of Business Integrity
- Vice President Responsible Business.

Whatever the title, the first task of the 'Ethics Manager' is likely to be a review of the organisation's code of conduct.

## Determine Code of Conduct Requirements

The starting point and bedrock for any ethics programme is the organisation's code of conduct. Otherwise known as a 'code of business conduct', 'code of ethics', 'ethics policy', etc., the purpose of this document is to:

- clarify an organisation's mission and purpose and bring to life its values and principles;
- provide guidelines to link these core values to the standards of conduct expected of employees;
- assist employees to make ethical decisions and comply with the law by providing real-life scenarios and comprehension aids;
- serve as a central reference for related policy documents and provide details of resources available for further support and advice;
- communicate to all stakeholders the covenant the organisation has made to uphold its core values in its dealings with its customers and suppliers, business partners and shareholders, the environment and its communities; and
- help ensure the organisation meets its various governance and legal requirements.

115

Studies have shown that enterprises exhibiting a pronounced emphasis on ethics and trust have higher employee retention rates and attract more prospective employees.[8]

It is worthwhile, therefore, taking the time to translate your values and guiding principles into a well-thought-out code of conduct. This will not only help to communicate the culture and guiding principles of your organisation but makes business sense in that you will attract the brightest and the best. Current best practice in code of conduct development, as proposed by Corpedia, the Corporate Governance of the New York Stock Exchange, is set out below.

## CODES OF CONDUCT: BEST PRACTICE[9]

### Tone from the Top
- Communicate clearly the executive team's support for the code.
- Personalise with an introduction from the CEO.
- Communicate the code's applicability across the organisation.
- Explain its role within the broader ethics programme.
- Reference reporting channels and highlight the non-retaliation policy.

### Readability, Tone and Learning Aids
- Ensure the code is an appropriate length (between 8,000 and 10,000 words, with more rule-heavy topics migrated to a policy manual).
- Adopt a warm, inclusive tone to engage employees, using 'We' and 'Us' instead of the dictatorial 'the Company' and 'You'.
- Focus on expected behaviours rather than prohibition; it should not read like the 10 commandments.
- Tailor the complexity of the material to your target audience, i.e. avoid legal jargon and keep sentences short and simple.
- Liberally sprinkle the Code with sector-specific terminology and buzz-words for consistency with other enterprise-wide communications.
- Supplement the code with learning aids and ensure these are relevant.

### Non-retaliation and Reporting
- Clearly communicate resources for asking questions or making reports.
- Make a firm statement of the non-retaliation policy.
- Provide information on the complaint resolution process.
- Put this section near the front.

| Value Statements and Stakeholder Commitments |
|---|
| • Clearly and enthusiastically communicate the organisation's values. |
| • Outline the commitments employees hold to key stakeholders, e.g. the organisation, customers, suppliers, the community, etc., why they exist and why they should be fulfilled. |

| Risk Coverage |
|---|
| • Ensure the risks covered are commensurate with the organisation's scale, sector and structure.<br>• For clarity, define the terms and concepts used within each risk area.<br>• Clearly communicate behavioural expectations for each risk area.<br>• Reference corresponding company policies.<br>• Communicate how the code relates to other laws and regulations and other company policies. |

A table of contents for a code of conduct is set out below, providing a flavour of the typical topics covered and provisions included. Please note that this is not exhaustive; organisations may put their own label on code provisions and content can vary substantially based on culture, sector, location and regulatory environment.

## Code of Conduct: A Sample Table of Contents

- Introductory Letter from the CEO
- Introduction
- Core Values and Principles
- Available Ethics Resources
- Good Faith Reporting Channel and Non-retaliation

Employment Practices
- Workplace Health & Safety
- Illegal Drugs and Alcohol
- Equal Opportunity, Diversity and Non-discrimination
- Fair Treatment of Staff
- Bullying and Harassment
- Use of Organisation's Property

Protecting Assets and Information
- Proper Use of Assets
- Intellectual Property

- Insider Dealing
- Data Protection, Retention and Privacy
- Accounting and Business Records
- Social Media & External Communications

**Bribery, Corruption and Fraud**
- Gifts and Hospitality
- Government Customers
- Political Lobbying and Contributions
- Money Laundering
- Export Controls
- Fraud

**Conflicts of Interest (including disclosure)**
**Relationships with:**
- Vendors: procurement practices
- Business partners: due diligence and contractual commitments
- Customers: product quality and fair advertising
- Competitors: competing fairly

**Environmental, Community and Political Activities**
- Commitment to the Environment
- Charitable and Community Initiatives
- Political Involvement and Activities

The list above should provide a flavour of the typical topics and provisions covered in an organisation's code of conduct. A fundamental feature of any code of conduct is that it should resonate strongly with employees, so that when they pick it up the 'look and feel' already seem familiar.

## OUR CODE, OUR PEOPLE

An early assignment as an independent consultant was to assist a growing organisation to redevelop its code of conduct from a legalistic document into a more interesting and informative guide for its increasingly global workforce. We spent considerable time getting the tone and content right, to accurately capture and convey the core values and unique culture of the company.

We simplified the language, eliminating all jargon, using simple, concise sentences consistent with the 'house style'. We added lots of realistic 'FAQs', included pointers for further guidance as well as summary lists of 'dos and don'ts' to aid understanding. Finally, we used high-quality contemporary images of employees, representative of different genders, ages and ethnicities across a global enterprise.

We then presented the new code to the board, who declared it a huge step forward. "Just one thing though", said the CEO, "I don't think we have anyone that good-looking working for our company!" The photographs we had used (stock images of airbrushed, attractive, highly groomed executives) did not reflect the reality of the company's average employee. We immediately set about organising photographs of real employees from a variety of locations. Though less glossy, the final effect was much more realistic and impactful. It was a valuable lesson in the overriding necessity and value of authenticity.

An example of a particularly compelling code of conduct that does a really effective job of capturing the essence of the company's culture and values is Vodafone's "Working in The Vodafone Way". Note the tone, clarity and simplicity of CEO Vittorio Colao's introduction to the code in the following extract[10]:

Being an admired company is not just about our performance and achievements, it's also about acting in a responsible, ethical and lawful way. As one of the world's leading international companies, we need to earn the trust of our customers, colleagues and the communities where we work.

Our Code of Conduct sets out our business principles and how every single person at Vodafone needs to apply these. We call this Working in The Vodafone Way.

I am proud about working for a company that has the highest standards of integrity and which passionately protects its people, assets and reputation. Please take the time to understand our Code of Conduct, to speak up when you have any concerns and always work in The Vodafone Way.

Vittorio Colao
Vodafone Group Chief Executive Officer

## Determine Supporting Policy Requirements

Depending on the organisation's size, scale and sector, it may or may not be possible to provide employees with sufficient guidance in the code of conduct alone. Important risk areas will often require a supplementary policy or set of guidelines. The risk-assessment process described above will help guide the development of policies that may be required to supplement a basic code of conduct. This is especially the case for large, multinational and operationally diverse organisations.

A typical suite of ethics-related policies might address the following topics (although again the list is not exhaustive):
- Anti-Bribery
- Anti-Fraud
- Anti-Money Laundering
- Ethical Procurement
- Competition Law
- Insider Dealing
- 'Know Your Customer'
- Employee Health & Safety
- IT Security & Data Protection
- Digital Media
- Gifts, Hospitality & Donations
- Social Responsibility
- The Environment
- Good Faith Reporting ('Whistleblowing').

There may also be additional documents including, for example:
- Supplier Code of Conduct
- Mergers & Acquisitions and Joint Venture Due Diligence Programme
- Lobbying Protocols.

It is beyond the scope of this book to prescribe the contents of the documents listed above. Suffice to remember that those affected by such policies should be involved in drafting them, to keep them simple and clear, and provide contact details for further questions or support. Good practice when formulating policy documents is to include the following key headings:

- Objective
- Applicability
- Roles and Responsibilities
- Clear Policy Statement

- Policy Standards
- Roll-out and Communication
- Monitoring and Assurance
- Breach Reporting
- Approval for Departures (if applicable)
- Definitions
- Advice and Support

## Design Ethics Training Programmes

Question:

Which large multinational had an award-winning, 64-page code of conduct?

Answer:

Take-away: codes and policies are useless if they sit in a drawer. The only meaningful way of bringing them to life is through training, which needs careful consideration and planning. Let's take a look at the 'Why, Who, How, What and When' of business ethics training.

**Why Teach Business Ethics?** According to the former CEO of Porsche, Peter Schultz, "You hire character and you train skill". If that is true, why bother teaching ethics? Can it be taught at all? If the 'bad apple theory' is correct, then people are either good or bad and organisations are powerless to change them.[11] (This may be a convenient truth because unethical behaviour can be blamed on a few rogue individuals who can then be discarded from the barrel.) However, as Linda Trevino and Stuart Youngblood point out, while people may have predispositions to behave ethically or unethically, getting rid of a few 'bad apples' will not necessarily solve the problem if there is something rotten inside the organisation that is spoiling them in the first place.

Good character alone simply does not prepare people for the unique ethical problems they are likely to encounter in the workplace. It is perhaps more correct to paraphrase Schultz: 'You hire character *and* you train skill and character'. It is only with special training that employees can be prepared to anticipate and recognise ethical dilemmas and be provided with frameworks for thinking about and resolving them.

In providing ethical training, the course objectives should be to:
* inform staff about relevant laws, regulations and standards, as well as company code and policies;
* explain the employees' relevant obligations in relation to these external rules and internal requirements;
* teach some basic 'dos and don'ts' for compliance;
* facilitate practical applied learning scenarios involving ethical dilemmas;
* provide a framework and method for evaluating these dilemmas and making decisions;
* provide information regarding when and where to get help or raise concerns;
* reinforce the organisation's core values and guiding principles.

**Who should be Trained and by Whom?** All employees will require ethics training to a greater or lesser extent, and on a range of different topics, depending on their role and level in the organisation. For example, a new employee will need a different type and level of training than a senior manager; likewise, an hourly employee may need training only on selected topics. Most companies provide a basic code of conduct level of training to all employees and, then, using a risk-based approach, provide further instruction to specific staff on selected topics germane to their function or responsibilities.

In deciding who should deliver the training, the options include the following:
* professional in-company trainers or HR managers;
* external consultants;
* business unit managers.

The best option is likely to be a combination of all three. The most important contributor here is the business unit manager, who should provide context, highlight real-life examples, set the 'tone from the top' and provide leadership by explaining the right behaviours and standards to follow in order to live the organisation's core values. (Where employees are more dispersed, a CEO video or a streamed presentation can be an effective means of bridging the gap and delivering the tone at the top perspectives to more remote locations.)

As well as encouraging, even pressuring, managers themselves to become aware of the organisation's value and principles, their involvement will guarantee a more genuine and impactful training session.

**How should Ethics Training be Delivered?** With advances in communications technology, come more options to cascade engaging ethics training throughout the organisation cost-effectively. Options include customised online training programmes delivered to the participants 'PCs, podcasts on specialist topics, intranet-based group chats led by subject-matter experts and smart phone apps providing instruction and easily accessible frameworks for employees to consult, e.g. in the area of gifts and hospitality.

Sometimes, however, there is no substitute for face-to-face human interaction, e.g. a traditional 'classroom' setting with smaller groups, in which dialogue and debate are encouraged and a more lasting learning experience is facilitated. The choice is between cost, benefit, risk and reward. A combination of a number of different channels may work best, including an online approach for basic instruction covering a wide population and in-person sessions for more complex issues for select employee groups.

**What Should be Taught in Ethics Training?** In relation to content, what does 'good' look like? This is perhaps best explained by way of example. Consider the following as sample material from a training programme aiming to explain the basics of competition law:

### Scenario A

The following is prohibited as incompatible with EU competition law: all agreements between undertakings, decisions by associations of undertakings and concerted practices that may affect trade between Member States and that have as their object or effect the prevention, restriction or distortion of competition within the internal market, and in particular those which:

(a) directly or indirectly fix purchase or selling prices or any other trading conditions;

(b) limit or control production, markets, technical development, or investment;

(c) share markets or sources of supply;

123

(d) apply dissimilar conditions to equivalent transactions with other trading parties, thereby placing them at a competitive disadvantage;

(e) make the conclusion of contracts subject to acceptance by the other parties of supplementary obligations which, by their nature or according to commercial usage, have no connection with the subject of such contracts.

Summarise below the key prohibitions in relation to undertakings, decisions and practices as set out in EU competition law.

Lost interest already? Compare Scenario A with the following:

## SCENARIO B

As Flooring Sales Manager for Floors & Walls, you are working on a price quote for a school project that includes various types of tiles, including a proprietary roof tile ('TuffTex') with a fire-resistance rating much higher than the roof tiles you can supply.

The general contractor (GC) will only deal with one supplier for all tiles. You call a supplier of TuffTex to request a quote on that one item. He says:

> "Coincidentally, the GC asked me for a quote on the whole job, too. But all that other floor and wall tiling isn't really my thing. I figure you guys have the best shot at the job, anyway. Tell you what, if you'll commit to getting all the TuffTex material from me, I won't quote for the whole contract."

Discuss at your group table and share your thoughts with the class. Reference any relevant laws, regulations, codes, policies, guiding principles, etc., in your answer. Please also outline who you would call for advice and to report this conversation.

The main difference in approach is that Scenario B is:
• specific
• applied
• contextualised
• relevant

- interactive
- directive
- memorable.

If you tick all these boxes in relation to content of your materials, your ethics training programme should deliver the required results.

**When and how often should Ethics Training be Delivered?** If the ethics message is to be kept alive, it is essential that training is regularly refreshed. Annual basic training is recommended, with a potentially longer cycle for more advanced classroom sessions, perhaps with an interim online refresher. We will discuss 'Moments that Matter' in **Chapter 7**, where specific events in an employee's career or the organisation's operating cycle trigger a need for specific dialogue and training, including:
- induction;
- promotion;
- foreign assignment;
- before a reorganisation or restructuring;
- following a breach of company policy or a high-profile national or industry violation of the law. As well as demanding urgent communication to assure employees, such violations present a compelling opportunity to remind employees of core organisational values and what happens when they are ignored or forgotten. We will also discuss managing through ethical crises in **Chapter 7**.

Finally, ethics training should be incorporated into leadership development programmes so that it becomes fully integrated into normal progression plans and the management culture of the organisation. You might find the following table useful in planning and tracking ethics training programmes:

| Course | Delivery Method | Course Outline | Employee Population | Time-table |
|---|---|---|---|---|
| **Code of Conduct** | | | | |
| **Anti-bribery & Fraud** | | | | |
| **Competition Law** | | | | |
| **Anti-money Laundering** | | | | |
| *Etc.* | | | | |

| Junior Management Training Programme | | | | |
| --- | --- | --- | --- | --- |
| Senior Management Development Programme | | | | |
| *Etc.* | | | | |

Having assessed the risks and identified mitigating policies and procedures, you then need to take action to communicate those policies, deliver the training modules, as well as keeping the ethics message alive through effective two-way communications systems. Then you are in 'Monitor' mode, i.e. establishing appropriate monitoring and reporting tools to check ethics programme effectiveness before proceeding to 'Evaluate' and, of course, improve. We will now look in turn at each of these steps in completing the creation of the ethics and compliance framework.

## 3. Act

### *Effective Communication*

For an ethical approach to really 'stick' in an organisation, values must become part of communications from senior executives and functional leaders alike, to both external and internal audiences.

The world is used to hearing about the quality of what you produce or provide. Why not also wear your values as a badge of honour, on your headed paper, e-mails and in promotional literature, and start to build 'reputational capital' with your stakeholders? The code of conduct should also have a prominent position on the company's website, clear for all stakeholders to see. Likewise, the annual report is an ideal opportunity to showcase core values, where possible pointing to specific examples of the company's principles in practice.

Many companies now choose to supplement the traditional, financially driven annual reporting cycle with a specific account of their responsible business practices. Usually coming under the 'Sustainability' banner, these often quite elaborate reports highlight how the company is positively impacting society and the communities in which it operates. Examples from some of the most admired companies in the field include:

- BMW's annual Sustainable Value Reports[12];
- Adidas's annual Sustainability Progress Reports[13];
- Reckitt Benckiser's annual Sustainability Reports.[14]

According to a report by EY and the Center for Corporate Citizenship at Boston College, this trend in additional voluntary disclosure is here to stay.[15] Citing a Global Reporting Initiative (GRI) source and noting that a full 95% of the world's top 250 companies now issue sustainability reports (up from 50% 10 years ago), the report comments:

> "Where once sustainability disclosure was the province of a few unusually green or community-oriented companies, today it is a best practice employed by companies worldwide. A focus on sustainability helps organisations manage their social and environmental impacts and improve operating efficiency and natural resource stewardship, and it remains a vital component of shareholder, employee and stakeholder relations."[16]

This is entirely consistent with the growing support for the concept of 'whole company' or 'integrated' reporting, as promulgated by the International Integrated Reporting Council, which aims to develop more holistic corporate reporting norms reflecting "how an organisation's strategy, governance, performance and prospects, in the context of its external environment, lead to the creation of value in the short, medium and long term".[17]

The story being told within the organisation's four walls must match and mirror its message to the outside world. With regard to the internal audience, as we know, employees learn in a variety of different ways, so it is good to 'mix it up' a little in terms of media. A multiplex approach works best, exploiting the full range of available formal and informal communication channels, including:

| Company Magazine | Intranet | Speeches | Recruitment Literature |
|---|---|---|---|
| Newsletters | Employee Handbooks | Meeting Agenda | Wallet Cards |
| Calendars | Brochures & Posters | Merchandise | Blogs |

That old chestnut about effective communication, 'tell them what you are going to say, then say it, then tell them what you said', applies equally to communicating about ethics with an important addendum: 'then tell them again'! While regular, consistent information is required, use different approaches from time to time to keep it fresh. Also, avail of more informal channels to reinforce specific aspects of more official policy or training modules, providing readily accessible bite-size guidelines.

Consider the topic of competition law compliance, for example, one that certainly requires regular airtime. Your policy document on its own will not be sufficient, so you may want to consider a themed newsletter on the subject, which could summarise relevant laws and recent cases and highlight employees' key responsibilities in this area. To make it really resonate, this bulletin could incorporate wallet cards as a convenient and accessible reference for executives on the move to check for what they can and cannot do in any exchanges with counterparts in competing companies. You could also include valuable 'Dawn Raid Survival Tips' (see below) to remind employees of what they should and should not do in the event of an unexpected early morning visit by the competition authorities as part of an investigation of any suspected cartel activity or similar competition law breach.

## DAWN RAIDS: SURVIVING THE FIRST HOUR

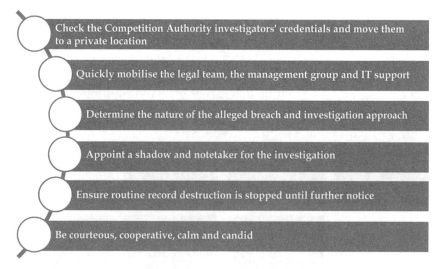

Check the Competition Authority investigators' credentials and move them to a private location

Quickly mobilise the legal team, the management group and IT support

Determine the nature of the alleged breach and investigation approach

Appoint a shadow and notetaker for the investigation

Ensure routine record destruction is stopped until further notice

Be courteous, cooperative, calm and candid

We will cover the important topic of communication in more detail in **Chapter 7,** particularly the very special role the ethical leader has in using all available channels to communicate clear expectations and create an open culture. Central to this is the recognition that communication, to be effective, should be two-way; while employees might be on the receiving end of communications most of the time, they must have open channels available to them through which they can ask questions or report ethical concerns, i.e. good faith reporting channels.

## Good Faith Reporting Channels and Investigation Protocols

According to the Association of Certified Fraud Examiners, over 40% of all corporate fraud cases detected come from tip-offs, many more than are detected by internal or external audit reviews.[18] We discussed 'whistleblowing' as part of the case for ethical leadership in **Chapter 1** and concluded that the age of the whistleblower has well and truly arrived. Corporate retaliation, however, remains a problem and is still one of the main reasons an employee will choose to look the other way.[19] Another factor contributing to reticence in reporting is confidentiality agreements, or 'gagging clauses', that some companies ask their employees to sign. A third is the employee's overriding concern that they either will not be listened to or taken seriously, or that the confidentiality of their report will not be respected.

While it is the leader's job to create a culture in which employees feel free to speak openly about ethical issues, this must be backed up at an organisational level with the provision of accessible, credible channels through which they can report concerns. The first step is to draw up a good faith reporting policy. This should clearly set out:
- the types of issues that should be reported;
- the options or channels for reporting;
- an outline of the investigation process;
- the likely timeframe for resolution.

The policy should also explicitly state that retaliation will not be tolerated, that all matters will be investigated and that confidentiality will be respected as far as possible within the law.

It may also be advisable to state that routine HR issues are better addressed directly with line managers or with a HR representative, although not to unduly limit the scope. Sometimes, disgruntled employees will use this channel not only to register their dissatisfaction with the world at large and generally rail at the unfairness of it all but also to take the opportunity to vent their frustration with a particular manager and 'dish the dirt'. It might be reported thus: "I am not paid enough, my boss is so mean – and you should also know he is stealing from the company". These complaints should not be dismissed out of hand.

Again, policies can be wordsmithed to perfection but be entirely useless if employees are unaware of their existence. A simple poster, displayed in prominent areas, is a simple way to draw attention to the relevant guidelines and reporting options, while also serving as a subliminal reminder of the organisation's intolerance for inappropriate conduct and its firm ethical stance.

Consider the following example of information used by AkzoNobel to communicate the who, how and what of its 'SpeakUp' channel:

For most large enterprises operating in multiple jurisdictions and through many different languages, it is necessary to engage a third party to provide a 24/7 'hotline' service as a conduit for accepting reports and then directing them through to the ethics office. In smaller enterprises, concerns should ideally be channelled directly to someone independent of executive management, e.g. a non-executive director or, if this is not possible, then someone who is and is perceived to be objective and impartial, such as whomever is charged with managing compliance issues, for example, the HR manager, or equivalent.

The need for objectivity and independence should be carried through to the investigation procedure. A 'One Step Up and One Step Out' principle can be invoked, i.e. whoever is charged with investigating the issue should be at a level above the person reporting the problem and in a different area of the business, i.e. removed from the individual's daily work environment and certainly not their direct manager. Investigation protocols should be established to guide the process, from triaging the reports received in terms of their type and seriousness to determining and assigning resources, the investigation and analysis of the findings, to the implementation and reporting of corrective actions based on agreed recommendations. Care must be taken to ensure confidentiality is maintained throughout the process. Finally, it is important that the person reporting in good faith is updated regularly on the status of the investigation as it proceeds through the various stages.

Typical investigation protocols for receiving, assessing and resolving reports received in a good faith report are as depicted in **Figure 4.12** below:

FIGURE **4.12:** INVESTIGATION PROTOCOLS

Receive
- receive the report via letter, call, web, etc.
- triage and categorise by gravity and subject matter
- escalate if urgent

Reflect
- determine necessary resources, internal and external
- assign investigation team and leader
- notify management as necessary

Research
- conduct interviews
- review relevant documentation
- write up report

Communicate with reporter

Resolve
- assess report and resolve any queries
- discuss fully with investigation team
- determine follow-up action required

Report
- implement corrective action
- report to board and executive management
- retain documents as required

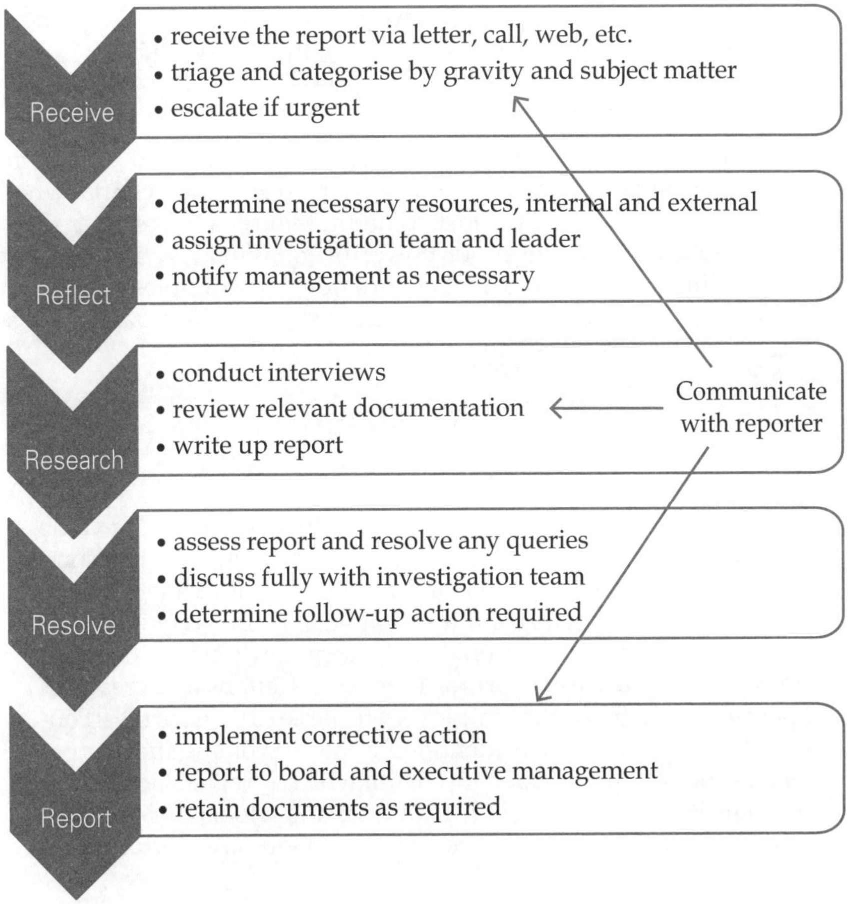

## Adapting Processes and Procedures

Effective communications and fair systems for reporting and investigating ethical issues are critical components of an ethical culture. There are a number of other processes that also warrant attention to ensure values fully permeate the decisions made and procedures followed during the working day.

**Performance Management** Performance management refers to all the processes around articulating goals for the business and the employees' goals, agreeing performance metrics, assessing performance accordingly and then aligning the reward system to recognise each employee's contribution. These are some of the most important processes to get right if the performance of employees is to match the ethical expectations of the organisation. As the old adage goes: 'What gets rewarded gets done'.

At the heart of performance management is understanding:
• what the organisation wants to achieve; and
• how performance towards those goals can be motivated.

In **Chapter 2** we saw the harmful effect that ill-conceived goals can have on ethical behaviour, so you need to really understand what drives your employees. The most common failure is to consider only financial metrics, ignoring more powerful, non-financial motivators. Linda Trevino and Katherine Nelson provide two examples of companies that expressly link their performance systems to the organisation's values: American Express and Lockheed Martin.[20]

### AMERICAN EXPRESS

American Express has two clear goals: to create shareholder value over the long term and to be "an employer of choice". The company's code of conduct states the expectation that "leaders will be ethical role models who exhibit the highest standards of integrity, develop employees, communicate the company's ethical expectations and their own support for those expectations and create an open environment so that employees feel free to express their concerns". The company has identified a number of specific competencies for its senior leadership team, which it regularly assesses through 360-degree reviews (i.e. an assessment tool where all who observe and who are affected by an individual's performance

provide feedback (including subordinates, peers, superiors, as well as self-assessment). These competencies include explicit examples, such as:
- treats others with respect at all times, is fair and objective;
- actively listens and incorporates input from others;
- acts with integrity;
- inspires the trust of the team, is reliable and consistent;
- talks openly and honestly – says it as it is.

Examples of poor performance, for example 'breaks promises', 'is inconsistent', 'fails to show respect for others', are also included for assessment and comment.

Ratings of positive competencies are given substantial weight in promotion and compensation decisions. Finally, the company has invested resources to address and remediate under-performance or negative ratings so that leaders are equipped with the requisite skills to drive performance consistent with the company's values.

## LOCKHEED MARTIN

The performance management system at Lockheed Martin also rates employees not only on financial results, such as increased sales or profits, but also on 'how you got there', through attributes including ethics, excellence, integrity, people and teamwork, all of which are explicitly defined. For example, 'ethics' is defined as "is honest and forthright; embraces truthfulness; knows regulations, rules and compliance requirements, and actively demonstrates compliance".

For each attribute, managers are asked to provide examples of how they behaved and to justify their salary increase recommendations on this basis.

Incentive systems can be used to dramatic effect where a change of behaviour is mandated. Take Siemens, for example. In 2009 (i.e. the year following the major bribery case – see **Chapter 2**), some 17% of management bonuses were weighted on active participation and support for the compliance system.[21]

In companies with no such issues, explicitly including values and ethical competencies in reward strategies sends a very clear message to employees that these things matter to the company and should matter to them. Admittedly, measuring achievements across these more intangible qualities is more challenging than determining required percentage increases in turnover, EBITDA or RONA. Perhaps it is less important 'to get it done right' than 'to get right done'.

**Decision-making and Due Diligence** We have already discussed the primary schools of ethics and posed some questions or tests that leaders can use to generally assess the ethical dimensions of a particular decision. We will prescribe an even more practical tool, the 'ETHIC' framework, in **Chapter 8**. However, to complement personal accountability for making the right decision, organisations also need to hard-wire a dimension of ethical responsibility into their formal decision-making systems, along the lines of the McKinsey useful '7-S' model discussed earlier.

This kind of joined-up thinking requires that all documented deliberations incorporate a distinct evaluation of how each decision reflects shared values. This approach can extend to:
- reports regarding new product launches or service offerings;
- investment decision analyses;
- research supporting new market entry;
- evaluations of prospective business partners;
- procurement and sourcing comparisons;
- site location or expansion plans;
- recommendations for new employment practices.

In the next chapter, we will examine issues around some of these decision-making processes in more detail in an international context. In particular, we will look at how to formally introduce ethical considerations into mergers and acquisitions due diligence and as part of global sourcing considerations to assess the bona fides of potential business partners.

As with performance measurement, the trick is not to be over-reliant on quantitive analysis to the exclusion of a more qualitative narrative. We saw in **Chapter 2** how a blinkered, wholly numbers-led analysis prevented the Ford Pinto from being recalled, which ultimately cost multiple deaths. Decisions must reflect 'the bigger picture', i.e. not just the hit to profits or cash flow but the impact on people and perceptions.

## 4. Monitor

The 'three lines of defence' were outlined earlier in this chapter in the context of delivering on ethics and compliance responsibilities, i.e. line management within business units, the support functions (compliance, legal, risk, etc.) and internal audit. Each also has a role to play in monitoring the effectiveness of the programme.

## Line Management

Of the three lines of defence, the involvement of line managers in monitoring is more passive and likely to entail completion of a questionnaire aimed at assessing the breadth and depth of their involvement in and support for the ethics & compliance programme. Usually, it will ask if the manager has:

- issued and followed the code of conduct and related policies;
- ensured all employees have completed required ethics training;
- adhered to recommended procedures, e.g. for new product decisions, sourcing requirements, third-party due diligence, etc;
- followed protocol in relation to reporting cases of misconduct or policy breach;
- communicated good faith reporting channels to employees;
- addressed any additional specific risk areas.

To avoid this questionnaire being a mere 'box-ticking' exercise, include blank spaces so that managers can elaborate on how they have set the right tone in their teams, ideally providing examples of how they have done so during the period under review. One will quickly get a sense from such responses, or the lack thereof, as to whether the manager 'gets it'. It is also useful to organise a follow-up meeting to discuss the manager's feedback and determine together if and how the bar needs to be raised.

Another control worth considering is to have managers annually document their review of their overall compliance status in the formal minutes of the company. While an in-house questionnaire may be completed in haste and without much thought, requiring a manager to formally document their opinion of the overall ethical health of their business unit in company's records should focus the mind a little more and evoke a more thorough reflection.

## The Compliance, Legal and Risk Functions

In line with the principle of the segregation of duties, relying on people reviewing their own work is fraught. The lead ethics manager should keep track on progress and the overall status of programme initiatives with the aid of suitably defined KPIs. The risk heatmap approach may be helpful to employ here, highlighting specific ethical issues or business areas, depending on the inherent risk and strength of the mitigation strategy. An ethics and compliance dashboard might look something like that in **Figure 4.13** below, with priorities categorised as high, medium or low.

FIGURE **4.13**: SAMPLE ETHICS & COMPLIANCE DASHBOARD[22]

| Governance Framework | Risk |
| --- | --- |
| • Structure | Low |
| • Policies/controls | Low |
| • Integration into enterprise risk management | High |
| Operating Business Metrics | |
| • Feedback from senior business leaders | Low |
| • Regulatory violations compared to industry average | Medium |
| • Efficiency of regulatory approvals | Low |
| Functional Metrics | |
| • Allegation and investigation case-cycle time | Low |
| • Compliance costs per € million relative to peers | Medium |
| Employee/Cultural Metrics | |
| • Employee perceptions or corporate culture | High |
| • Percentage of employees who fear retaliation | Medium |

## Internal Audit

The internal audit function has an important monitoring role in the provision of balanced and independent assurance on the effectiveness, or otherwise, of the ethics framework by:
• checking and benchmarking management questionnaires;
• testing of self-certification reports;
• including ethical considerations and compliance risks into the standard internal audit work programmes;
• through 'themed audits' addressing the more pervasive and far-reaching ethics-related risks and related controls;
• as well as periodically assessing the strength of the ethics and compliance function itself.

In smaller companies this level of organisation and monitoring will not be feasible. However, it is possible to engage with managers to assess their awareness of and engagement with the ethics framework. The ethics manager should also track the progress and effectiveness of their own work. Regardless of the scale or complexity of the organisation, employees are ultimately the most important arbiter on who is 'walking the talk' and should not be overlooked when assessing the real strength of the company's ethical framework.

In terms of monitoring of the company's compliance with its ethical standards, the board is the ultimate line of defence. We will discuss in some detail how the board can best discharge its oversight responsibilities in **Chapter 6**.

## 5. Evaluate

Having tackled everything outlined in Steps 1 to 4 above, it is tempting now to breathe a sigh of relief and file it all away under 'E'. But ethics is not a once-off project or a year-long initiative. It is a long-term commitment and way of working that requires periodic assessment, overall evaluation and improvement to ensure its continued relevance and resonance.

There are a number of ways to appraise your ethics programme, including self-assessment methods or by conducting an external benchmarking exercise. The most effective and honest way to accurately gauge current ethical norms in the organisations is to conduct asking employees about their:

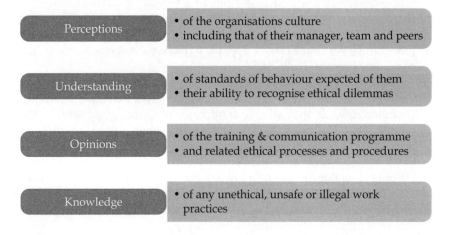

In order to work properly, employee surveys should be carried out by a third party on an anonymous basis to encourage trustful responses. Simplicity is also key: ask clear, candid questions to elicit equally frank and forthright answers and, as with the management questionnaires above, leave some blank spaces so that employees can provide more detailed commentary. Repeat the process regularly so that base-line information can be compared over time to measure progress or changing attitudes.

The 'Credo' survey is Johnson & Johnson's ethics-related employee census. Carried out over a two-year cycle and on an anonymous basis across all its locations, employees are given the chance to rate how well the company is living up to the tenets of its Credo, by answering c. 100 questions, including such basic but searching inquiries as: "Do you feel proud to say you work for Johnson & Johnson?"

The final point to note, of course, is that generally, when you ask for feedback you get it and those providing it will expect a response. So you may need to brace yourself for some 'no-holds-barred' perspectives. Be prepared to address the key points being relayed to you and take the time and courtesy to communicate your proposed actions back to the attendant group. That is a sure way to simultaneously improve your programme while building employee trust.

## References to Chapter 4

1  Schein, Edgar H., *Organisational Culture and Leadership* (Jossey-Bass, 2010).
2  Hofstede, Geert, Hofstede, Gert Jan and Minkov, Michael, *Culture and Organisations: Software of the Mind* (3rd Edition, McGraw-Hill Education, 2010).
3  Johnson, Gerry and Scholes, Kevan, *Exploring Corporate Strategy: Text and Cases* (Prentice Hall, 2007).
4  An edited version of a chapter that explains the use of the cultural from Gerry Johnson and Kevan Scholes (eds.), *Exploring Public Sector Strategy* (Prentice Hall, 2001). Available at http://www.strategyexplorers.com/whitepapers/Culture-Web.pdf (accessed February 2016).
5  See: http://www.mckinsey.com/insights/strategy/enduring_ideas_the_7-s_framework (accessed February 2016).
6  Deloitte Development LLC, *Compliance Risk Assessments: The Third Ingredient in a World-class Compliance and Ethics Programme* (2015).
7  See Trevino, L.K. and Nelson, K.A. *Managing Business Ethics: Straight Talk About How To Do It Right* (Wiley, 2011).
8  See, e.g. http://www.gsb.stanford.edu/insights/mba-grads-corporate-responsibility-trumps-salary
9  NYSE-Corpedia, "Best practices in Code of Conduct Development". Available from the American Bar organisation at http://www.americanbar.org/content/dam/aba/administrative/litigation/

materials/2014_sac/2014_sac/best_practices_in_code_of_conduct_development_2013.authcheckdam.pdf

10 Available at https://www.vodafone.com/content/dam/sustainability/pdfs/vodafone_code_of_conduct_2012.pdf

11 See Trevino, L.K. and Youngblood, S.A., "Bad Apples in Bad Barrels: A Causal Analysis of Ethical-Decision Making Behaviour", (1990) *Journal of Applied Psychology*, Vol. 75, No. 4, 378–385.

12 See http://www.bmwgroup.com/com/en/responsibility/svr_2014/index.html

13 See http://www.adidas-group.com/en/sustainability/reporting-policies-and-data/sustainability-reports/

14 See https://www.rb.com/our-responsibility/policies-and-reports

15 *The Value of Sustainability Reporting; A Joint Study by EY and the Boston College Center for Corporate Citizenship*, available from EY.com at http://www.ey.com/Publication/vwLUAssets/EY_-_Value_of_sustainability_reporting/$FILE/EY-Value-of-Sustainability-Reporting.pdf (accessed February 2016).

16 *Ibid.* p. 2.

17 See International Integrated Reporting Council, *The Integrated Reporting Framework*, available at http://integratedreporting.org/wp-content/uploads/2013/12/13-12-08-THE-INTERNATIONAL-IR-FRAMEWORK-2-1.pdf

18 Association of Certified Fraud Examiners, *Report to the Nations on Occupational Fraud & Abuse – Global Fraud Study 2014.* Available at http://www.acfe.com/rttn-summary.aspx (accessed February 2016).

19 See Navex Global, *2015 Corporate Governance and Compliance Hotline Benchmarking Report.* Available at: http://trust.navexglobal.com/rs/020-ZPR-995/images/FINAL_TNW_2015GRC_Benchmarking-Report_Web_120415.pdf (accessed February 2016).

20 See Trevino, L.K. and Nelson, K.A., *Managing Business Ethics: Straight Talk About How To Do It Right* (Wiley, 2011).

21 "The Compliance Programme at Siemens", presentation by Nadeem Anwer, Regional Compliance Officer Siemens LLC, UAE, at the Strengthening Integrity in the Private Sector Conference, organised by UNDP, MENA-OECD, Bahrain, March 2010. Available at http://www.oecd.org/mena/investment/44927648.pdf

22 Sample compliance dashboard, produced by the Corporate Executive Board. Available at: http://www.executiveboard.com/exbd-resources/pdf/legal-risk-compliance/compliance-ethics/CEB%20Compliance%20and%20Ethics%20360%20Assessment.pdf

# 5

## Leading with Integrity, Everywhere:
### *The International Dimension*

*There are times when a leader must move out ahead of the flock, go off in a
new direction, confident that he is leading his people the right way.*

**Nelson Mandela**

- Introduction
- Doing the Right Thing, Everywhere
- International Due Diligence
- Ethical Sourcing Strategies
- Aligning the CSR Agenda with your Growth Strategy

# Introduction

Technology is shrinking the globe and enabling access to world markets at unprecedented speed. If you decided in the morning to develop your business internationally, you could probably be more or less up and running by late afternoon. 'Going global' has never been easier. From an ethical perspective, however, it has never been more fraught. How can an organisation expand internationally while adhering to its 'home-grown' core values?

In this chapter we will look at the challenges of running an enterprise ethically in an international context, specifically at those posed by 'abnormal norms' in areas such as corruption, labour practices and human rights. Our analysis will focus on a number of key issues, including due diligence, sourcing decisions and the case for having a corporate social responsibility (CSR) strategy that is fully aligned with a more global footprint.

## Doing the Right Thing, Everywhere

Let's say you have conquered your domestic market and branched out across Europe and North America and your export programme to the Middle East has been reasonably successful. You are now contemplating your next move, find the emerging markets of South-east Asia compelling and are keen to develop a foothold in the region. However, from initial discussions with peers already operating there, you are starting to question the wisdom of this strategy. Your eyes have been opened to the very real risk of having to contend with any or all of the following:

- having to pay bribes to secure operating licences and move goods through customs;
- questionable employment practices, including issues around child labour, working hours, fair wages, etc.;
- lack of legal certainty and the associated risk that supply contracts may not be honoured;
- the fact that intellectual property is not protected and is routinely stolen;
- limitations in the reliability and transparency of publicly recorded financial information and related problems for due diligence;
- having to contend with very different, sometimes very difficult, political regimes;
- being able to uphold even basic human rights.

Caution is justified. Many companies have bravely ventured forth only to find themselves out of their depth, struggling to adjust, having to compromise their values in navigating unfamiliar and unethical territory. Google's experience in China is instructive.

## GOOGLE IN CHINA[1]

Gu Ge (roughly translated as 'harvesting song') is the name Google gave to the mainland Chinese version of its Internet search engine. Mainland China is the biggest market of Internet users in the world and yet is also home to the most sophisticated state censorship. The Chinese Government sanitises search pages by filtering out keywords, pictures and news reports, while also recording individuals' every keystroke made and website accessed.

In 2006, Google decided to cooperate with the Chinese Government's demand to block Chinese Internet users' sites that included information deemed off-limits to its citizens, such as democracy, human rights and "the three Ts": Tibet, Tiananmen Square and Taiwan.

Google was excoriated by critics for its decision, for "enabling evil" with its "sickening collaboration" and even accused of violating the Universal Declaration of Human Rights. Despite admitting to compromising its values, Google maintained that it would serve a more useful role in China through participation and that withdrawing the service entirely would be a "greater evil". CEO Eric Schmidt said that the company "had a responsibility to abide by the law in every country where it does business". "We had a choice to enter the country and follow the law, or ... not to enter the country. I think it is arrogant for us to walk into a country where we are just beginning operations and tell that country how to run itself."

However, in 2010, in a dramatic turnaround, the company decided to close Google.cn and redirect Chinese users to its uncensored Hong Kong website. Precipitated by the hacking of a number of e-mail accounts of Chinese human rights activists that the company linked with government censorship, Google stated: "These attacks and the surveillance they have uncovered – combined with attempts of the past year to limit free speech on the Web – have led us to conclude that we should review the feasibility of our business operations in China." At a significant loss to shareholders, the company subsequently exited China, a move that some experts suggested was a statement by the company that 'enough was enough'.

Google's new stance was praised by human rights activists and international civil liberties specialists, who have commented that "It helps realign Google's business with its ethos" and that "no company should be forced to operate under government threat to its core values or to the rights and safety of its users".

(In September 2015 it was reported that Google would return to the mainland of China with a Chinese version of its Google Play mobile app store.[2] It will be interesting to gauge reactions to what could be perceived as another U-turn by the company, one that may compromise its views on censorship in the pursuit of market growth.)

While interesting, the censorship problems Google encountered in China are more political in nature and less common than the typical challenges faced by most companies when trying to expand overseas, which will most likely include:
(a) having to pay bribes to facilitate business transactions; and
(b) contending with unfamiliar, possibly unsavoury, labour practices and human rights issues.

Environmental issues also regularly arise and we will address such concerns in discussing the CSR agenda later in this chapter. More recently, international tax policy has also come under the spotlight as a real political 'hot potato' for any business in determining where it should locate its assets and profits. We briefly discussed this new challenge in **Chapter 1** and will leave it to the experts to advise further as the 'BEPS' (Base Erosion and Profit Shifting) project gathers momentum. For now, we will focus on the issues of corruption and international labour and human rights practices.

## *Bribery and Corruption*

Though increased legislation and enforcement activity worldwide is helping to tackle corruption and level the global 'playing field', in certain countries bribery is still very much alive and well. To facilitate analysis and awareness of corruption, non-governmental organisation Transparency International ("the global coalition against corruption") produces an annual Corruptions Perceptions Index (CPI) that "ranks countries/territories based on how corrupt a country's public sector is perceived to be".[3] This is depicted in **Figure 5.1** below, from the pale green of very 'clean' countries to the dark teal of countries that are perceived to be the highly corrupt. The countries of Western Europe and North America tend to be paler green, whereas corruption hotspots of Sub-Saharan Africa and some of the contiguous Russian states feature in the darker teal.

FIGURE 5.1: DEPICTION OF THE TRANSPARENCY INTERNATIONAL
CPI FOR 2015

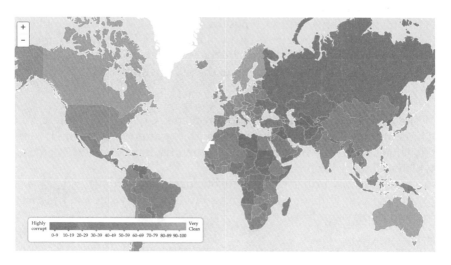

Scores range from zero (highly corrupt) to 100, where there is a perception of high degrees of integrity and low corruption. The 2015 index analysed 175 countries. The five countries with the lowest levels of corruption were:
1. Denmark
2. Finland
3. Sweden
4. New Zealand
5. The Netherlands.

On the low end of the scale, the bottom five countries were:
171. South Sudan
172. Sudan
173. Afghanistan
174. North Korea
175. Somalia.

As you can see from the top five, all are countries with stable, demo-cratically elected governments. The bottom five, on the other hand, are all either war-torn or have undemocratic governments, or no govern-ment at all.

As well as countries being risky, some *sectors*, by virtue of their com-petitive realities and operating norms, are considered more prone to corruption than others. Again, Transparency International provides a useful tool. As well as ranking "28 of the world's largest economies according to the perceived likelihood of companies from these coun-tries to pay bribes abroad", the 'Bribe Payers Index' "captures per-ceptions of bribery across business sectors", including bribery among companies.[4] Historically, the index has identified construction, mining and defence as among the most troublesome sectors, while agricul-ture, civilian aerospace and IT are relatively clean from a corruption standpoint.

Awareness of when and where corruption is most likely to occur is key to understanding the relative risks of operating in a given indus-try or region. *How* corruption becomes manifest is another dimension to consider. As well as the obvious involvement of cash, bribery can take more subtle and insidious forms, such as excessive hospitality, unearned rewards, campaign contributions, charitable donations, even nepotism.

Tackling the root causes of corruption, therefore, requires a skilful and nuanced approach. Imperiously waving international or domestic laws is unlikely to prevent it. In fact, bribery is probably already illegal in the location, though the law may not be fully enforced. The trick is to work out practical ways to make the law stick.

### EXAMPLE: GETTING REAL IN INDIA

I recall an assignment with an international group which involved training their management teams across India on anti-corruption policies. After enduring an hour of baleful stares while I rattled on about 'adequate procedures' under the UK's Bribery Act, I even-tually got the message. I shut down my PowerPoint presentation and we discussed the challenge of doing business without bribery in India. We agreed that the management team could not change the world overnight. However, we were also unanimous that they should at least try. So, for example, with regard to all-too-common requests for facilitation payments (i.e. 'grease payments', kickbacks or small bribes), we devised the general rule that if asked by a corrupt government official for, say, a 1,000 Rupee 'administration fee' or similar, that the manager would create at least "1,000 rupees worth of hassle". Tactics would include:

- requesting a copy of the official's ID;
- asking to speak with his or her superior;
- demanding a receipt for the payment;
- pointing to the section of the company's policy prohibiting such payments;
- explaining that the request is in breach of local and international law;
- confirming the incident would be reported on www.IpaidaBribe. com or similar (see **Chapter 1**);
- simply saying you don't have enough cash.

While it's possible that the official would be completely unimpressed by any or all of the above, he might also decide, because you're such a nuisance, to wave you on and seek a bribe from the next guy instead. The general conclusion of the training session was that if you don't start somewhere, you will never get anywhere.

## Labour Practices and Human Rights

As well as bribery, a company contemplating overseas expansion may grapple with the ethics of internationally diverse labour practices and whether it should:

- pay a higher wage to raise the living standards of its workforce;
- refuse to hire children, even when it is legal to do so;
- hire women or members of a discriminated-against race or ethnicity;
- limit the number of working hours to acceptable 'western' norms, but in the process possibly deny local staff overtime opportunities;
- refuse to engage local suppliers and contractors whose practices may be unethical or unsafe.

The following hypothetical scenario is designed to show how complex these issues can be:

## EXAMPLE: DAMNED IF YOU DO

The CEO of multinational company 'CottonOn', which prides itself on the fair labour practices and policies with which it operates at its manufacturing plants in India and Pakistan, is shocked to learn that as part of a routine CSR audit, nine-year-old twins (brother and sister) have been found working in one of the company's facilities in India's Andhra Pradesh province. The CEO immediately issues an instruction that controls must be comprehensively reviewed so that this can never happen again and, of course, the nine-year-olds must not be allowed work in the factory until they have reached the legal minimum age. A few months later the CEO learns that the children's family could no longer find the means to maintain their home, while the girl had been sold into prostitution and the boy was now begging and scavenging recyclable plastic from the local dump for a pittance.

What would you have done as CEO if you could have anticipated the devastating impact on the family? Who could condone child labour? But is that better than the, albeit unintended, consequences of the alternative? The clothing manufacturer Levi Strauss & Co. faced a similar issue with apparel workers in its factory in Bangladesh and a case study the company has published on its website describing its enlightened approach in dealing with the problem is reproduced below.[5]

## LEVI STRAUSS AND THE ISSUE OF CHILD LABOUR

### "Case Study: Child Labor in Bangladesh

Shortly after our Terms of Engagement (TOE) were implemented, factory assessors discovered that two factories in Bangladesh were employing workers under the minimum working age. While a clear violation of the TOE, Levi Strauss & Co. (LS&CO.) management found itself in a difficult situation when it came to addressing the problem.

The issue of underage labor is a complicated one in Bangladesh — a country where it is not uncommon for a child (defined in the TOE as a person younger than 15 or younger than the mandatory schooling age) to support an entire family on his or her wages. Further, many children born in Bangladesh are not issued birth certificates and due to malnutrition, many people can look younger than their age.

Other companies facing the issue of child labor at the time simply instructed their contractors to fire underage workers. LS&CO. management decided to take a different approach — one that would be informed and guided by the company's values: empathy, originality, integrity and courage.

Several LS&CO. managers and consultants met with the contractors to develop an agreement on what to do in the immediate situation and how the contractors would operate going forward.

Under the agreement, the factories agreed to continue to pay the already employed underage workers their salaries and benefits while they attended school and offer them full-time jobs when they reached the legal working age. LS&CO. agreed to pay for the students' tuition and books. If there was no room in the nearby public school, LS&CO. and the factories would rent space and hire a teacher for the students.

The factories also agreed that, going forward, their personnel would require any youth who applies for a job to present a school certificate stating that the applicant is 15 years old or older. In the event an applicant appears much younger, a dental examination may be used to establish the worker's age.

Our approach to this difficult situation earned LS&CO. the praise of Bangladeshi and U.S. government officials, academics and several nongovernmental organizations (NGOs). Subsequently, the Bangladesh Garment Manufacturers and Exporters Association along with other groups set aside approximately $1 million for the education of about 75,000 underage girls who previously worked in factories."

Levi Strauss is praised regularly for its progressive practices, not only in relation to labour relations, worker conditions and safety but for its entire approach to sustainable, responsible business.

In some industries, companies join with their peers to agree voluntary codes of conduct, prescribing minimum standards with the intention of improving the sector as a whole. For example, in the apparel sector a group of companies have sponsored the 'Sweatfree' and 'Clean Clothes' codes of conduct, which cover labour relations, health & safety, freedom of association, terms of employment, etc. Similar initiatives have been developed in many other sectors from IT to toys, from baby formula to footballs.

The UN Global Compact is the "world's largest corporate sustainability initiative". It is a "call to companies to align strategies and operations with universal principles on human rights, labour, environment and anti-corruption, and take actions that advance societal goals." Derived from the Universal Declaration of Human Rights, the International Labour Organization's Declaration on Fundamental Principles and Rights at Work, the Rio Declaration on Environment and Development and the UN Convention Against Corruption, the UN Global Compact sets out 10 principles for sustainable business[6]:

1. protection of internationally proclaimed human rights;
2. non-complicity in human rights abuses;
3. support for the freedom of association;
4. elimination of forced and compulsory labour;
5. effective abolition of child labour;
6. elimination of employment and workplace discrimination;
7. supporting a precautionary approach to environmental challenges;
8. undertaking initiatives to promote greater environmental responsibility;
9. development and diffusion of environmentally friendly technologies;
10. working against corruption in all its forms, including extortion and bribery.

More than 8,000 participating companies and 4,000 non-business participants have already signed up to the principles of the UN Global Compact. Joining such networks, groups and compacts can be a straightforward way to obtain up-to-date, unbiased information, access best practice tools and even avail of mentoring opportunities to assist in approaching new, overseas territories with the requisite knowledge and confidence to answer some of the questions raised above.

## 'When in Rome ...'?

In his essay, "When in Rome, do … What?", business ethics expert Thomas Donaldson, writes:

> "When in Rome, we should not simply do as the Romans, nor exactly as we do at home. We should allow for differences in customs, even as we remain true to our own deeper values at home; and doing this well means preparing for our trip to Rome in advance."[7]

Beware therefore of 'cultural relativism', the idea that no culture's ethics are better than any other's and that there are no international rights and wrongs (i.e. 'when in Rome'). As Donaldson notes in another article: "Cultural relativism is morally blind. There are fundamental values that cross cultures and companies must uphold them."[8] At the other end of the spectrum, and one to be equally avoided, is 'ethical imperialism', "which directs people to do everywhere exactly as they do at home".

> "There is no Esperanto of global ethics."
>
> Michael Walzer

Donaldson concludes that if for cultural relativists nothing is sacred and nothing is wrong, and for ethical imperialists most things that are different are wrong, neither approach is adequate: the answer must be between the two extremes. Companies should determine a single "ethical threshold" for business conduct both at home and abroad, based on the golden rule ('do unto others as you would have them do unto you') and in turn guided by three principles:

1. respect for core human values that determine the absolute moral threshold for all business activities;
2. respect for local traditions; and
3. the belief that context matters when deciding what is right and wrong.

The idea of an absolute ethical threshold, or a set of cross-cultural common values, is also at the heart of an article titled "Up to Code: does your company's conduct meet world-class standards?", published in the *Harvard Business Review* in 2015.[9] By reviewing code of conduct development worldwide, the authors identified eight principles representing emerging best practice in providing guidelines for good conduct internationally, which are set out in **Figure 5.2** below:

## FIGURE 5.2: EIGHT PRINCIPLES TO GUIDE GOOD CONDUCT INTERNATIONALLY

| | | |
|---|---|---|
| **Fiduciary** (acting in the best interest of stakeholders) | **Respect for Property** | **Reliability** (trust and promise-keeping) |
| **Transparency** (importance of honesty, truth and openness) | **Dignity** (respect for people) | **Fairness** (in distributing rewards and burdens) |
| **Citizenship** (respect for the law, shared resources and contribution to society) | **Responsiveness** (to stakeholders concerns) | |

In helping managers to distinguish between practices that are merely locally different and those that are fundamentally wrong, these universal principles need to be supplemented with localised guidelines and detailed procedures. These, in turn, should be informed by an appreciation of what Erin Meyer calls "the invisible boundaries of global business".[10] As she points out, "the interconnected systems of the global economy are in full swing", so whether we communicate by e-mail, Skype, video conference or in person, "cultural awareness across nations is becoming a must for all, managers and employees alike". This, Meyer believes, can be achieved by understanding an eight-scale framework of national culture, each scale described as a continuum between opposing positions in relation to:

1. **Communicating** Are they simple and clear, or rich and deep in meaning?
2. **Evaluating** For example, is negative feedback given directly or discreetly?
3. **Leading** Are people in groups egalitarian or do they prefer hierarchy?
4. **Deciding** Are decisions made top-down or by consensus?
5. **Trusting** Is trust based on how well people know each other or work together?

6. **Disagreeing** Are disagreements tackled directly or is confrontation avoided?
7. **Scheduling** Is time perceived as absolute linear points or as a flexible range?
8. **Persuading** Do they like to hear specific cases or holistic explanations?

These are supported by engaging stories and explanations, for example as to:

- Why the Chinese expert keeps quiet at a crucial meeting on his topic.
- How the Japanese 'read the air' to interpret what you really mean.
- How a Dutchman can inform his colleague that his proposal is daft and then share a beer with him the same day.
- What an Englishwoman really means when she says, "Perhaps you could think about doing it this way?"

By taking the time to decode how and why people are culturally predisposed to behave in a certain way, colleagues can be better equipped and adapted to work multinationally.

The table below includes some of these lessons and outlines top 10 tips for a company to consider when moving into overseas markets and how best to adapt its domestic values, ethics and culture for foreign application to successfully and ethically reap the rewards of international growth.

## TOP 10 TIPS FOR INTERNATIONAL ETHICAL LEADERSHIP

| |
|---|
| 1. **Understand the Risks** Venture forth, but do your homework and keep your eyes wide open. Before you make a move, scour country reports, World Bank analyses, sectoral publications, consult the Transparency International website, establish contacts with companies with operations in the location, seek advice and regular updates from professional firms with experience on the ground. Only merge, acquire, buy from, sell to or partner with those that share your standards and conduct full ethical due diligence before signing on the dotted line. |
| 2. **Don't Let your Values get Lost in Translation** Keep ethics communications simple. Use plain words, straightforward structures and short sentences. Avoid metaphors and humour (at best, it doesn't translate and, at worst, it insults.) Don't just fire off missives from head office. Include overseas operations in the normal review cycle and visit regularly. Time some of these trips to coincide with a national holiday and celebrate with the local team. |

3. **Establish Exchange Programmes and Develop Cultural Competencies** Create in-house ambassadors through an international exchange programme to integrate the different cultures. Ensure that 'expats' are trained and their families fully supported during the transition so that it is a positive, enriching experience for all. Complement this programme by arranging cross-cultural training for employees who interact with colleagues overseas and sponsor foreign language courses both at home and abroad.

4. **Explicitly Address Ethical Awareness** Ensure that all who work internationally are trained on the ethical issues likely to arise (employment practices, corruption, worker safety, environment, etc.). Ensure that they understand relevant law, regulations and codes of practice. Overseas employees should also be fully trained on your values, ethics and culture ('the way we do things around here'). Provide a dedicated resource or helpline to provide further guidance and answer concerns. Employ local expertise to assist in the design of these training modules, to provide context and credibility.

5. **Flex Ethical Policies and Procedures to Fit** Be wary of 'one-size-fits-all' compliance rules – they generally don't. Take gift giving, for example, traditional in certain national business cultures and occasionally involving the exchange of expensive items. While these could be toned down (putting your company's logo on the gift is an easy way of converting it into a token), banning such gifts outright is not recommended. Regarding gift limits, €50 is different depending on whether you are in Zurich, Glasgow or Delhi. Besides, some governments prescribe their own limits on the value of a gift received, which will always trump an in-house policy. Allow local input to influence the development of pragmatic guidelines and train employees to help them differentiate between what is acceptable and what is inappropriate.

6. **Apply One's Own Standards Consistently** While an adapted, tailored approach works best, this must be balanced with a clear understanding that when local norms conflict with the company's 'domestic' standards, the higher standard will always apply. Maintain strict discipline to show clearly that reputation will not be compromised just because it's easier to let things slide to a lower common denominator. More importantly, explicitly reward employees for operating within the rules, making it clear that it is acceptable to walk away from business if it cannot be secured through ethical means, e.g. if it would have required the payment of a bribe.

7. **Plan for Differing Responses to Ethics Initiatives** Seniority rules in Japan, Ramadan is not the time to launch a new initiative in the UAE, a French whistleblower is a rarity, *'guanxi'* (connections) underpin Chinese business, in Latin America firms are run like families, the list goes on. Understand cultural nuances and plan for varied responses, being careful not to stereotype. Again, helplines or similar dedicated resources will help to bridge the gap.

8. **Align the CSR Agenda** Investing in your international communities and on issues close to the hearts of your overseas staff is the responsible and also the smart thing to do. (We will review this in more detail below.)

9. **Don't Expect International Ethical Leadership to come Cheap** Competing to win business when brown envelopes are expected is challenging. Paying fair wages and not hiring minors undermines your competitive advantage relative to those with no such scruples. Making the workplace safer likewise increases relative costs. Ensuring standards are upheld through training and communication costs money and consumes valuable management time. Doing the right thing will not be the cheapest option, so budget for it accordingly.

10. **Make Local Alliances and Put your Reputation on the Map** Accept that you cannot change the world alone; partner with like-minded companies in your industry and join associations that aim to improve labour standards, support fair trade and stamp out corruption. While visiting your locations overseas, meet local government, trade officials, chambers of commerce, etc. Explain your approach and ensure that your name is synonymous with integrity.

In addition to these general tips, there are a number of particular areas that require the application of a more focused ethical lens in order to ensure you can run your business with integrity internationally. These include the requirement for due diligence in international merger and acquisition transactions and in selecting overseas business partners, in developing ethical sourcing strategies and the increased case for an aligned CSR agenda.

## International Due Diligence

### Mergers and Acquisitions (M&A)

*"Just so as we are clear: you buy a company you buy their problems. If they have lawsuits, investigations, illegal conduct going on, it's now your problem. And there's no insulation that I know of."*

Walter G. Ricciardi, formerly Deputy Director of the
Division of Enforcement of the US Securities and
Exchange Commission[11]

If ever there was a case for *caveat emptor*, it is in international mergers and acquisitions (M&As). Deal-making across borders can be problematic, particularly transactions in the more corrupt countries. Information can be opaque and records unreliable, with language barriers further impeding proper financial, legal and reputational analysis. A joint venture may be the only available or permitted route to market in some of these countries, and involves a big leap of faith, effectively staking your company's reputation on the anticipated conduct of a relatively unknown partner.

Furthermore, if you buy a foreign business with a history of corruption, you may overpay for it in three different ways:
1. The asking price is likely to be determined based on a multiple of EBITDA or profit. These numbers will be tainted by revenues from contracts illegally obtained through bribery, meaning that any consideration will entail paying a multiple of those tainted earnings.
2. As the new owner, presumably intent on conducting only clean business, inherited contracts might not be capable of renewal without payment of bribes, meaning that the business model may no longer be sustainable.
3. Finally, you may be liable to the authorities for fines, disgorgement of profits and even criminal sanctions should the bribery be brought to their attention.

Increased legislative requirements both at home and overseas have heightened the risk of criminal and civil penalties for individuals and companies. There have been many examples of the perils of ignoring these corruption risks in M&A transactions, including the famous case of "wilful blindness" involving millionaire investor Frederick Bourke.[12] In this 2009 case the US Department of Justice secured a conviction against Mr Bourke in relation to a consortium investment in the privatisation of the State Oil Company of Azerbaijan. The court found that he knew or *should have known* that improper payments were made to government officials, failed to conduct due diligence and ignored red flags. He was sentenced to over a year in prison, so had plenty of time to consider what he should have known and could have done about it.

Despite such caveats and cases, many companies either do not undertake corruption due diligence or just skim the surface, allocating insufficient time and resources for a forensic review. The checklist below provides a simple but practical method for high-level **initial** anti-corruption screening in international M&A.

### INITIAL CHECKLIST FOR M&A CORRUPTION DUE DILIGENCE

| | | Yes | No |
|---|---|---|---|
| 1. | Does the target business operate in a country with a Transparency International Corruptions Perceptions Index score of 50 or less? | | |
| 2. | Does it operate in a high-risk industry, as per the Transparency International Bribe Payers' Index? | | |
| 3. | Does the business depend on licences from, sell to or contract with government officials or state-owned enterprises? Are any of the deal principals politically connected? | | |
| 4. | Is the target reliant on agents or other intermediaries? | | |
| 5. | Does it operate in a new product or geographic market? | | |
| 6. | Does the target, its principals or the industry have any history of sanctions for anti-corruption and/or competition law violations? | | |
| 7. | Is there evidence of an existing compliance infrastructure, e.g. audit committee, codes of conduct, policies, good faith reporting channels, due diligence procedures, etc.? | | |

| 8. | Do the values and culture of the target, its board and management team appear to be consistent with ours? | | |
|---|---|---|---|
| 9. | Is this a joint venture? | | |
| 10. | Is the target subject to the UK's Bribery Act and/ or the US FCPA, e.g. by virtue of its ownership structure or legal nexus? | | |

Based on the answers to the above, further analysis may be required, particularly to address any 'Yes' responses, and specialist legal assistance engaged to conduct further required due diligence. The conclusions of the due diligence process will in turn:

- impact the deal negotiation process;
- determine if the transaction should proceed or not;
- be reflected in the acquisition documents, especially the representations and warranties clause of the sales and purchase agreement;
- inform the post-acquisition compliance integration plan.

The following example illustrates how this might work in practice.

### EXAMPLE: A FIRST INVESTMENT IN KAZAKHSTAN

- This is a first, large-scale acquisition by your company in Central Asia.
- One of the principals is a locally well-known, politically-connected entrepreneur.
- The business was formerly a state-owned enterprise (SOE).
- The target has a good code of ethics and an effective compliance framework.

Given the size of the deal and location of the target business, the political connections of the principal and the fact that the company was formerly an SOE, a substantial ethical compliance due diligence exercise is required with the assistance of third parties well-versed in researching transactions in this part of the world.

159

Let's say this reveals a number of issues, including the fact that one of the board members has been the subject of an extended corruption investigation and is in settlement negotiations with the local authorities; there is also some evidence of unusual payments to agents in offshore locations. Do these findings mean the end of the deal?

Not necessarily. Here are some steps that could be taken to de-risk the transaction and potentially clear the way for it to go ahead:

- Consider renegotiating the transaction as an asset deal (rather than equity), as in share deals all legal responsibilities and potential liabilities are automatically inherited, which is not the case in a transaction for the acquisition of assets.
- If that is not possible, then as part of the deal terms, the corrupt board member should exit the company on deal signing.
- A full due diligence of all third parties should be commissioned and contracts with corrupt agents cancelled. Reporting responsibilities should be reviewed.
- The principal's political connections should be examined in detail and any payments or arrangements with them or their associates scrutinised.
- A robust schedule of representations and warranties should be agreed.
- The escrow* could be negotiated upwards.
- A comprehensive post-integration compliance plan should be developed, building on the existing infrastructure (a mitigating factor in the deal), correcting any inappropriate practices and mindful of the country risk factors and potential for corruption.

In reality, with fuller legal and financial due diligence, more comprehensive deal analysis, much board discussion and debate, etc., there may be other reasons why a transaction of this nature would not proceed. It might simply fail 'the smell test', i.e. where, despite having passed the various due diligence hoops, the board votes against it given the possibility of the company's reputation being sullied simply by association with a market so synonymous with corruption. However, the main point of the example is that it *is* possible to enter riskier emerging markets as long as one is wide awake to potential hazards and mitigates them accordingly.

---

* Funds held by a third-party escrow service on behalf of the two parties in a transaction until it receives instruction that certain obligations have been fulfilled.

## *Overseas Business Partners (Third Parties)*

While important at home, in operating abroad extra vigilance is necessary in the selection of business partners. In **Chapter 2**, we saw in the Walmart Mexican bribery case how trying to maintain a veneer of respectability by delegating 'dirty work' to third-party agents is not acceptable. Under most international and, increasingly also national, legislation, business partners or third-party agents are now considered *pari passu* with employees in terms of the requirement to ensure they are not engaged in corrupt activities. Such third parties typically include:

| | |
|---|---|
| • Agents | • Intermediaries |
| • Consultants | • Distributors |
| • Sub-contractors | • Lobbyists |
| • Project partners | • Deal makers |

Operating in overseas markets, the risks are even higher with third parties because a company is likely to rely more heavily on these relationships than at home to facilitate business, negotiate contracts or extend existing ones.

The only way to ensure that a third-party relationship is genuine, value-adding and on the right side of the law is to complete proper due diligence prior to selection. Because companies operating internationally may engage hundreds, if not thousands, of third parties annually, it can and should only focus on those requiring closer scrutiny, so the adoption of a risk-based approach is both wise and speedy. The process is not dissimilar to that employed in the context of international M&A and consists of the five steps shown in **Figure 5.3** on the following page:

## FIGURE 5.3: STEPS IN A RISK-BASED APPROACH TO BUSINESS PARTNER DUE DILIGENCE

| | |
|---|---|
| **Risk Triage** | • identify and categorise third parties based on perceived risk and assign a 'relationship owner' |
| **Research** | • gather data relevant to the risk assessment |
| **Review** | • review the information and decide whether or not to engage |
| **Ratify** | • agree contractual terms and any other conditions, e.g. certification, training, etc. |
| **Reassess** | • monitor changes, reassess risk and re-certify |

We can note the following with regard to the specific steps above.

**Risk Triage** The level of perceived risk may be influenced by such factors as:
- the location of the third party, again with reference to the 'Corruptions Perceptions Index' (CPI – see above);
- the amount and type of direct engagement with government officials;
- the third party's brand, reputation, scale and experience;
- the contract terms and the quality of records and compliance.

Examples of third parties that may be considered low and high risk respectively are set out below.

| Low Risk | High Risk |
|---|---|
| • is in a country with a low CPI;<br>• operates globally under a recognised, established brand;<br>• does not interact with government officials;<br>• charges a time-based fee, in line with industry standards;<br>• is paid by cheque. | • has its only office in a country with a high CPI score;<br>• operates on a success-fee basis;<br>• interacts regularly with government agencies in relation to product approvals;<br>• requires payments to be made offshore or in cash. |

**Research and Review** The information required will depend on the spectrum of risk categorisation above. Here are some practical suggestions of the kinds of information to review at different risk levels.

---

**Low to Moderate Risk**
- **Internal Questionnaire addressing:**
  - third party type, contact information, location and business description;
  - company type, structure, ownership and date and place of establishment;
  - CVs for senior management;
  - summary financial statements, press releases and online information;
  - information re any prior violations;
  - information on known government or other third-party affiliations;
  - local legal requirements.
- **External Search (discretionary)**
  - reputational and financial references;
  - media search and government database inquiry.

**Moderate to High Risk**
- **Internal Questionnaire addressing all points above plus:**
  - interviews with senior management and CVs for staff involved in the engagement
  - full business profile, license review and detailed financial check
  - report from facility visit
  - compliance programme plan
- **External Search (mandatory) to include the above and also:**
  - embassy consultation
  - public records search
  - industry source interviews.

---

**Ratify** Contractual terms will naturally vary from one third party to the next, but standard provisions typically address the following:
- full indemnification in the event of any corruption violation;
- any such violation being considered a material breach of contract and grounds for cessation of all payments;
- full co-operation with any compliance investigation;
- written approval from the principal prior to the recruitment of any sub-vendors or agents;

- the right to regularly audit relevant accounting records and compliance procedures;
- acknowledgement of compliance with the principal's code of conduct and any relevant legislation.

Depending on the risk profile of the third party and whether the relationship is considered strategic for development of the business in the location, some companies go beyond due diligence and legal checks and, as mentioned above, require such third parties to be trained in the company's values and code of conduct, even require an annual certification of compliance.

Consider how a leading consumer technology manufacturer determines the extent of follow-up work required for its various distributors and agents across the globe in the example below.

### EXAMPLE: THIRD-PARTY RISK ASSESSMENT AND ACTION PLAN

| Requirement | Lower-risk Distributor | Higher-risk Distributor | Agent |
|---|---|---|---|
| **Contact with Anti-bribery T&Cs** | *Required* | *Required* | *Required* |
| **Business Conduct Expectations** | *Required* | *Required* | *Required* |
| **Full Application/ Due Diligence** | *Not Required* | *Required* | *Required* |
| **External Background check** | *Not Required* | *Discretionary* | *Required* |
| **Escalated Approval** | *Not Required* | *Not Required* | *Required* |
| **Live Training Session** | *Not Required* | *Not Required* | *Required* |
| **Application Recertification** | *Not Required* | *Required (annually)* | *Required (semi-annually)* |
| **Activity Reports** | *Not Required* | *Not Required* | *Required (semi-annually)* |

Finally, the following extract from the guidance to the UK's Bribery Act 2010 is a helpful example of the third-party due diligence process outlined above, highlighting some of the commercial red flags to be alert to throughout.

## EXAMPLE: DUE DILIGENCE OF AGENTS[13]

"A medium to large sized manufacturer of specialist equipment ('G') has an opportunity to enter an emerging market in a foreign country ('H') by way of a government contract to supply equipment to the state. Local convention requires any foreign commercial organisations to operate through a local agent. G is concerned to appoint a reputable agent and ensure that the risk of bribery being used to develop its business in the market is minimised.

G could consider any or a combination of the following:
- compiling a suitable questionnaire for potential agents requiring, for example, details of ownership if not an individual; CVs and references for those proposed in performing the proposed service; details of any directorships and third-party relationships and any relevant judicial or regulatory findings.
- Having a clear statement of the precise nature of the services offered, costs, commissions, fees and the preferred means of remuneration.
- Undertaking research, including internet searches, of the prospective agents and, if a corporate body, of everyone having a degree of control over its affairs.
- Making enquiries with the relevant authorities in H to verify the information received in response to the questionnaire.
- Following up references and clarifying any matters arising from the questionnaire of any other information received with the agents, arranging face-to-face meetings where appropriate.
- Requesting sight or evidence of any potential agents' own antibribery policies and, where a corporate body, reporting procedures and records.

- Being alert to key commercial questions, such as:
  - Is the agent really required?
  - Does the agent have the required expertise?
  - Are they interacting with or closely connected to public officials?
  - Is what you are proposing to pay reasonable and commercial?
- Renewing due diligence enquiries on a periodic basis if an agent is appointed."

## Ethical Sourcing Strategies

While companies should monitor the 'downstream' activities of third parties such as their agents, distributors, etc., the following newspaper headlines remind us of the importance of also focussing on ethics 'upstream' in the supply chain.

| "Building Collapse in Bangladesh leaves Scores Dead" |
|---|
| *The New York Times* |
| "'Mass suicide' protest at Apple manufacturer factory" |
| *The Telegraph* |
| "Child labour on Nestlé farms: chocolate giant's problems continue" |
| *The Guardian* |
| "Horses for main course: a scandalously delicious meat" |
| *The Irish Times* |

In the 1980s and 1990s, more and more multinationals chose to outsource production to parts of the globe with entirely different worker safety standards and employment practices. Companies such as Nike, one of the worst offenders, have had to spend the decades since reforming labour practices, restructuring supply arrangements and rebuilding customer trust.

As recent as 2012, however, another corporate giant, Apple, was hit by a tsunami of criticism for working conditions at its Chinese manufacturer FoxConn, which it was claimed contributed to the suicides of 14 employees.[14] Then, in April 2013, the Rana Plaza disaster in Bangladesh happened, in which more than 1,100 people died in the collapse of a garment factory.[15] International outcry prompted genuine efforts to improve conditions, however it seems that there is still much to do to embed social responsibility and ethical behaviour throughout international supply chains. In the meantime, there are real risks to the reputation of companies and the health, even the lives, of their overseas employees as long as these issues are not taken seriously.

A pragmatic way to get suppliers to share and uphold your values and standards is to have them sign up to a suppliers' code of conduct as a pre-condition of contracting with you. A good example is the McDonald's Supplier Code of Conduct, which sets out the minimum standards the company expects throughout its supply chain, and can be read on their corporate website, www.aboutmcdonalds.com, under 'Sustainability', then 'Sourcing'.[16]

McDonald's is also another company that has had to step-up its efforts in product provenance and supply-chain transparency, having no doubt suffered indigestion itself from having to swallow the worst kind of publicity in the movie *Super-size Me* and the book *Fast Food Nation*. An enhanced supplier code was one such initiative, part of a series of due diligence steps that each procurement manager, supplier and facility must follow in order to ensure the integrity of the entire supply chain.

As with the selection of business partners, a risk-based approach is also common in carrying out due diligence on prospective suppliers. Suppliers (including procurement agents) may be categorised as high or low risk based on a number of factors, including, for example:
- their location, or the location of their source of supply;
- the value of the annual supply or service contract;
- whether they are a regular, strategic supplier to the business or an occasional, casual provider of certain goods or services;
- the strength of the supplier's own ethical practices and its CSR pedigree.

Depending on the assessment of relative risk, the supplier will then be required to engage in a series of checks, from basic requirements like signing a code of conduct or completing a self-assessment analysis for lower risk suppliers to an extensive external CSR audit for those suppliers carrying a high level of inherent procurement risk.

Finally, in the management and maintenance of an ethical sourcing pro-gramme it is vital to ensure that:
- those in charge of sourcing and procurement decisions are sensitised to the issues and fully trained, understand the process and what is expected of them;
- the sourcing environment is carefully monitored and updated for new or changed supplier circumstances, and for any new legislative requirements or CSR best practices;

- there is regular assessment of the programme and relevant, timely reporting to executive management and, if appropriate, the board on its overall effectiveness.

## Aligning the CSR Agenda with your Growth Strategy

Finally, let's discuss CSR. It is not the sole preserve of international companies, as social responsibility obligations apply to all companies, big and small, whether operating domestically or across borders.[17] However, there is no doubt that when a company makes the move overseas, the expectations for it to develop a more focussed CSR agenda intensify.

Corporate social responsibility could demand a chapter in its own right, so this relatively brief section will introduce the topic, highlight the key elements of an international CSR programme, provide two examples of companies that do a good job of integrating their social programmes within their overall strategic frameworks, and conclude with a nod to emergent best practices in the area.

In *Cannibals with Forks: The Triple Bottom Line of 21st Century Business*, John Elkington introduced the need for a more holistic perspective on company performance.[18] Using the metaphor of the 'triple bottom line', Elkington argued that businesses should have performance and related reporting responsibilities along three dimensions: profit, people and planet (see **Figure 5.4**).

FIGURE 5.4: THE THREE 'PS' OF THE TRIPLE BOTTOM LINE

Profit
- the traditional, default measure of performance, reflecting the responsibility to shareholders and providers of capital

People
- representing the obligations to employees, society and the wider stakeholder group

Planet
- being the company's responsibility for environmental stewardship

His principal thesis is that the corporation is a member of the moral community and as such has certain social responsibilities. CSR has a similar premise and finds that corporations also have responsibilities analogous to any other citizen in a community, and that these are of an ethical, legal, economic and philanthropic nature.

As a concept, it has developed over time, undergoing a number of name changes in the process: 'corporate citizenship', 'social responsibility', 'sustainability' and, more recently, the concept of 'responsible leadership' and a "shared value approach". These are all more or less interchangeable terms for an organisation's strategies and programmes to operate in a socially and environmentally sustainable way, though often with a slightly different emphasis or focus, depending on sector, location, etc.

The broad range of business responsibilities that CSR embraces is nicely summarised in the 'mind map' in **Figure 5.5** below, reproduced from Sheila Killian's *Corporate Social Responsibility: A Guide with Irish Experiences*:

## FIGURE 5.5: RESPONSIBILITIES OF A BUSINESS[19]

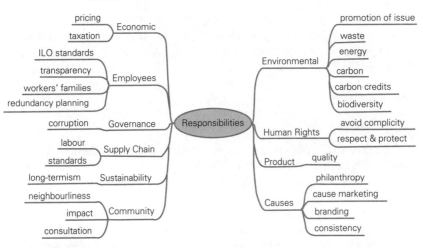

We have already discussed a number of these topics, including corruption, labour and human rights, and the supply chain. The environment and community are also key CSR areas and the following are examples of what true leadership on these issues can look like. First, the personal perspectives of the late Anita Roddick, founder of The Body Shop.

## Extracts from an Interview with Dame Anita Roddick[20]

"When Anita Roddick founded the Body Shop in 1976, it was out of an emerging need to support herself, and she didn't expect the endeavor to last more than a few years. Originally, Roddick sold 20 products inspired by recipes and natural ingredients she had picked up in her travels around the world. Integral to the Body Shop was an ethic of concern: incorporating environmentally sound ingredients and practices into the products and using the shops and items to raise consciousness and inspire activism among consumers. With their simple reusable bottles and no-frills packaging, the public soon caught on, launching the Body Shop into one of the most successful beauty products chains in the world."

**"What were some of the guiding principles when you started the Body Shop?**
People assume that we were campaigning, that we were environmentalists. We couldn't have spelled the word environment in those days. We were social activists. In America you had the anti-war movement. In England, we had mostly the student union movement and the anti-atomic bomb movement. The guiding principles, I think, were never to tell lies, never cheat. We were learning so much from the Quakers—they're great businesspeople. And the cooperative movement, Scandinavian business practices, the Amish. Those were the good practices we were looking for, our founding principles—go back to the community and protect the workers."

...

The other principles were that no product, no ingredient was ever animal tested. That was a major building block. The other was very much human rights. We dedicated the Articles of Association and Memoranda, which in England is the legal definition of the purpose of your company, to human rights advocacy and social and environmental change. So everything the company did had that as its canopy. We used our ideas to corral millions of customers into the shop to change the world [with respect to] animal testing or to help human rights activists or prisoners of conscience. You could have 2,000 shops fighting against certain issues. I mean we did the most amazing campaigns. On political prisoners around the world—30 political prisoners, 17 were released. I think that was the single most courageous thing we did. We turned our shops into little [activist] stations, where the guiding principle was that we had to clean up our own mess.

**When you talk about cleaning up your own mess—how?**
We made our own boxes, and recycled them. We have our own compost system which was copied from Ben Cohen of Ben and Jerry's, where all the water from our cleaning processes went into and was recycled into the products. And we invested 40 percent of our energy in a wind power station in Wales.

Also we were looking at community initiatives, so that if you make skin and haircare products, it's not a matter of life and death. We found we could balance these by defining trade; by having conversations with farmers or growers or cooperatives around the world, asking them, "You grow this, harvest it, we will buy from you." We call it community trade, and we have some projects around the world, supporting thousands of families. It's a very honorable exchange. We see the results: in schools and latrines that are built; cooperatives; HIV/AIDS workshops; livestock.

We have a wonderful project in Nicaragua where we work with sesame farmers. For five years I've been trying to get Avon, who is huge, to purchase some of their sesame oil, which is wonderful on the skin. To this day I have not managed to get any cosmetic house to [do this.]

**Well that comes to my next question. As the pioneer behind the Body Shop, how do you see the relationship between sustainability and a successful business, or consumerism, really? Can they co-exist?**
That's a difficult question. I think there's a myth that says to grow is the way to go. I don't think you need to grow that way to be successful. You can honor [the idea] of a livelihood and run an honorable enterprise. I keep saying now to young entrepreneurs, "Don't take up the traditional business model. Look at the work. Even if it's a small version of a large company, you're still going to have the thinking of a large company."

One of the biggest mistakes I made was to go public and on the stock market. If I had had the knowledge then, and the patience, I would not have. It's such a sickness when you're successful, to keep growing and growing—and it's bullshit. But you don't know that, you're just so excited. Going public is really a way of saying that your financial bottom line is your motivator, and how you treat the community doesn't matter. That's never part of a business measure—it should be, but it isn't. It's always about maximizing profits, and we were always being contrary to that—doing things that the financial journalists were very wary of; acting like a nonprofit group and putting part of the profit back into the community.

But you're right—unless you can have a model in terms of sustainability, [where you're] increasingly aware of what you take out and put back in/on the planet... The biggest dilemma for me is water because in cosmetics you use so much. So we came out with a line about five years ago, which at minimum has less than five percent water in it. And I thought it was the most innovative product we ever did, but nobody bought it. Maybe it was the wrong time, maybe the Body Shop should take it up now. It's always a [matter] of the right time."

**"What are some of the more shocking things that you've learned?**
Indifference in humans. Human frailty. I went to give a major speech at an international chamber of commerce, and I'd been in Mexico and seen children born with no genitalia because of pesticides in the tobacco fields, and I was sharing this with the people who could do something about it, these heads of huge corporations, [who were] absolutely [indifferent]. That shocked me to the core. And suffering of kids: when you see kids or young people working 20 hours a day—20 hours a day—being beaten, being forced to take contraceptives, forced to take an abortion pill if they're pregnant—just to get a cheap product out the door. That completely outrages me. Because in this new millennia, still we can't dialogue. We don't put a penny towards peace initiatives; why can't we bloody sit down and dialogue?"

The CSR strategy and programmes of the Indian conglomerate, the Tata Group, is another example of what really good can look like.

> "The Tata philosophy of management has always been and is today more than ever, that corporate enterprises must be managed not merely in the interests of their owners, but equally in those of their employees, of the customers of their products, of the local community and finally of the country as a whole."
> J.R.D. Tata

## THE TATA WAY

Founded by Jamsetji Tata in 1868 and headquartered in India, the Tata Group employs over 600,000 people in more than 100 countries in sectors as diverse as steel, power, chemicals, communications, beverages, hotels and motors and with a mission "To improve the quality of life of the communities we serve globally, through long-term stakeholder value creation based on Leadership with Trust". 66% of the group is held by philanthropic trusts endowed by members of the Tata family.

Although better known in Europe as owner of the Jaguar and Land Rover marques, Tata has won accolades globally for its outstanding achievements in corporate citizenship. In a case study in the *Ivey Business Journal*,[21] Anant Nadkarni and Oana Branzei expose some of the secrets of the 'Tata Way', including:

- that Tata employees share the values of their leaders, which act as a guide for every new project in the group;
- that all Tata companies have evolved a collective commitment to aligning pro-social and environmental values with excellence in business endeavors.

These strengths have been carefully cultivated through two ground-breaking initiatives:

1. **The Tata Index for Sustainable Human Development** A pioneering effort to direct, measure and enhance the community work that assists Tata companies in their CSR initiatives, while seeding new benchmarks and motivating innovation across its operations.

   Within each Tata firm, a Head of CSR manages a cross-functional team in charge of community development, environmental management and volunteering. For each project, a leader is responsible for understanding the specific concerns of each community, defining beneficiaries and sustainability payoffs and identifying how the firm's core capabilities contribute to the stated need. Companies must self-assess their performance based on system, people and programme metrics, with clear KPIs for accountability, commitment, leadership, training and risk management.

2. **The Tata Leadership for Corporate Sustainability Profile** A set of guidelines for leaders who, having widened their leadership through Index for Sustainable Human Development projects, are then given specific 'roadmaps' for further developing

their competencies to set new standards for what their business can achieve.

Two of the best examples of this holistic approach to value creation include:

- the Computer-based Functional Literacy Project: a multimedia-based programme that helps adults learn how to read in just 40 hours;
- the Tata 'Swach', a compact, low-cost, in-home water-purification device, development of which was prompted by the 2004 tsunami which left thousands of people without clean drinking water.

Finally, Nestlé is a good example of a traditionally hard-nosed company making real headway with a 'shared value' approach.

## Nestlé and Shared Value

The subject of a *Harvard Business Review* article by Michael Porter and Mark Kramer,[22] 'shared value' is all about reconnecting company success with social progress in three distinct ways, specifically: "by

- reconceiving products and markets
- redefining productivity in the value chain
- and building supportive industry clusters at the company's locations."

In the case of Nestlé, this meant a redesign of its coffee-procurement processes, "working intensively with small farmers in impoverished areas who were trapped in a cycle of low productivity, poor quality, and environmental degradation." The company also began to provide advice on better farming practices, helping growers to secure better seeds, fertilisers and pesticides, and paying them a higher price for premium beans. "Higher yields and quality increased the growers' incomes, the environmental impact of farms shrank, and Nestlé's reliable supply of good coffee grew significantly. Shared value was created."

While these companies are at the leading edge of sustainable business practices worldwide, there are other notable emergent trends in CSR, including:

> The move by CEOs of the world's largest organisations to define their success in terms that have conventionally been the realm of political leaders and NGOs, recognising that there is a limit to what governments can achieve on their own and that collaboration with a more globally integrated and economically significant private sector is needed to effect real change.
>
> For example, Unilever CEO Paul Polman announcing the company's 2020 strategy as including the goal of halving the water associated with the consumer use of its products.[23]

> Decisions by some of the world's wealthiest individuals to donate sizeable portions of their fortunes to philanthropic and social causes in the course of their lifetimes, including the signatories of some 80-plus billionaires to 'The Giving Pledge'.[24]
>
> For example, in December 2015, Mark Zuckerberg promised to give away 99% of his shares in Facebook to a new organisation with two core goals: advancing human potential and promoting equality.[25]

> Similar altruism is increasingly apparent in the general employee population, especially among the millennial workforce, who are keen to volunteer to make a positive impact on society or even endure personal privation – were you one of the millions who took part in the Ice-Bucket Challenge in the summer of 2014 in aid of several motor neuron disease charities?
>
> For example, according to the Head of Social Impact at LinkedIn, by the end of 2014, more than 3.5 million LinkedIn members had indicated on their profile that they want to serve on a non-profit board or use their skills to volunteer.[26]

> The growing practice among companies, large and small, to partner with each other and/or NGOs and community groups to advance their causes locally.
>
> For example, NGO Canopy partnered with the Canadian publisher of Harry Potter, Canadian Raincoast Books, to print the fifth book in the series on 100% recycled paper. By the time the final book was published in 2007, it was printed on ecopapers in 24 countries.[27]

The demand for more transparent reporting by engaged stakeholder groups, including progressively influential 'socially responsible investment funds'.

For example, the Global Reporting Initiative (see www.globalreporting.org) is fast becoming the accepted industry standard for CSR reporting, feeding strong demand for information on sustainable and ethical performance, which is now being formally assessed by rating agencies such as FTSE4Good, Ethisphere, GIRS, EIRIS, etc.[28]

New topics are also appearing on the CSR agenda beyond purely environmental and social responsibilities, including, for example, genuine ethical governance, as well as continued traction and support for initiatives specifically focussed on empowering girls and women, from education and technology access programmes to supply-chain diversity initiatives.[29]

Finally, CSR is also good for business. Research over the last decade has revealed the measurable payoff that CSR initiatives yield both for companies and their stakeholders. These include:
- reduced costs through less waste of resources;
- improved competitive advantage through innovation and brand differentiation; and
- the development and maintenance of reputational capital through meaningful engagement with customers, employees and shareholders.[30]

One highly respected researcher in the field concludes that a typical company, through sustainability efforts, can raise its profits by 51% to 81% within five years.[31] While this seems ambitious, even implausible that a CSR payback can be accurately quantified to the nth degree or definite percentile, for companies struggling to reconcile competing resource allocation decisions CSR will almost always represent a 'win–win' investment or the perfect marriage of doing good and doing well. Why aim for just one bottom line when you can aspire to three (profit, people, planet)?

*"A business that makes nothing but money is a poor business."*
Henry Ford

## Conclusion

Company leaders should embrace the opportunities that international development can bring, but also take the time to appreciate the recurring ethical dimension of developing a global footprint, then form appropriate alliances and adapt the organisation so that it is competent in accommodating new cultures, has the confidence to apply its own high standards and is responsive to changing compliance requirements. We will look at the individual competencies required of the ethical leader in an international growth strategy in **Chapter 7**. Before that, in **Chapter 6** we will turn our attention to the board's role as a fundamental pillar in the organisation's ethical framework, whether operating at home and/or abroad.

## References to Chapter 5

[1] This account is summarised from the case study, "Google Goes to China", provided by Renee Flemish and Linda Trevino in their chapter on "Managing for Ethical Conduct in a Global Business Environment" in Trevino, Linda and Nelson, Katherine, *Managing Business Ethics: Straight Talk About How To Do It Right* (Wiley, 2011).

[2] Matthews, Chris, "Google is heading back to China", *Time Magazine*, 4 September 2015. Available at http://time.com/4023367/google-china/ (accessed February 2016).

[3] See http://www.transparency.org/

[4] See http://www.transparency.org/whatwedo/publication/bpi_2011

[5] Levi Strauss & Co., "Case Study: Child Labor in Bangladesh". Available at http://www.levistrauss.com/wp-content/uploads/2014/01/Case-Study_Child-Labor-in-Bangladesh.pdf

[6] See https://www.unglobalcompact.org/what-is-gc/mission/principles

[7] Donaldson, Thomas, "When in Rome Do ... What? International Business and Cultural Relativism" in Minus, Paul M. (ed.), *The Ethics of Doing Business in a Global Economy* (Kluwer, 1993).

[8] Donaldson, Thomas, "Values in Tension: Ethics Away from Home", (1996 September–October) *Harvard Business Review*.

[9] Paine, L., Deshpande, R., Margolis, J.D. and Bettcher, K.E., "Up to Code: does your company's conduct meet world-class standards?" (2005 December) *Harvard Business Review*, 122–133.

[10] Meyer, Erin, *The Culture Map: Breaking Through the Invisible Boundaries of Global Business* (PublicAffairs, 2014).

[11] See http://www.pwc.com/us/en/foreign-corrupt-practices-act/assets/fcpa_managing_risk.pdf

[12] See Transparency International UK, *Anti-bribery Due Diligence for Transactions: Guidance for Anti-Bribery Due Diligence in Mergers, Acquisitions and Investments* (2012) p. 22.

[13] Ministry of Justice, *The Bribery Act 2010: Guidance about procedures which relevant commercial organisations can put into place to prevent persons associated with them from bribing*, Appendix A, Case Study 6 – Principle 4 (March 2011). Available at https://www.justice.gov.uk/downloads/legislation/bribery-act-2010-guidance.pdf.

[14] See Chan, J., "A Suicide Survivor: the Life of a Chinese Worker" (2013) *New Technology, Work and Employment*, 28(2) 84–99. It is heartening to see that Apple has since joined the Fair Labor Association (www.fairlabor.org/affiliate/apple) and CEO Tim Cook is in the process of implementing new workplace standards for application throughout its entire supply chain – see the "Apple Supplier Responsibility: 2015 Progress Report". Available at https://www.apple.com/supplier-responsibility/pdf/Apple_Progress_Report_2015.pdf

[15] See "Bangladesh factory death toll passes 1,000", BBC News 10 May 2013. Available at http://www.bbc.com/news/world-asia-22476774 (accessed February 2016).

[16] See http://www.aboutmcdonalds.com/content/dam/AboutMcDonalds/Sustainability/Library/Supplier_Code_of_Conduct.pdf

[17] For further reading, I recommend Sheila Killian's *Corporate Social Responsibility: A Guide with Irish Experiences* (Chartered Accountants Ireland, 2012), a concise guide written from a uniquely Irish perspective and with very practical advice for SMEs in particular.

[18] Elkington, John, *Cannibals with Forks: The Triple Bottom Line of 21st Century Business* (Capstone Publishing Ltd, 1999).

[19] Killian, Sheila, *op. cit.*, above, n.17.

[20] Extracts from "A Dame of Big Ideas: The *Satya* Interview with Anita Roddick", *Satya* January 2005. Available at http://www.satyamag.com/jan05/roddick.html

[21] Nadkarni, Anant, G. and Branzei, Oana, "The Tata Way: Evolving and Executing Sustainable Business Strategies" (2008) *Ivey Business Journal*, March/April.

[22] Porter, Michael and Kramer, Mark, "Creating Shared Value" (2011) *Harvard Business Review*, January–February. Available at https://hbr.org/2011/01/the-big-idea-creating-shared-value (accessed March 2016).

[23] See Gitsham, Matthew, "The Changing Role of Global Leaders", *Harvard Business Review*, 14 February 2012.

[24] See http://givingpledge.org

[25] Staunton, Denis, "Give it to them, baby: Mark Zuckerberg's philanthropy", *Irish Times*, 5 December 2015. Available at http://www.irishtimes.com/business/give-it-to-them-baby-mark-zuckerberg-s-philanthropy-1.2454648 (accessed February 2016).

[26] McPherson, Susan, "Eight CSR Trends to Watch Out For in 2015", *Forbes*, 31 December 2014.

[27] Ryecroft, Nicole, "Four World-changing Examples of NGO-Brand Partnerships", posted on SustainableBrands.com, 28 August 2013, and available at http://www.sustainablebrands.com/news_and_views/collaboration/four-world-changing-examples-ngo-brand-partnerships (accessed February 2016).

[28] See Strasser, Kurt, *Myths and Realities of Business Environmentalism: Good Works, Good Business or GreenWash?* (Edward Elgar, 2011).

[29] See McPherson, Susan, *op. cit.* above, n.26.

[30] See Carroll, Archie B. and Shabana, Kareem M., "The Business Case for Corporate Social Responsibility", posted on The Conference-Board.org and available at: https://www.conference-board.org/retrievefile.cfm?filename=1156_1307550372.pdf&type=subsite

[31] Willard, Bob, *The New Sustainability Advantage: Seven Business Case Benefits of a Triple Bottom Line* (New Society Publishers, 2013).

# 6

# Ethical Corporate Governance:
## *A Better Board*

*"Governance and leadership are the yin and the yang of successful organisations. If you have leadership without governance you risk tyranny, fraud and personal fiefdoms. If you have governance without leadership you risk atrophy, bureaucracy and indifference."*

**Mark Goyder, Tomorrow's Company**

- Introduction
- Responsibilities and Expectations of the Board
- Doing the Right Things
- Asking the Right Questions
- Board Dynamics
- Hallmarks of an Effective Board

## Introduction

In this chapter we will examine the role of the board as a fundamental pillar of an organisation's ethical governance framework.

As we established in **Chapter 3**, a strong, self-aware and authentic leader with high 'EQ' is necessary for a culture of integrity in any organisation. Supporting compliance systems (see **Chapters 4** and **5**) are then required to give effect to the values and guiding principles of the business, on which its leader has the privilege of putting his or her own personal stamp.

However, the CEO's position can be daunting and challenging. He or she needs support at the highest levels of governance to sustain the desired standards of responsible business conduct as well as continuous challenge to ensure compliance risks are being addressed and that the ethics programme is operating effectively. This is the function of the board: to stand squarely behind the CEO and collectively set the tone from the top while providing independent oversight on the organisation's ethical culture and compliance infrastructure.

We will start by reviewing the obligations, responsibilities and expectations of the board to ensure that the business is run ethically. We will then look at how best it can deliver on these requirements by doing the right things and asking the right questions. We will explore how a board's dynamics impacts its effectiveness in this regard and review the critical role of non-executive directors (NEDs), especially the chair and the importance of his or her relationship with the CEO. Finally, we will distinguish and catalogue the style, structures and skillsets that are the hallmarks of a truly effective board, one that supports the CEO and management in pursuing long-term shareholder value while safeguarding the organisation's integrity and reputation.

## Responsibilities and Expectations of the Board

The obligations and responsibilities of directors to follow and require ethical and compliant business practices derive from a number of sources, including those shown in **Figure 6.1** below.

## Figure 6.1: The Drivers of Ethical Responsibility in the Boardroom

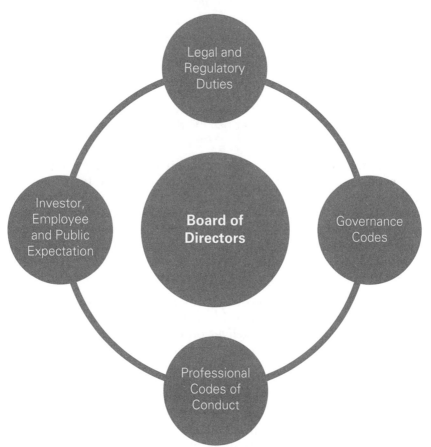

### Legal and Regulatory Duties

In Ireland many of the statutory and indeed some of the common law duties of a director in relation to ethics and compliance have been codified in the 2014 Companies Act to include the following:

1. to act in good faith in what the director considers to be the interests of the company;
2. to act honestly and responsibly in relation to the conduct of the affairs of the company;
3. to act in accordance with the company's constitution and exercise his or her powers only for the purposes allowed by law;
4. not to use the company's property, information or opportunities for his or her own or anyone else's benefit;

5. not to agree to a restriction of his or her exercise of independent judgement;
6. to avoid any conflict of interest between the director's duties to the company and his or her own interests;
7. to exercise the care, skill and diligence that would be exercised in the same circumstances by a reasonable person;
8. to have regard to the interests of the members of the company, as well as the interests of the company's employees.

For all PLCs and companies with a turnover exceeding €25 million and a balance sheet total exceeding €12.5 million, the directors must include in the Directors' Report a 'Directors' Compliance Statement' acknowledging their responsibility for securing compliance of the company with its obligations (including certain company law requirements and tax law).

Interestingly, the UK's Companies Act 2006, although not imposing a compliance statement obligation, goes a little further in relation to stakeholders and also codifies a 'tone from the top' element. Specifically, section 172(1) requires a director to act in good faith to promote the success of the company for the benefit of its members as a whole, while having regard to (among other matters):
- the interests of the company's employees;
- the need to foster the company's business relationships with suppliers, customers and others;
- the impact of the company's operations on the community and the environment; and
- the desirability of the company maintaining a reputation for high standards of business conduct.

Apart from company law, there are other areas of law that impact on directors' responsibility to ensure levels of probity at their companies. These include, for example, stakeholder legislation (including anti-corruption and anti-competition law and regulations governing consumer protection, data privacy, health and safety, etc.), activity legislation (i.e. laws relating to copyright, the environment, planning, licensing, charities, telecommunications, transport and so on) and also employment law.

Taking a closer look at anti-bribery legislation in particular, the Criminal Justice (Corruption) Bill represents a significant step-up in the enforcement of white-collar crime in Ireland. If and when enacted, the new bill will:
- outlaw both giving and receiving bribes;
- cover both the public and commercial sectors;

- make corporate bodies liable for the corrupt actions of directors, employees and agents; and
- require those companies to "take all reasonable steps" and "exercise all due diligence" to prevent corrupt practices.

Directors and managers who "wilfully neglect" the commission of an offence under the bill will also be criminally liable, with sanctions including potentially unlimited fines and penalties of up to 10 years in prison.

In addition to Irish legislation, EU law and laws of certain other countries add to the responsibilities of some Irish directors (and not just Irish directors but the directors of Irish companies and the activities of those companies at home and abroad). Examples relevant for our purposes include the UK's Bribery Act 2010, the FCPA and the Sarbanes–Oxley Act in the US and EU competition law. The United States Federal Sentencing Guidelines also apply to all companies doing business in the US (whether incorporated there or not) and prescribes the standard for compliance and ethics programmes, with boards clearly charged with the task of ensuring that the company "promotes a culture that encourages ethical conduct and a commitment to compliance with the law".[1]

Case law has also established and emphasised some of the primary duties of a director, including the general obligation to carry out their functions with due care, skill and diligence and also the fiduciary duty to exercise their powers in good faith and to avoid conflicts of interest or to personally profit from their position as director.

Finally, additional governance and compliance-related responsibilities may be set down in the company's own constitution. These should be tailored and updated as appropriate to the organisation's particular circumstances. Consider, for example, the scandal at Tallaght Hospital in the late 1990s arising from the backlog of some 58,000 unreported X-rays and unopened GP referral letters.[2] One of the principal findings of the reviews commissioned by the Health Service Executive (HSE) and then the Health Information and Quality Authority (HIQA)[3] in the wake of the allegations was that the hospital's charter was not in line with modern corporate governance principles. At a more profound level, the reviews revealed serious deficiencies in terms of the lack of arrangements to properly direct and govern the hospital and overall highlighted a board that was far from functioning effectively.

In 2012 the hospital found itself once again at the centre of findings of sub-standard patient care, with patients left uncared for on trolleys for long periods, this time resulting in the death of an elderly man. Commenting on the subsequent investigation, the chief executive of the Health Information and Quality Authority (HIQA) said that it "found a history of long-standing challenges in leadership, governance, performance and management at board and executive level of the hospital".[4]

It is incumbent on all company directors to ensure they are fully *au fait* with the legal compliance landscape applicable to the companies they direct so that they can begin to properly understand and discharge their duties. It is also important for directors to fully appreciate that, while they may take into account the perspectives of one or many stakeholders, case law has firmly established the precedent that their *primary* duty is to the company itself.

> "Directors have but one master, the company."
>
> Lord Cullen in *Percival v. Wright* (1902)

## Corporate Governance Codes

As introduced in **Chapter 1**, in addition to the 'hard law' requirements above, organisations of a certain size or in a particular sector or jurisdiction are also subject to 'soft law', i.e. codes of corporate governance that also prescribe responsibilities and duties with an ethical dimension. For example:

- All companies listed on the London Stock Exchange are subject to the provisions of the *UK Corporate Governance Code*,[5] with additional specific requirements applicable for companies in the FTSE350.
- As well as the UK *Corporate Governance Code*, companies listed on the Irish Stock Exchange are also subject to the "Irish Corporate Governance Annex", a supplementary code to the *UK Corporate Governance Code*.[6]
- The *UK Stewardship Code*, which sets out best practice for engagement between institutional investors and companies.[7]
- In 2011 the EU issued a green paper *The EU Corporate Governance Framework*, which sets out corporate governance guidelines for European entities.[8]
- The Central Bank of Ireland has also issued its own corporate governance requirements applicable to credit institutions and insurance undertakings (see http://www.centralbank.ie/regulation/pages/codes.aspx).[9]
- In the not-for-profit sector, a *Code of Practice for Good Governance of Community, Voluntary and Charitable Organisations in Ireland* has been developed on a voluntary basis by a grouping of charities.
- The term 'state bodies' refers to enterprises that are beneficially owned, either completely or mostly, by the Irish Government. The Department of Finance has issued guidelines for state bodies in its *Code of Practice for the Governance of State Bodies* (2009) which sets out

provisions covering internal governance practices of such bodies and their external relations with the government, relevant departments and ministers.

Although compliance with many of the corporate governance codes above is voluntary, best practice and stakeholder expectation usually dictate full compliance. Furthermore, under the 'comply or explain' principle enshrined in most of these codes, if an organisation chooses *not* to comply with any of the prescribed provisions, then it must explain its alternative approach and the reason for the departure.

For example, both the Irish and UK Listing Rules require companies with securities listed on the Main Securities Market (Irish Stock Exchange) or having a Premium Listing (London Stock Exchange) to report on a 'comply or explain' basis on their application of the *UK Corporate Governance Code*.

Even when an organisation does not come with the ambit of any of these codes, for example private companies, it may adopt their provisions to demonstrate a professional approach to corporate governance, to help inform development of governance structures that respond to the expectations of finance providers and stakeholders, and to signal clear intent to run their business in an ethical manner. Indeed, in response to such a demand, in 2010 the European Confederation of Directors Associations (ecoDA) published *Corporate Governance Guidance and Principals for Unlisted Companies in Europe* as a practical tool for unlisted companies seeking to improve their governance structures and policies.[10]

Some of the principal ethics-related board responsibilities common to many of the governance codes outlined above include the following:
- To set the company's values and apply high ethical standards and have regard to the interests of stakeholders, i.e. to set 'the tone at the top'.
- To monitor the effectiveness of the company's governance practices.
- To ensure compliance with the law, regulations and relevant standards.
- To take responsibility for determining the nature and extent of the significant risks the organisation is willing to take to achieve its strategic objectives.
- To maintain sound risk management and internal control systems, including monitoring the effectiveness of external and internal audit.
- To establish 'good faith reporting' (whistleblowing) procedures for employees to raise concerns about financial reporting irregularities or other matters and ensure meaningful follow-up.

(The audit committee, typically comprised exclusively of non-executive directors, is usually charged with a specific responsibility in relation to the two latter provisions.)

## *Professional Codes of Conduct*

Alongside the law and codes of governance, certain professional bodies also prescribe standards to help guide the behaviour of their members. Over half of the *Code of Professional Conduct* of the Institute of Directors (IOD), for example, relates to ethical expectations, as outlined below.

**CHARTERED DIRECTOR CODE OF PROFESSIONAL CONDUCT: SUMMARY OF ARTICLES[11]**

| Article | (note: all references to the masculine gender include the feminine) |
|---|---|
| 1. | Exercise leadership, enterprise and judgement in directing the company so as achieve its continuing prosperity and act in the best interests of the company as a whole. |
| 2. | Follow the standards of good practice set out in the Institute's *Good Practice for Directors – Standards for the Board* and act accordingly and diligently. |
| 3. | Serve the legitimate interests of the company's shareholders. |
| 4. | Exercise responsibilities to employees, customers, suppliers and other relevant stakeholders, including the wider community. |
| 5. | Comply with relevant laws, regulations and codes of practice, refrain from anti-competitive practices and honour obligations and commitments. |
| 6. | At all times have a duty to respect the truth and act honestly in his business dealings and in the exercise of all his responsibilities as a director. |
| 7. | Avoid conflict between his personal interests or the interests of any associated company or person and his duties to the company. |
| 8. | Not make improper use of information acquired as a director or disclose or allow to be disclosed information confidential to the company. |
| 9. | Not recklessly or maliciously injure the professional reputation of another member of the IOD and not engage in any practice detrimental to the reputation and interests of the Institute or of the profession of director. |

| 10. | Ensure that he keeps himself abreast of current good practice. |
|-----|----------------------------------------------------------------|
| 11. | Set high personal standards by keeping aware of and adhering to this Code, both in the spirit and the letter, and promoting it to other directors. |
| 12. | Apply the principles of this Code appropriately when acting as a director of a non-commercial organisation. |

Based on the code developed by the International Federation of Accountants (IFAC), Chartered Accountants Ireland also provides a *Code of Ethics* for its members. In broad terms, the *Code of Ethics* establishes the fundamental principles of ethics for professional accountants and provides a conceptual framework for them to apply in order to:
* identify threats to compliance with the fundamental principles;
* evaluate the significance of the threats identified; and
* apply safeguards, when necessary, to eliminate the threats or reduce them to an acceptable level.

The fundamental principles are:
* **Integrity** – to be straightforward and honest in all professional and business relationships;
* **Objectivity** – not to allow bias, conflict of interest or undue influence of others to override professional or business judgements;
* **Professional competence and due care** – to maintain professional knowledge and skill at a level required to ensure that clients or employers receive competent professional service;
* **Confidentiality** – to respect the confidentiality of information acquired as a result of professional and business relationships and, therefore, not disclose any such information to third parties without proper and specific authority, unless there is a legal or professional right or duty to disclose, nor use the information for the personal advantage of the professional accountant or third parties; and
* **Professional behaviour** – to comply with relevant laws and regulations and avoid any action that discredits the profession.

## Stakeholder Expectations

Finally, the expectations of a range of stakeholders also demand that directors are fully engaged in relation to the ethical culture of their organisations. In **Chapter 1**, we discussed the power of large institutional and activist shareholders, the growing relevance of socially responsible investment indices, such as the FTSE4Good, and the increasingly influential NGO community. Such stakeholders can ultimately hold a board accountable for its company's social, ethical and environmental performance. Likewise, an organisation's employees will look to its board to set the 'tone' or ethical culture for the enterprise in relation to *how* it operates and seek cues from directors (particularly executive directors) to guide their own conduct.

So, given the multitude and range of competing requirements from 'hard' to 'soft' law and the demands of stakeholders, how should a board ensure it meets all of its ethical and compliance responsibilities? The Financial Reporting Council (FRC) has provided some useful guidance for board effectiveness in this regard.[12] Written to assist companies in applying the *UK Corporate Governance Code*, an extract from the FRC's *Guidance on Board Effectiveness* is provided below:

"An effective board develops and promotes its collective vision of the company's purpose, its culture, its values and the behaviours it wishes to promote in conducting its business. In particular it:
- provides direction for management;
- **demonstrates ethical leadership, displaying and promoting throughout the company behaviours consistent with the culture and values it has defined for the organisation;**
- creates a performance culture that drives value creation without exposing the company to excessive risk of value destruction;
- makes well-informed and high-quality decisions based on a clear line of sight into the business;
- creates the right framework for helping directors meet their statutory duties ... and/or other relevant statutory and regulatory regimes;
- is accountable, particularly to those that provide the company's capital; and
- thinks carefully about its governance arrangements and embraces evaluation of their effectiveness."[13]

In order to focus on its key ethical remits around culture, values and behaviours, the board can think about its role as having the following practical elements:
- doing the right things; and
- asking the right questions.

## FIGURE 6.2: THE CORE ELEMENTS OF THE BOARD'S ETHICAL REMIT

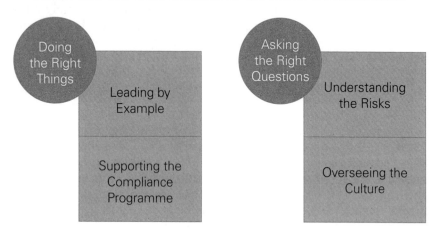

## Doing the Right Things

### *Leading by Example*

Unless individual directors and the board are seen to possess and actively demonstrate the highest standards of integrity, then codes of conduct and value statements are worthless. When considering new board appointments, therefore, the values and integrity of each candidate should be carefully assessed, based on their track record, in-depth interviews, peer assessments and 360 reviews, and even psychometrics. As Simon Webley of the Institute of Business Ethics notes, "recruiting the right board members who have the knowledge and ethical acumen to support the organisation is a good way to ensure that ethics is part of the language of the board."[14]

It has also been well observed that employees tend to follow the example of their immediate managers, even when such behaviour may be at odds with documented procedures. In a 2013 PwC survey of its 'Fraud Academy' membership, all of whom have responsibility for managing fraud, corruption and integrity risk in their organisations, 43% of respondents "said that on the occasions where 'Tone from the Top' had been undermined it was due to the fact that leadership actions did not reconcile with the ethical messages being delivered".[15]

In order to set the right tone, therefore, the board must clearly exhibit appropriate behaviours. To put it more simply: the board must 'walk the talk' and set an example, not become one.

One of the greatest areas of risk for a director in this regard arises when their other business dealings, financial interests or relationships conflict with those of the company. When this happens, or even if the potential for such a conflict arises, it should be disclosed and thereafter the directors should absent themselves from any discussions or decisions on related matters. It is common practice for directors to be required to provide information on an annual basis on their business associations, financial interests and relationships, so that such conflicts of interest can be identified and managed before they become a problem. The duty to avoid conflicts of interest has also been codified in the Companies Act 2014.

## Supporting the Ethics and Compliance Programme

As well as being role models for the stated values of the organisation, the board needs to fully support its ethics and compliance programme and framework. A few suggestions for a board to demonstrate this sponsorship include:
- ensuring that ethics and compliance is on each board agenda;
- discussing ethics and compliance challenges at formal and informal meetings with management (a powerful way to convey to those running the business that these things really matter);
- active involvement in the development and review of ethics policies and initiatives, e.g. when the code of conduct is being updated;
- taking part in ethics and compliance training programmes (not being 'above it all');
- ensuring the ethics manager/team and their efforts are adequately resourced;
- meeting regularly with the ethics manager to understand current risks, the state of compliance, any violations, etc. (ideally, schedule a meeting once a year in the absence of all executives for a full and frank discussion about any pressing issues or concerns);
- requiring explicit (usually annual) statements of accountability by the board, management and employees to comply with the code of conduct;
- encouraging open channels for good faith reporting (sometimes the NEDs may be the nominated recipients for such reports, providing independence from the executive or management line);
- not expecting 'fields of green' or 100% perfect scores across the board in compliance reporting, or rushing to blame in the event of a breach, but constructively reviewing any compliance failures, their route cause and remediation proposals;
- checking that investigation protocols are appropriate and enforcement is fair and consistent.

While some of the above tasks are often delegated to the audit committee, issues of fundamental importance to the organisation's values and ethical performance should be discussed by the full board.

## Asking the Right Questions

### *Understanding the Risks*

In **Chapter 4** we discussed the elements of an ethics and compliance risk-assessment process. The board needs to be especially in tune with risks of an ethical nature. Indeed, many of the governance codes referred to earlier explicitly require this engagement.

A key feature of a board's role in relation to these risks is to ensure that the company's interactions with external stakeholders and key counterparties are above reproach. With the supply chain, for example, this means that the company is not transacting with suppliers using child labour, or with partners with a track record of polluting the local environment or whose working conditions endanger the lives of workers. (Most of the 1,100 people who died in the Bangladesh clothing factory collapse of 2013 were working on orders for western high-street retailers.)

Tax is another area requiring board oversight and considered analysis, in terms of compliance with various tax laws but also in managing reputational risk. Specifically, the board should take care that when corporate tax bills are minimised, albeit legally, it is not done to the point that the company is seen to be getting a 'free ride' in the jurisdiction in which it is either incorporated or earns significant profits. (In 2015, for example, Starbucks, Apple and Amazon, among others, came under fire in the media for 'tax shaming'.) In terms of mergers and acquisitions, the board should also see itself as the gatekeeper of the organisation's reputation, ensuring that only those acquisitions or mergers that involve a genuine meeting of minds on ethical issues are approved, as outlined in the previous chapter.

Ethics and compliance risks may be greater or lesser, depending upon the sector or the countries in which the company operates or into which it would like to expand. Related ethical decisions usually involve trade-offs between short-term profit and longer-term interests, may be costly to implement and require a degree of courage on the part of the directors. However, such decisions cannot be taken lightly or the risks ignored, given the real possibility that the board will be collectively or individually pursued for their effects or outcomes. Wilful neglect or tacit acquiescence is viewed by the authorities as seriously as the blatant endorsement of unethical choices. Thus, being aware of the risks and asking the right questions is vital.

## *Overseeing the Culture*

Astute directors will leverage their understanding of the risk factors discussed above when overseeing the effectiveness or otherwise of management in reinforcing a culture of integrity throughout an organisation. Specific items on which they may seek assurance include:

- the regularity and scope of the ethics and compliance risk assessment;
- how and when employees receive ethics training;
- when, why and how the code of conduct and related policies are updated (see **Chapter 4**);
- how compliance with code of conduct requirements is monitored and enforced;
- ethics and compliance programme communication strategies;
- the number and nature of violations of the code of conduct, and how they are reported, e.g. through the reporting line or to helplines;
- pending litigation in relation to any ethical breaches, including, for example, corruption or collusion;
- ethical challenges in the supply chain or distribution network and how these are being managed;
- ethics due diligence carried out for any M&A proposals;
- the extent to which ethical behaviour is impacted by and promoted through the company's performance management and incentive schemes.

A powerful way for the board to take the organisation's 'temperature' from a cultural perspective is to sponsor an employee-wide ethics survey. Done properly through a confidential third party, this can be a real eye-opener and highlight:

(a) the level of awareness of ethics and expected standards of behaviour;
(b) confidence in the CEO and his or her team's integrity, and whether these business leaders are really 'walking the talk';
(c) the prevailing cultural norms in the organisation, whether it is one of openness or fear, etc.

To assess if management are handling key relationships in the right way and in line with organisational values, the following sources of information may be useful to request and review:

- 360-degree reviews on senior management;
- employee turnover statistics;
- customer satisfaction results;
- complaints registers; and
- any ethical concerns or similar subject matter in correspondence with large shareholders.

In his book *The Fish Rots from the Head*,[16] Bob Garratt describes a tele-communications company whose board's perception of values was so different from that of the rest of the organisation that the chairman had to require each board member to spend a day per week "up poles or down holes", meeting staff and customers and getting to grips with the business before a credible value statement could be created to which the staff would subscribe. Garratt suggests some ways board members could actively test the consistency of stated values with actual behaviours, including:

- phoning the organisation's switchboard posing as a customer and trying to buy a product or service;
- trying to make a complaint, or even calling the company's ethics hotline, and following through on what happens.

With a particular focus on the board's responsibility to thoroughly assess their organisation's ethical culture and practices, Praesta and Chartered Accountants Ireland in *The Art of Ethical Leadership* suggest 10 questions for leaders to ask and periodically assess if they are committed to steering their organisations 'true north'.

### 10 QUESTIONS FOR PERIODIC REVIEW BY BUSINESS LEADERS[17]

1. "What are the ethical issues facing the organisation now or in the future?
   - Are there potential risks to reputation?
   - What is their significance and potential impact?

2. How are ethical issues detected and monitored?
   - What is the organisation's approach to managing these ethical issues?
   - How successful are the approaches taken?
   - Why do they work? Or not?
   - How can they be improved?

3. What are the key ethical values of my organisation, e.g. integrity, objectivity, confidentiality, professional behaviour?
   - Are the ethical values of the organisation clear?

4. Is there an Ethics Code?
   - How long has it been in existence?
   - Are there policies and procedures in place that support the code?
   - Are the employees and Board of Directors aware of the ethics code?

- Do they have to confirm in writing their compliance with the code?
- How is the code enforced?
- When was the code last reviewed?
- If there is no own business code, is there an appropriate code of ethics or guidelines that my organisation can use (e.g. Professional Code of ethics?)

5. Is there adequate ethics training?
   - Do employees and directors receive ethics training on joining the organisation?
   - Is there continuing ethics training for employees and directors?

6. How does my organisation compare with benchmarks?
   - How are my competitors approaching ethics?

7. How well do we communicate on ethics?
   - Does the organisation communicate its ethics standards to shareholders and other stakeholders?
   - If so, how?
   - Is it effective?

8. Do we lead by example?
   - How can I and the Board of Directors infuse a high ethical standard throughout the organisation?

9. Do I have my own ready reckoner for ethical decision-making?
   - According to the Institute of Business Ethics, a CEO facing an ethical decision might try to answer the following questions when making a decision:
   - Transparency: am I happy to make my decision public – especially to the people affected by it?
   - Effect: have I fully considered the harmful effects of my decision and how to avoid them?
   - Fairness: would my decision be considered fair by everyone affected by it (consider all the stakeholders – the effects of decisions can be far-reaching).

10. How much attention do I give to these questions and to the ethical implications of all my decisions and actions?"

We will allow the last word on asking the right questions and ethical oversight to someone you would not expect to credibly comment on such matters: Andrew Faston, former CFO of Enron. As he himself admits, "It's like inviting Kim Kardashian to talk to your daughters about chastity!"[18] However, having spent five years in prison for securities fraud, he has had time to reflect on the subject. In an address to the Canadian Society of Corporate Secretaries (by Skype, as the Canadian authorities would not issue a visa to a convicted felon), and referring to his previous role at Enron as "Chief Loophole Officer", he admitted that he simply did not think about the ethical implications of what he was doing:

> "I wasn't sitting in a dark room with a bunch of sinister guys thinking, 'How can we break the law?' I was thinking that what I was doing was great. We were rocket scientists coming up with every new accounting twist and turn, every new loophole."

Faston believes that part of the problem with oversight can be attributed to the typical attitude of boards which, when presented with a new proposal or practice, will usually ask, "Is it allowed?" He urges boards to ask a different question:

> "If this company was privately owned and I were leaving this company to my grandchildren, would I make this decision?"

If answered honestly, this question could have prevented many of the ethical failures that we have witnessed in recent years. What might frustrate this compellingly simple check? Board dynamics? Quite possibly.

## Board Dynamics

In discussing the "reality of the boardroom", Bob Tricker refers to "How people, power and politics affect practice".[19] In this section, we will look at the board as a working group and how the relationships between individual members and their collective boardroom behaviour can impact on its effectiveness in leading the organisation with integrity and on the quality of their ethical decision-making.

From **Figure 6.3** below, pick which 'C' best describes the role to which you typically default.

FIGURE 6.3: THE EIGHT BEHAVIOURAL TYPES ON BOARDS

| Change Agent | Counsellor | Challenger | Consensus Builder |
|---|---|---|---|
| Critic | Conformist | Controller | Cheer-leader |

(Hopefully you may have picked a descriptor from the top line ...)

Based on their research in Canadian boardrooms, Richard Leblanc and James Gillies describe the eight behavioural types set out in **Figure 6.3** as impacting the ability of a board to form a cohesive group, which in turn significantly impacts their aggregate performance.[20] The four types in the boxes in the top row enhance board effectiveness, whereas the four in the bottom row hinder it. The implication is that every board should be comprised of directors with 'enhancing' characteristics. However, as Leblanc and Gillies readily acknowledge, given the available pool of directors, wide variability in selection processes and the complexities of human nature, the real world seldom delivers this.

Another factor that can impact on board behaviours and effectiveness, is the style and competence of the chair, who is responsible for creating the right culture for a board to truly flourish as a team. Adrian Cadbury describes the chairman's role "as coming nearest to the conductor of an orchestra".[21] It involves listening, encouraging debate, managing dissent, keeping on topic, integrating context and opinions, drawing conclusions, as well as running board meetings efficiently and with the right information.

The Financial Reporting Council recognises the special nature of the chairman's role by requiring listed companies to keep the position separate from that of the CEO. Following a 2009 review of its corporate governance code, it also included a specific requirement for the chair "to lead the board and foster a culture of openness". This approach to having separate CEOs and chairmen roles is different from the US model where the two have historically tended to be combined and authority over the board and the executive vested in the same person, which seems contrary in turn to the general understanding that 'absolute power corrupts absolutely'.

An example of the dynamic and effect that a single-minded, autocratic CEO can bring to a boardroom is provided in Walter Isaacson's biography of Steve Jobs.[22] Jobs invited Arthur Levitt, former Chairman of the SEC, to join the Apple board. Levitt, a self-confessed 'Apple-nut', was delighted and planned a trip to Cupertino to meet Jobs and agree the details of his appointment. Meanwhile, however, Jobs came across a speech written by Levitt in which he argued that boards should have a strong and independent role. Jobs promptly called Levitt and told him to cancel his flight. According to Levitt, Jobs said, "Arthur, I don't think you would be happy on our board, and I think it best if we not invite you. Frankly, I think that some of the issues you raised, while appropriate for some companies, really don't apply to Apple's culture."

The complementarity of the relationship between the chairman and the CEO is as important as its separation. Likewise, the respective roles of the chair, the executive and the NEDs must be clearly defined and understood, yet also work in harmony. According to research by John Roberts of the University of Cambridge, three conditions support the development of these key board relationships[23]:

1. the NEDs, especially the chairman, must be clear as to their non-executive role;
2. the chairman must be willing to develop his or her knowledge of the company and to create similar processes for the other NEDs to do likewise;
3. the board's complementary skills and knowledge need to be brought together through skilfully managed and rigorous processes of board accountability, both formal and informal.

Working with two other academics, McNulty and Stiles, Roberts distilled these findings still further, listing the following as critical characteristics for NEDs to effectively create accountability in the boardroom[24]:

1. engaged but non-executive;
2. challenging but supportive;
3. independent but involved.

Thus, the chairman and NEDs should support the CEO, act as an informed sounding-board for ideas and problems, but not get so close as to compromise their independence, nor should there be any competition for executive authority. Anglo Irish Bank again provides a good example of how not to do it, show-casing the wholly unwise practice of having an ex-CEO appointed chairman (Sean Fitzpatrick), thereby removing the normal checks and balances that the chairman/CEO relationship should embody (see Anglo Irish Bank, *Annual Report and Accounts 2004*, p. 5).

The importance of the NED position has also increased as corporate governance codes have evolved, leading to a much bigger role for non-executive directors in challenging and developing strategy. It is now well accepted that a strong cohort of credible, independent and engaged NEDs is critical if decisions are to be considered comprehensively and constructively challenged. This should help to avoid comments such as that of Michael Grade, who at an Institute of Directors dinner once wryly remarked:

> "A non-executive is a bit like the bidet in your bathroom: nobody is quite sure what they are for, but they add a touch of class."

The key point is that a board is a group of people working together and like any team it needs a common goal, trust among its members, leadership, the right balance of personalities and a diversity of skills, perspectives and experience. Bob Tricker's 'Six Cs' model (see **Figure 6.4** below) provides some insight into the characteristics of a functional board and a fitting conclusion this discussion on boardroom dynamics.

## FIGURE 6.4: THE 'SIX CS' OF BOARD BEHAVIOUR[25]

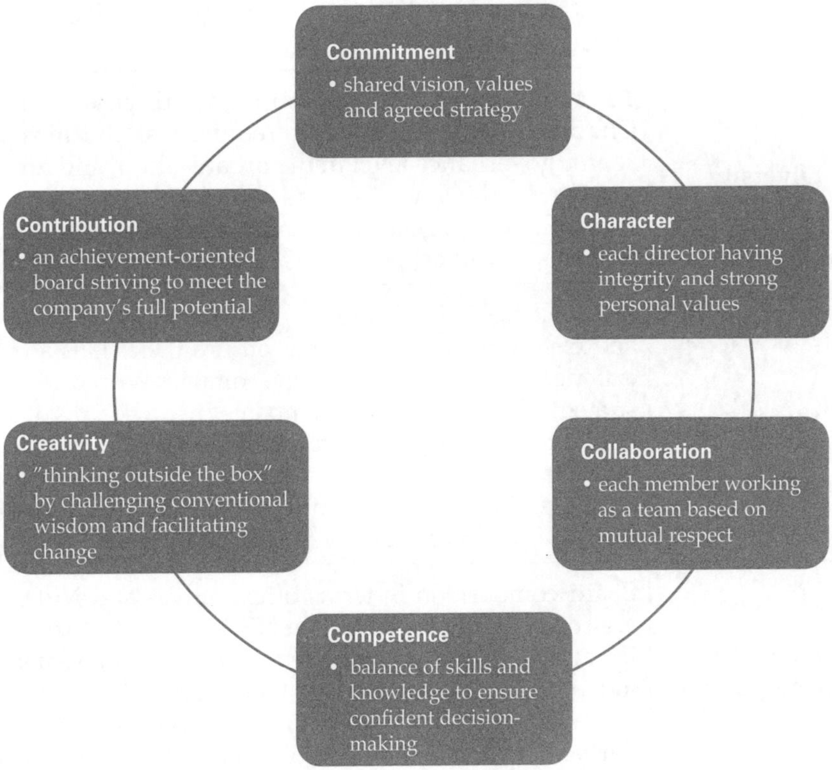

Commitment
- shared vision, values and agreed strategy

Contribution
- an achievement-oriented board striving to meet the company's full potential

Character
- each director having integrity and strong personal values

Creativity
- "thinking outside the box" by challenging conventional wisdom and facilitating change

Collaboration
- each member working as a team based on mutual respect

Competence
- balance of skills and knowledge to ensure confident decision-making

## Hallmarks of an Effective Board

As we have seen, there are a number of characteristics in the make-up and modus operandi of a board that will better enable it to effectively fulfil its roles, including its ethics and compliance responsibilities, and which, if absent, will almost certainly derail such efforts. Many of these characteristics are prescribed by codes of corporate governance while others are plain common sense. Some of the principal hallmarks of an effective board are summarised below, grouped under relevant headings.

| SIZE, SKILLS AND COMPOSITION | |
|---|---|
| The Right Size | While there is no magic number, for an average-sized company, eight to 10 directors is generally accepted as optimal, being enough to provide a sufficient range of resources and skills, and efficient task performance and delegation, but small enough to facilitate inclusive discussion and decision-making, i.e. to maintain efficient coordination and meaningful involvement of each member.[26] |
| Diversity | To avoid the kind of groupthink discussed in **Chapter 2**, real diversity is required at the most senior governance level in the organisation, and not just gender diversity but in all of its forms, including race, ethnicity, age and probably most importantly, in terms of values, perspectives and experiences. |
| Mix of Skills | The challenge is to tap into the pool of available talented and experienced directors and ensure their skills and experiences are aligned with the company's needs and strategic direction.[27] Many companies use a board skills matrix for this purpose, documenting all requisite skills and the extent to which each director possesses these attributes. Ethical acumen must feature high on this list if ethics is to become part of the board's vernacular. |
| Balanced Composition | Board composition in terms of executives and NEDs is also key. Best practice is that NEDs are in the majority and that one is appointed to the role of senior independent director to act as their representative and a sounding-board for the chairman and other directors, particularly in times of crisis or a board dispute. |

| APPOINTMENT, INDUCTION AND STRUCTURE | |
|---|---|
| Professional Recruitment | Unfortunately the 'tap on the shoulder' approach is still common in board appointments, but there is a move to a more professional process being employed for NED recruitment. In larger companies, the task is generally undertaken by the nomination committee (excluding the CEO), now a requirement for FTSE 350 companies and becoming generally accepted best practice. It is also incumbent on the new director to carry out their own extensive due diligence prior to joining a board. |
| Proper Induction | Once recruited, a new NED should undertake a comprehensive induction process, including visits to company facilities and meetings with key executives so that he or she comes fully au fait with the business and its strategy. For a new executive director, the focus will be more on the regulatory responsibilities of directors and the ethical dimensions of their new role. |
| Appropriate Structures | Separate board committees should be established when the scale or complexity of the business requires a dedicated focus on functions such as nomination, audit, remuneration, acquisitions, risk, etc. The board and its committees should have clear terms of reference so that there is full agreement on responsibilities and the division of labour. It is important to recognise that while a committee may undertake some in-depth analysis and work on certain issues on behalf of the board, the board does not delegate its collective responsibility in that area to the committee. Fundamental issues such as values, ethics and reputation should always demand the attention of the full board. |
| TIME, AGENDA AND INFORMATION | |
| Sufficient Time | Each board member should ensure that he or she has sufficient time to carry out their role effectively. A single directorship is estimated to take circa two days per month.[28] Add to that any committee work and multiply it by a factor in the event of a crisis. Depending on the size of the company or its sector, additional governance codes recommendations may apply. |

| | |
|---|---|
| The Right Agenda | Increasing compliance duties have added to a board's workload, tipping the agenda towards governance matters to the detriment of robust engagement on strategy and risk. "The basic argument for boards' intense focus on compliance is to prevent the loss of shareholder value that corporate misdeeds create. But ... boards cannot afford to become so mired in compliance that they ... fail to live up to their larger obligation: to help their companies grow and prosper, not just in the next quarter but the next decade and beyond."[29] |
| Quality Information | A board should be "supplied in a timely manner with information in a form and of a quality appropriate to enable it to discharge its duties" (FRC). Board papers should be about quality not quantity, relevant and reliable, timely, forward-looking and focussed, with context, comparability and completeness. Information asymmetry also needs to be carefully monitored, i.e. where executives naturally have more information at their disposal than the NEDs, for whom information may be sanitised, drip-fed or even withheld. |
| INDEPENDENCE, SUPERVISION, EVALUATION | |
| Independent Challenge | One of the most important features of an effective director, especially a NED, is their ability to bring objectivity to and create accountability in the boardroom. Independence is a critical board asset and should be protected by annual review of directors' interests and regular refreshment of the composition of the board to facilitate new thinking. Furthermore, NEDs must not have been an employee within the last five years or have any material business relationships with the company, should not hold cross-directorships, represent a significant shareholder or have been on the board for more than nine years. |

| | |
|---|---|
| 'Nose in; Finger out!' | The board must be clear about its main responsibilities, "setting the company's strategic aims, providing the leadership to put them into effect, supervising the management of the business and reporting to shareholders on their stewardship" (Cadbury Report). It should not, however, meddle in detailed operational issues best left to executive management. |
| Honest Evaluation | The board should regularly review its effectiveness, both collectively and at individual director level so as to continuously improve its performance. External evaluation is often the best approach, providing rigour and objectivity, and works well as long as it is seen as a positive process and embraced as such by executive directors and NEDs alike. |

## References to Chapter 6

[1] See http://www.ussc.gov/guidelines-manual/2011/2011-8b21 (accessed September 2015).

[2] Donnellan, Eithne, "Tallaght doctors had warned managers of X-ray 'scandal'", *Irish Times*, 20 November 2010. Available at http://www. irishtimes.com/news/tallaght-doctors-had-warned-managers-of-x-ray-scandal-1.679146 (accessed March 2016).

[3] *Report of the Review of Radiology Reporting and the Management of GP Referral Letters at Adelaide and Meath Hospital (Dublin), incorporating the National Children's Hospital (AMNCH) [Tallaght Hospital]* (HSE 2010) and *Report of the investigation into the quality, safety and governance of the care provided by the Adelaide and Meath Hospital, Dublin incorporating the National Children's Hospital (AMNCH) for patients who require acute Admission* (HIQA 2012).

[4] Stack, Sarah "Tallaght Hospital HIQA report: Nobody was accountable for patients on trolleys", *Irish Independent*, 17 May 2012. Available at http://www.independent.ie/irish-news/tallaght-hospital-hiqa-report-nobody-was-accountable-for-patients-on-trolleys-26854457. html (accessed March 2016).

[5] Financial Reporting Council (September 2014).

[6] Irish Stock Exchange, *Main Securities Market Listing Rules and Admission to Trading Rules*, Appendix 4 (2010).

[7] Financial Reporting Council (September 2012).

[8] EU Green Paper COM (2011) 164 final Brussels, 5.4.2011.

[9] See www.centralbank.ie

[10] See http://ecoda.org/uploads/media/GUIDANCE_-_2010_CG_for_ Unlisted_-_EU.pdf

[11] Chartered Director Code of Professional Conduct (Institute of Directors, 2012). Available at http://www.iod.com/developing/chartered-director-qualifications/chartered-director/chartered-director-code-of-professional-conduct (accessed February 2016).

[12] Financial Reporting Council, *Guidance on Board Effectiveness* (FRC, March 2011). Available at https://www.frc.org.uk/Our-Work/Publications/ Corporate-Governance/Guidance-on-Board-Effectiveness.pdf (accessed February 2016).

[13] *Ibid.,* para. 1.2 (emphasis added).

[14] Webley, Simon, "The Role Boards Play in the Ethical Performance of Companies" in *The Art of Ethical Leadership* (Praesta/Chartered Accountants Ireland, 2012). Available at http://www.charteredaccountants. ie/Documents/Ethics/Chartered_Accountants_Praesta_Ireland_ Ethics_31.1.13.pdf (accessed February 2016).

[15] PwC, *Tone from the Top: Transforming words into action* (2012).

[16] Garratt, Bob, *The Fish Rots from the Head* (HarperCollinsBusiness, 2010).

[17] Praesta and Chartered Accountants Ireland, *The Art of Ethical Leadership* (2012), p. 35.

[18] Peritz, Ingrid and McFarland, Janet, "Former Enron CFO speaks of convictions, offers business advice", *The Globe and Mail*, 18 August 2015. Available at http://www.theglobeandmail.com/report-on-business/ international-business/us-business/former-enron-cfo-speaks-of-convictions-offers-business-advice/article26009702/ (accessed February 2016).

[19] Tricker, R., *Corporate Governance; Principles, Policies and Practices* (Oxford University Press, 2012).

[20] Leblanc, Richard and Gillies, James, *Inside the Boardroom: How Boards Really Work and the Coming Revolution in Corporate Governance* (John Wiley, Ontario, Canada, 2005).

[21] Cadbury, Adrian, *Corporate Governance and Chairmanship: a Personal View* (Oxford University Press, 2002).

[22] Walter Isaacson, *Steve Jobs* (Simon & Schuster, 2011).

[23] Roberts, John, "Building the Complementary Board. The Work of the PLC Chairman" (2002) *Long Range Planning*, 35(5) 493–520.

[24] Roberts, J., McNulty, T. and Stiles, P., "Beyond agency conceptions of the work of the non-executive director: Creating accountability in the boardroom" (2005) *British Journal of Management*, 16, 5–26.

[25] See Tricker, R., *op. cit.* above, n.16.

[26] Hickman, G.R. and Creighton Zollar, A., "Diverse Self-Directed Work Teams: Developing Strategic Initiatives for 21st Century Organizations" (1998) *Public Personnel Management* 27, 187– 200.

[27] See Duffy, David, *A Practical Guide to Corporate Governance* (Chartered Accountants Ireland, 2014).

[28] Hanson Green, *Life in the Board Room: Chairman and Non Executive Director Survey 2012* (The median number of days spent by NEDs working for companies with turnover of £30–£100 million was 23.)

[29] Lorsch, Jay W. and Clark, Robert, C., "Leading from the Boardroom" (2008 April) *Harvard Business Review*, 105–111.

# III

# Mastering the Art of
# Leading with Integrity

# 7

# The Leading with Integrity Toolbox

*"Try not to be a man of success. Rather become a man of value."*

**Albert Einstein**

- Introduction
- Setting the Tone and Leading by Example
- Communicating Clear Expectations: 'Moments that Matter'
- Creating an Open Culture
- Supporting the Ethics Programme
- Disciplining and Rewarding
- The Ethical Leader Abroad
- Leading with Integrity in Times of Crisis

## Introduction

In the next three chapters, comprising the third and final part of the book, we will bring together the concepts and ideas discussed in **Parts I** and **II** and focus on their practical application in day-to-day ethical leadership.

This chapter leverages the groundwork study of ethical behaviour and leading with integrity from **Part I** (particularly **Chapter 3**) with the structural foundations outlined in **Part II** to provide a set of tools with which to apply ethical leadership within these supporting frameworks.

The objective is to fully equip you to set the 'tone at the top' and inspire ethical conduct throughout your organisation, in good times and through the challenging periods. We will highlight the need for leaders to clearly communicate their expectations regarding ethical standards and to create genuine accountability. We will identify 'moments that matter', those critical points in an employee's career when a leader can make a lasting impression on their ethical journey and at those decisive points in the development of the organisation which can define the true character of its leadership. Related to this, we will briefly review the leader's role in recruitment, discipline and reward, and discuss how best he or she can create an open, honest culture.

We will then discuss the journey of the ethical leader abroad and how to adapt leadership style in order to confidently address the unique challenges of operating cross-culturally and enjoy the rich rewards of leading with integrity, always and everywhere.

The chapter concludes with an ethical crisis survival guide, recognising that sometimes, despite best efforts, ethical lapses can happen, and what to do if they reach crisis proportions, including how to go about rebuilding trust.

Let's begin, however, by examining how to establish a culture of trust in the first place, by setting the right tone.

## Setting the Tone and Leading by Example

Setting the ethical tone of an organisation has two main elements:

FIGURE 7.1: SETTING THE TONE – PRINCIPAL ELEMENTS

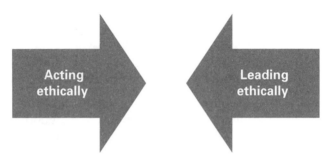

The leaders of an organisation make many decisions every day: what target markets to pursue, where resources should be allocated, who gets promoted, what merits reward, and so on. While not all of these decisions will have a significant ethical dimension or warrant in-depth analysis, every decision you make as a leader should be consistent with your stated values and those of your organisation. A simple way to check if a decision is ethical in the sense of fitting with 'the way we do things' is to ask the following four questions:
- Is it consistent with my values and those of my organisation?
- Would I be happy to be held accountable for it?
- Is it legal, ethical and fair?
- Is it the right thing to do for the business?

You may prefer to apply the 'golden rule' we discussed in **Chapter 3** as a way to gauge the integrity or otherwise of a decision, i.e. would you be happy being on the receiving end of the decision or action? Or you may want to satisfy 'the light of day test', i.e. 'Would I be happy if others knew of my decision?' Whatever your approach to ethics, as a leader you need to consistently demonstrate the ethical backbone underpinning your everyday assessments.

As well as *acting* ethically, you must also *lead* ethically. Once you assume a leadership position, you become a de facto role model. Employees will look at your demeanor and will often unconsciously mimic your behaviour. What you do always trumps what you say. As a former ethics lead at a large US corporation once remarked:

> "We could have had all the ethics workshops in the world. We could have even had Jesus, Moses, Mohammed and Buddha

come and speak at them. But if after all that, someone in a leadership position behaved in a way contrary to our standard, that instance would teach more than all the experts combined."

In **Chapter 3** we discussed the three core competencies necessary for ethical leadership, of which **Figure 7.2** serves as a reminder.

**FIGURE 7.2: THE CORE COMPETENCIES OF ETHICAL LEADERSHIP**

How, in practice, do you translate these core competencies into actions and behaviours that will inspire others to follow your lead? From observation and research, the key ways in which these competencies become manifest are outlined below, together with specific examples, many from outside the corporate sphere and from the worlds of sport, politics and religion.

**PRACTICING ETHICAL COMPETENCIES – LEADING WITH INTEGRITY**

---

Set aside your ego for the good of the organisation
- A self-aware leader will be comfortable enough to step back and let others take the initiative and centre-stage from time to time.
- A secure CEO will allow others to develop his or her ideas and let them take the glory.
- He or she will also know instinctively when to adjust their behaviour in line with unspoken expectations, understanding the organisational *zeitgeist* (e.g. forgoing a bonus in especially lean times).

Prime example: Joe Schmidt Highly competent and focused, yet self-effacing Head Coach of the Irish Rugby team, who always celebrates in the collective while taking personal accountability for any loss.

---

Create an environment of respect and trust
- A leader with a strong sense of values will seek to translate these to the workplace. They will start with respect, which is about getting the basics right: give employees the tools, resources, time and freedom to do their job. Honour work–life balances. Provide a safe working environment. Recruit fairly, embrace diversity, reward justly and promote impartially. Say thank you, often.
- Then they will build trust, which is the "lubricant" that allows companies and their stakeholders to work together with "minimal friction and maximum harmony", trust thrives in open, inclusive environments where traditional hierarchies are eschewed in favour of collaboration and teamwork.[1]

Prime example: Joe Gebbia, Co-founder of Airbnb  For an interesting perspective on building trust, take a look at the TEDtalk by Joe Gebbia, "How Airbnb designs for trust". As well as having a whole department dedicated to 'Trust & Safety', they have had to literally hard-wire the design of their websites to build "olympic trust between people who have never met".

Treat everyone fairly, all the time
- While all men may not be created equal, everyone has equal worth and deserves to be treated so. Employees care about outcomes, but more so, they want to be treated fairly in the process.
- Customers and suppliers also need to be treated fairly. If you are known as being upfront and honest, that reputation will attach to your organisation and other businesses will be drawn to work with you.[2]

Prime example: Tim Cook, Apple CEO  While Apple does not have a perfect track record in labour practices, especially in Asia, Tim Cook has moved the company forward in leaps and bounds on social issues under the mantra, "Let's leave things better than we found them". Championing sustainability, supply-chain transparency and diversity, coming out as an openly gay CEO of the world's largest company was another brave exposition of his values.

Act as a beacon for values; inculcate ethical thinking and decision-making
An authentic leader will use genuine, considered communications to ensure integrity becomes part of the organisation's DNA, will actively sponsor its ethics programme, ensuring decision-making and reward structures are aligned, and will take a special interest in training (see further below).

**Actively seek opinions different from your own, embrace diversity, encourage challenge and debate and seek feedback, both positive and negative**
- Leaders with high emotional intelligence set a requirement for constructive challenge, take the time to become culturally sensitive and competent and make a real effort with diversity.
- Consider institutionalising ways for people to question your authority and survey your employee population regularly to measure how the behaviours of your lieutenants are aligned.

**Prime Example: Pope Francis** While the Church still has some way to go in terms of diversity, Jorge Bergoglio has in a short time and within rigid frameworks done much to open his organisation to constructive feedback and new perspectives, and demonstrated exceptional cultural competence, effortlessly making a connection with people of all faiths, ethnicities and persuasions.

**Expand your competence and continually learn**
- Recognise what you are *not* good at and work on it, or delegate it to someone who possesses that competence.
- Continually learn, re-examine your ethical stance and assess your leadership capabilities.
- An emotionally intelligent leader does not outstay their usefulness and avoids 'founder's syndrome', where they believe that by staying they are nurturing their 'baby' when in fact they are stifling it. Know when to go.

**Prime Example: Nelson Mandela** Having achieved racial reconciliation as President of South Africa, Mandela walked away from the halls of power when his one term ended in 1999, despite his iconic status. He would go on to find other ways to serve the causes dear to him, while paving the way for others to take their turn with the mantle of leadership.[3]

**Be responsible and accountable**
- In the long-term interests of the organisation, ethical leadership often involves doing what may be inconvenient, unpopular and even unprofitable (in the short-term).
- It involves straight dealing with the consequences of your actions, having the humility to admit mistakes and learn from them.

- It is about promoting responsibility in others, fairly and consistently disciplining misconduct, but also crediting and celebrating the right behaviours.
- It means never rushing to blame – doing so does not absolve a leader of responsibility.

**Prime Example: Willie Walsh, CEO IAG** With a reputation for saying things as they are and taking personal ownership of problems and challenges, Willie Walsh's straight-talking has enabled him to sway unions, bring around customers (remember the Terminal 5 debacle?) and win over governments and stakeholders, while remaining well-liked and highly respected.

**Don't take yourself too seriously**
- Maintain your perspective and sense of humour. Once you start to defend your leadership too vigorously and believe your own hype, your effectiveness and credibility as an ethical leader will start to diminish. Let your hair down occasionally, have some fun with your employees and customers, and smile.

**Prime Example: Michael O'Leary, CEO Ryanair** Any CEO willing to dress up as the Pope or Batman's sidekick, Robin, to promote their business could never be accused of taking themselves too seriously.

**Understand the power of leadership and use it well, sharing it when possible, never abusing it and exercising it only for good**
The appropriate use of power is one of the most important competencies of an ethical leader. Erich Fromm, in *Escape from Freedom*,[4] distinguishes between power *over* and power *to*. Power *over* is the ability to control others and to use them to achieve one's own ends. Power *to* is the capacity to accomplish one's goals without needing power over others. It can require their help and support, but this is not gained by coercion or for purposes of self-aggrandisement or self-advancement.

Ethical leadership is all about the power *to*. Authority is only legitimate if it advances a shared vision and power is a positive force used to mobilise the collective effort. Ethical leaders, therefore, encourage and mentor others to lead, increasing the 'ethical bandwidth' of the organisation and training the next generation of principled senior managers.

Leadership does not necessarily follow organisation charts or reporting lines; it can happen at all levels in a company. While the CEO sets the tone for the whole organisation, business unit managers, functional leads and supervisors shape the everyday work environment for staff.

If you work in a multinational company, this should resonate, i.e. the local operations management sets the values for behaviour in a much more immediate and tangible way than those in the 'C-suite' back in head office. The values of this cohort of managers must align fully with those of the CEO and translate into routine, daily exemplary behaviour so that the shared core values can cascade throughout the organisation. This advice is reflected by Thomas Peters and Robert Waterman in their classic book, *In Search of Excellence*:

> "An effective leader must be the master of two ends of the spectrum: ideas at the highest level of abstraction and actions at the most mundane level of detail. The value-shaping leader is concerned, on the one hand, with soaring, lofty visions that will generate excitement and enthusiasm ... On the other hand, it seems the only way to instil enthusiasm is through scores of daily events..."[5]

Finally, in leading by example, be aware that the price and privilege of leadership is a higher profile and a blurring of lines between one's personal and work life. (In the world of social media and camera phones, private behaviour can become public knowledge within seconds.) Leaders need to take special care to act with integrity in everything they do. Ethical leadership is a full-time job, or as C.S. Lewis once remarked: "Integrity is doing the right thing even when no-one is looking."

## Communicating Clear Expectations: 'Moments that Matter'

If you are acting ethically and leading ethically, you shouldn't be shy about it. Write down your values, share them with your team and use every opportunity to communicate them, setting clear expectations for standards of behaviour. The key to communications about ethics is to keep it simple and regular and not to overdo it. While you will be the best judge of what will work best for your team, generally, tailored, timely and truthful communications are more effective than a flood of information. Also, watch out for '**moments that matter**', i.e. occasions during the course of employees' careers with the organisation when it is fitting or opportune to inform them about its values or remind them of their responsibility for ethical conduct.

### Recruitment

According to Warren Buffett:

> "[I]n looking for people to hire, you look for three qualities: integrity, intelligence and energy. And if you don't have the

219

first, the other two will kill you. You think about it; it's true. If you hire someone without integrity, you really want them to be dumb and lazy."

He is right. Can you imagine how much trouble a clever, highly motivated and corrupt new hire would cause you?

It is important that ethical issues are addressed right at the start of the recruitment process. They should be incorporated into the brief for all positions and subtly reflected in the interview plan and questions. Rather than asking a candidate straight off if he or she is ethical, which really invites only one response, probe a little deeper with a more measured line of questioning to truly gauge their personal integrity. The following sample questions may help.

---

- What are your core values?
- What is your idea of an ethical organisation and what do you think can compromise the right culture?
- Have you ever had an ethical dilemma? How did you handle it and whom did you consult?
- Would you ever lie for me? (If they will lie for you, they will lie also to you. If this is too direct, you may prefer: Tell me about a time when you've had to go against company guidelines or procedures in order to get something done.)
- Have you read our Code of Conduct and if so, what resonated with you? (Assuming the material is readily accessible, e.g. on your website this answer will tell you that ethics are important to the candidate and whether or not they have done their homework on your organisation.)

---

## Induction and Mentoring

Successful at interview, a new recruit's next encounter with the company's value system should be its induction programme. Indeed, some companies require employees to sign up to their code of conduct as a precondition of employment. Whatever the approach, the code should be explained to new employees in some detail and it is much more powerful if a senior leader, ideally the CEO (depending on the size of the business) can deliver this in person for it to have real impact.

Consider assigning a mentor to each new team member. This can also facilitate their smooth transition into the company and provide a safe harbour for new hires to ask questions and quickly navigate the culture.

## Annual Performance Review

'Doing the right thing' should also be included in the annual performance review process, including completion of required training to show that acting with integrity is a key part of employees' performance evaluation and that there is no reward for breaking the rules. (Be especially careful not to reward questionable conduct, even if it produced a good result for the company.) The focus here should be on the means of achieving specific objectives, rather than evaluating the outcomes in isolation. You could also review if the employee demonstrated a willingness to challenge or report any unethical conduct that they may have witnessed during the year. For more senior management, assess how they have supported the ethics programme, reflected its requirements in their business plan and embraced core values in their communications with staff.

## Promotion

When someone is promoted it is timely to check in with them to ensure their values and those of the organisation are still aligned and that any training needs associated with the new position are being addressed. This is particularly relevant if the employee:
- is being promoted to a managerial role, will have staff reporting to them and relying on them to lead the way in terms of codes of conduct; or
- is being assigned overseas, where they will assume an ambassadorial role, representing the company abroad and maintaining international standards while also respecting local customs.

## Departure

Also, if a colleague decides to leave the company, spend a little time with them before they go. No longer vested and liberated from office politics, soon-to-be-ex-employees can provide reliable and candid accounts of the operational ethical norms. More properly conducted as 'exit interviews', an astute CEO or manager does not pass up the opportunity for a frank perspective on the cultural status quo from someone who has decided to move on to new pastures.

## Calendar-based or Event-driven Communications

As well as milestones in an individual employee's career, there are a number of regular events that punctuate the year when an organisation-wide ethics and compliance message is especially apt.

**New Year** New Year is an opportune time to emphasise the need to keep core values at the heart of every decision during the year ahead. One idea is to have desktop calendars printed and distributed to all staff, with a guiding business principle or ethics message from the CEO to accompany each calendar month.

**Budget and Reporting** During quarter-end or year-end reporting cycles, or at budget preparation time, be sure to highlight that integrity in financial reporting is expected and not cutting corners just to 'make the numbers'. Likewise, when summarising business performance, acknowledge the fact that good results only matter when they are based on responsible business practices.

**Regular Management/Staff Meetings** It is important that ethics and values are part of regular conversations among managers and their direct reports, so that they become embedded in everyday thinking and decision-making. Make ethics part of 'the grapevine', of what's really going on and what really matters. Again, consistency between word and deed are crucial.

Consider, for example, a company that has a strong anti-bullying policy. A manager is dismissed for bullying people in his department. For legal reasons, while the CEO may not be able to share the details of the case in a public forum, such as a town hall meeting, even an outline account will send a strong message, as the dismissal will have already spoken volumes about the company's stance on what is unacceptable behaviour. Doing nothing, i.e. retaining the manager, would have an equal but entirely opposite effect.

**Christmas** While not wanting to seem Scrooge-like, a timely reminder from the leadership team in the run-up to Christmas regarding the company's policy is advisable to maintain an appropriate attitude to the giving and receiving of gifts and hospitality. (See also **Chapter 4**.)

**Share-dealing Periods** In a PLC, a good time to highlight the company's insider-dealing policy is around reporting time, or 'closed' periods for share dealing.

**Company/Management Seminars and 'Town Hall' Meetings** Any company-wide gathering of all staff or management presents an ideal occasion for the CEO to convey some important tone from the top messages.

Consider the following, which could be woven into opening or closing remarks or adapted for a 'state-of-the-nation'-type address:

"My vision for 201X for our company is a simple one: to make it even better. Together we can do this – by harnessing the collective intellect in the room, working together as one team and inspiring excellence in our people everywhere.

The focus on performance will continue and may require some changes to how we do things. However, our core values: _____, _____ and _____ will prevail. These values have underpinned the success of our company. They must continue to be core as we embark on a new and exciting chapter in the company's history.

Rest assured, my door is always open. If you want to discuss any issue that concerns you, come and talk to me. I will listen to you and help as much as I can, whether the news is good, bad or ugly. Encourage your team to do likewise with you and earn their trust with transparency and discretion.

To everyone here today, let's commit to:
• keeping our core values front and centre in all our business dealings;
• fully understanding our responsibility to lead by example; and
• taking the time to ensure that every employee shares this commitment to the highest standards of business ethics.

Let's make sure that on our watch we will always do the right thing and set new standards for integrity as we forge a brighter future for our, better, company."

**Industry Events, Trade Association Meetings, etc.** Although offering excellent networking opportunities, any event that brings competitors in close contact with each other is fraught with the risk of their colluding, thereby breaching competition law and the company's code of conduct. It is a good idea for team members to be given summary competition law 'Dos and Don'ts' prior to attending such events.

## Times of Change

Other opportunities for values-related messages to management and staff include those involving significant corporate change. Examples include a reshuffle of the senior management team, or a business restructuring following an acquisition or a significant divestment, prior to the announcement of a new product launch, new market entry, cost-cutting initiative, etc. The communication's tone should be confident and reassuring, i.e. that while things may be changing or times are challenging, core values will prevail and integrity in all business transactions must be upheld as normal.

## Times of Crisis

Finally, in the event that the company suffers an ethical lapse or a breach of code of compliance procedures, particularly when this reaches the public domain, it is important that the CEO moves quickly to address staff. Edgar Schein notes that such moments, when a CEO is more likely to show his or her true colours, can act as powerful builders of an organisation's culture because of the "intensity of motion" involved.[6] If, at the height of the crisis, the leader makes values their touchstone, employees will truly understand that ethics matter. (This is discussed in more detail in the "Ethical Leadership in Times of Crisis" section at the end of this chapter.)

## Creating an Open Culture

Communication should be two-way. As well as communicating outwards, you should also invite comments, encourage dialogue and, most importantly, listen. Organisations, like societies, that are run with a police-state mentality simply create and reinforce a climate of fear. Command-and-control cultures will not work if we want employees to strive to do their best, instead of blindly following orders. Open, transparent cultures are the only way forward. The key to creating such environments and unlocking the potential of employees is for the leader to institutionalise ways for them to question your authority, ask questions and, in particular, to 'speak up' when things are not right.

In **Chapter 4** we saw how business misconduct tends to thrive in environments where employees fear retaliation (employees won't speak out if they are afraid that this will cause trouble for themselves). It is also the case that the vast majority of employees prefer to report misconduct directly to their manager rather than helplines or hotlines. To encourage employees to feel comfortable about discussing issues that concern them, they will need to be assured that:

(a)  they will not be retaliated against for speaking up; and
(b)  their report will be handled appropriately and with discretion.

Writing in the *Financial Times*, Stefan Stern has highlighted the importance of this issue:

> "The cost of behaving unethically needs to be significantly higher than the cost of failing to deliver expected returns and

the chance of being caught must be real. For that, companies must listen to and protect honest whistleblowers, whose ultimate confidant is the independent director."[7]

As well as ensuring that there are channels for communicating ethical concerns, Harvard professor Amy Edmondson argues, companies should strive to foster a culture of "psychological safety", in which employees are encouraged to take risks, report mistakes and ask questions without the fear of being blamed or ridiculed.[8]

The practical guidelines set out in **Figure 7.3** below are designed to help leaders foster this culture of openness in their organisation or team, and ensure that any ethical matter reported is triaged, investigated and addressed appropriately.

## FIGURE 7.3: STEPS IN THE INVESTIGATION OF GOOD FAITH REPORTS

**Remove fear of speaking up**
- Treat all employees with dignity and respect
- Keep an open-door policy and be approachable and empathetic
- Practice your active listening skills
- Clearly communicate good faith reporting channels
- Remind employees that the company does not tolerate retaliation

**Receiving Concerns**
- Thank the employee for coming forward
- Be aware of your tone and body language
- Reassure the employee regarding confidentiality and non-retaliation
- Take notes to ensure accurate information
- Outline the likely steps for an investigation and set a time for a follow-up discussion

**Dealing with Allegations**
- Determine if the concern is urgent
- Assess if it requires escalation to the board/legal counsel (see below)
- Decide if any corrective action is required immediately or put together an investigation plan with your compliance lead

**Escalation Criteria**
- Any infringements of the law
- Significant breaches of the code of conduct or related policy
- Any finding against a member of the senior management team
- Issues that could have a negative reputational impact on the company

## Supporting the Ethics Programme

In small enterprises what the leader says and does may be all that is required to communicate his or her ethical leadership. In larger organisations, however, with more diverse employees in several locations and with larger groups of stakeholders, the challenge to communicate and engage will be beyond the capacity of any one individual. It will require the creation of structures and systems to support the leader in 'spreading the word'. We discussed those structures in **Chapters 4** and **5** and in **Chapter 6** also explored the board's role in supporting the ethics programme and compliance.

The CEO and leadership team will be central to the effectiveness or otherwise of these systems and they need to visibly support them. It is not enough to 'print, post and pray' – the aim should be to make employees aware of ethical considerations and mitigate compliance risks, thereby minimising the chances of unethical behaviours occurring in the first place.

Core responsibilities in the area of ethics programme support can be summarised as follows:
- ensure that codes of conduct and related policies are well communicated and understood;
- hold your team accountable for their application;
- establish strong internal controls to facilitate their effective operation;
- participate in related risk-assessment reviews as required;
- address high-risk areas as a priority, including, for example, competition law, money laundering or bribery, as the sector or operating environment may demand;
- communicate good faith reporting ('whistleblowing') channels to employees;
- investigate all issues fully and fairly;
- ensure violations are reported to the board and any relevant regulatory authorities;
- ensure appropriate disciplinary actions are taken for breaches of codes and policies.

Ethics Training Ethical leaders must be demonstrably supportive in ethics training. Recommended practices that every leader can adopt to clearly signal this commitment are as follows:
- Send a personal invitation to your employees to the training session, confirming the importance of their participation.
- Introduce the session with some personal opening remarks.

- Highlight to attendees some ethical dilemmas that you experienced and how you resolved them. Invite discussion on typical ethical dilemmas relevant to your business.
- Stay for the full duration of the session – your full attendance will underscore its importance.
- Encourage active participation and ensure there is sufficient time for a Q&A session.
- Emphasise that staff should seek any further advice or express concerns of any kind to you, another manager or the ethics manager.
- Canvass feedback on the format and content of the training sessions.
- Consider sending a thank you to all attendees, summarising the key 'take-aways' and following up on any general questions/concerns.
- Ensure all ethics training is completed on a timely basis and discuss how training materials could be improved based on feedback received.

## Disciplining and Rewarding

Another important aspect of ethical leadership is to apply consistent and fair sanctions for breaches of codes or policies, and to credit ethical behaviour. Most companies are used to imposing sanctions but often neglect to acknowledge examples of personal or team integrity. Applying the useful parenting tip 'catch them when they are good' and publicly celebrating good behaviour is a much more positive and powerful motivator than the traditional 'stick' approach to misconduct. Here are some examples of how this might be done.

- Congratulate a sales executive for withdrawing from a bid process because it required making a questionable payment to the customer.
- Praise a member of the procurement team for seeking guidance on whether to accept a gift from a supplier.
- Commend a colleague for leaving a trade association meeting due to the collusive tenor of the discussions.
- Applaud a production operative for reporting an unsafe work practice.

A related suggestion is to encourage 'corporate story-telling' whereby stakeholders are invited to share their positive experiences of the company and its values with employees.[9] For example, Medtronic, a US medical technology firm, invites a group of patients and their doctors to their annual staff party to share their stories of how the company's products have helped them. One patient, with a long history of Parkinson's disease, told a story of how his life was transformed when he tried a new Medtronic device for deep-brain stimulation. Such stories help to reinforce the company's mission of serving others.[10]

A novel and powerful way to promote core values in an organisation is to set up an 'Ethics Awards Programme' to explicitly encourage and reward employees who espouse those values or inspire them in others. Staff are invited to nominate 'value ambassadors', colleagues who have shown outstanding commitment to ethical business conduct. The following is example of what this might look in practice.

## SAMPLE ETHICS AWARDS PROGRAMME

At Acme & Co we are deeply committed to our core values:
* integrity
* quality
* innovation
* courage
* collaboration.

This year I want to recognise employees who exemplify these values and I need your help to do so. If you work with someone who:
* actively demonstrates their commitment to these values;
* or inspires or leads others to translate these values into actions; or
* speaks up if they see or hear behaviour that conflicts with these guiding principles,

*please let us know.*

The Value Ambassador Nomination Form, together with further details on eligibility and the nomination process, is available from your HR Manager and on the intranet ...

If your nominee is a successful value ambassador, you are both invited to join us at a winners' dinner on ................. to celebrate and you will receive a token of our appreciation. You will also be initiated into our Values Hall of Fame ............ and your chosen charity will receive a donation of [XXX].

Thank you for your help and for ensuring that our values are lived, every day, everywhere by everyone.

---

*Chief Executive Officer*
*Acme & Co*

## The Ethical Leader Abroad

In **Chapter 5** we outlined some of the main challenges of operating a consistent set of values against the backdrop of variable, often unpredictable, business norms in another jurisdiction. We also examined some specific processes by which an organisation can be adapted and cross-cultural competencies embedded to facilitate a shared understanding of and compliance with home-grown ethical standards both domestically and overseas.

As an ethical leader abroad you are also a 'value ambassador', a role which requires you to draw deep on the competencies of ethical leadership, emotional intelligence, authenticity and your core values and to hone a number of specific qualities with which to achieve genuine 'cultural competence'. The qualities and skills that will enable you to successfully export your values-based approach and work successfully and ethically around the globe are:

- courage;
- communications;
- curiosity.

FIGURE 7.4: THE SKILLS AND QUALITIES OF THE
CULTURALLY COMPETENT LEADER

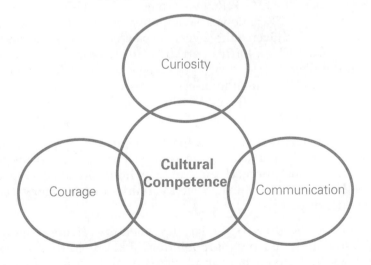

## *Courage*

I recall a conversation with the Latin-American Head of Compliance for a multinational and asking how she managed to keep everyone out of jail and ensure procurement and sales transactions in the region were above board. Her response was that the company was prepared to: (a) wait twice as long and (b) sometimes pay twice as much, rather than shortcutting the system and paying a bribe to expedite product delivery or to secure a contract. To survive and compete against those with no such compunction requires real courage. It also depends on being able to deliver real, sustainable, competitive advantage. Sometimes, however, as we noted in **Chapter 5**, the business model won't work and you need to just walk away.

Most of the time decisions may not be that 'black or white', but will require you, as the most senior representative on the ground, to make a call. Your chosen course of action at these moments may call on your core values, courage and conviction, and will be a defining chapter in the story of your international leadership. Mark Reilly is a good case in point[27]:

## GLAXOSMITHKLINE (GSK) AND 'OUR MAN IN CHINA': MARK REILLY[11]

In September 2014, Mark Reilly, former CEO of GSK's operations in China, and a UK national, having already been dismissed from his position, was given a three-year suspended prison sentence and deported from China for his part in "actively organising, promoting and implementing" a corrupt strategy, which included paying doctors over £300 million in bribes to prescribe GSK drugs. Part of an overall crackdown on graft by Chinese authorities, GSK was also fined a record £297 million for acting like a 'criminal godfather'.

It is likely that Mark Reilly knew that what he was doing was wrong. Chances are he was a loyal GSK executive. Perhaps he had adopted a 'when in Rome' approach motivated by his desire to develop and grow the business in China. What is certain is that he is now a convicted deportee.

CEO of GSK, Andrew Witty, has described the bribery within the Chinese unit as "deeply disappointing", but added that the company has "reflected deeply and learned from its mistakes", stressing that it remained "fully committed" to China despite its recent troubles.

At such times and in such circumstances, while in theory you may have the full backing of the head office 'back home', in practice, as 'our man in wherever', you are on your own. Do you compromise your ethics? Forget your values? Stoop to compete at abased levels? It's your call ...

## Communication

In addition to cases of expats falling foul of foreign regimes, many international marketing campaigns have been 'lost in translation'. The Swedish vacuum manufacturer didn't exactly nail the US market with its tagline, "Nothing sucks like an Electrolux". Conversely, the slogan of US beer manufacturer, Coors', "Turn it loose" didn't quite resonate with Spanish customers, translating literally as "Bring on diarrhoea"!

Take care to avoid similar cultural faux pas and craft messages that will resonate with your audience abroad. Be sensitive to the nuances in cross-cultural communication styles, know why they exist and respect the differences. As well as getting it right on paper, take time to visit; never underestimate the impact your presence will make. When there, you are centre-stage, so express yourself simply and genuinely and exercise a little humility. The latter can be easier than you think, as the warmth of the welcome and extent of the preparations can be incredibly humbling. When visiting Smurfit Kappa's international operations with Dr Michael Smurfit in the late 1990s, I noticed the soles of my shoes changing colour throughout the day. The factory had been freshly painted from ceiling to floor!

In her book *Say Anything to Anyone, Anywhere*, Gayle Cotton characterises successful cross-cultural communicating as including strategies to[12]:
* create proactive cross-cultural communication and avoid reactive communication;
* manage pre-existing cultural perceptions;
* understand cultural sensitivities and avoid conflict;
* build rapport in person, on the phone and by e-mail;
* understand how words, tone of voice and body language vary with every culture;
* increase self-awareness and adapt your style.

It is fair to say that the Irish communicate and travel across cultures particularly well. Irish people have tended to look beyond these shores for opportunity, are interested in people and find it easy to make alliances. If Irish executives can access these innate competences and marry them with the core competencies of ethical leadership, the future for our leaders overseas remains bright.

## Curiosity

Good communication is often borne of natural curiosity. Successful international leaders are adventurous in spirit, open to new ideas, tolerant of a degree of ambiguity and therefore more likely to be accepting of diverse cultures and customs. By taking the time to learn about the other person's beliefs and background, you will be able to interact with them in a more informed way. We have seen how emotional intelligence, or 'EQ', is a pre-requisite for ethical leadership. The ethical leader abroad needs to develop this to the next level and cultivate 'cultural intelligence', or 'CQ'. This has been defined as an outsider's "seemingly natural ability to interpret someone's unfamiliar and ambiguous gestures in just the way that person's compatriots and colleagues would, even to mirror them".[13] In their *Harvard Business Review* article on the subject, Christopher Earley and Elaine Mosakowski distinguish between EQ and CQ as follows:

> "A person with high emotional intelligence grasps what makes us human and at the same time what makes each of us different from one another. A person with high cultural intelligence can somehow tease out of a person's or group's behavior those features that would be true of all people and all groups, those peculiar to this person or this group, and those that are neither universal nor idiosyncratic. The vast realm that lies between those two poles is culture."

Despite cultural diversity, it is not always so difficult to bridge the gap between people and build relationships based on common interests and shared values. For example, most people are generally interested in either playing or watching a sport. Sometimes only basic social skills are all that is required to get the conversation going and start making genuine connections.

Even where business practices differ starkly, for example in locations where corruption is rampant, people still tend to value honesty and share common aspirations of decency and respect. (In **Chapter 1** we have seen an example of this in India's 'I Paid a Bribe' movement.) The distinction between *customs* and *values* is important and, once understood, can be leveraged to manage business abroad by appealing to common values instead of deferring to underlying, ingrained customs, such as corruption. As Linda Trevino and Katherine Nelson point out, the 'golden rule', i.e. the reciprocal Christian concept of 'do unto others as you would have them do unto you', also appears in the teachings of every major religion[14]:

Buddhism: Hurt not others in ways that you would yourself find hurtful.

Hinduism: This is the sum of duty: do naught to others which would cause pain if done to you.

Judaism: What is hateful to you, do not do to your fellow man.

Islam: No one of you is a believer until he desires for his brother that which he desires for himself.

This shared underlying belief suggests it is better to focus less on the differences that divide and more on the similarities that connect.

The experience of working and leading internationally will contribute to your growth as a person in ways you might never have imagined. It is likely to help you better appreciate all that you sometimes take for granted. Finally, and hopefully, it will increase your sense of responsibility as a leader and fuel your determination, not just to meet or set the bar but to raise the bar and help make the exciting world of business a better one by leading with integrity, always and everywhere.

## Leading with Integrity in Times of Crisis

Sometimes, despite best efforts and even in a company with the highest standards of conduct, ethical lapses will occur. More often than not these will have been identified in the risk-management process and can be dealt with using the response and investigation protocols discussed above. Occasionally, however, the issue will be of such magnitude as to warrant a crisis response.

The best way of responding to an ethical crisis, or indeed any crisis, is to be ready for it before it occurs. Have a clearly defined 'crisis response plan' in place to deploy when there is an ethical breach. The key elements of such a plan are set out below.

### KEY ELEMENTS OF A CRISIS RESPONSE PLAN

| | |
|---|---|
| Identify all potential crises | Brainstorm with the board and executive management team to identify crises that could hit the company, relevant to its business. Consider a number of headings, including: Product/Customer Safety, Financial, Health/Environment, Corruption, Operational Disasters, CEO Death/Exit, Hostile Bids, etc. |

| | |
|---|---|
| **Determine response team(s)** | A supervisory committee (e.g. CEO, CFO, Legal, Compliance, Communications and HR) 'to think', a project team (e.g. operations, finance and IT analysts) 'to do', with back-up members for each. |
| **Establish a crisis logistics database** | With contact details for all relevant stakeholders:<br>• Internal: key staff, management and board.<br>• External: advisors (PR, lawyers, auditors, bankers, insurers, consultants) and potential stakeholders (customers, government, stock markets, regulatory authorities, local community, NGOs, shareholders, unions, etc.).<br>• Select a 'situation room' (on-site and off-site).<br>• Decide who should be informed first. |
| **Draw up a responsibility matrix** | • Determine who will be responsible for what actions and at what points during the crisis.<br>• To avoid groupthink, build in safeguards to ensure decisions are challenged before taking action.<br>• It may not be possible to follow normal decision-making protocols. Document how, when and to whom authority may be delegated. |
| **Agree the communications plan** | • Appoint a credible primary and back-up spokesperson (the CEO or chairman is best). Ensure they are trained for dealing with media, especially in crisis situations.<br>• For crises that can be anticipated, prepare template press releases, stakeholder communications, internal memos and FAQs.<br>• Plan to leverage technologies for fast, effective messaging. |
| **Appoint media monitors** | Assign responsibility for monitoring the media, including digital media, for any negative messaging. |
| **Test, evaluate and improve** | Ensure the crisis response plan is tested for a range of crises, regularly updated and improved. At minimum, ensure that all included are informed and have a copy of it. |

When a crisis hits, and especially if it relates to ethical misconduct or a breach of trust, it is important to communicate effectively with all relevant stakeholders. Information so shared should be:

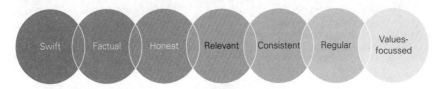

The most credible company source should be the communications lead. Again, this is most likely to be the CEO. Doing this well under stress is a real test of leadership at a time when it is most needed. The challenge is to dig deep and find the right balance of:

Don't worry if you don't have all the answers and cannot respond perfectly. As Harry Kraemer points out in *From Values to Action*,[15] the best antidote to fear is the conviction that no matter what, you will do the right thing and the best you can.

Above all, leading with integrity means being authentic. So, if the situation requires it, apologise. Don't let the lawyers dictate your ethical response. Phrases like 'it is regretful' don't resonate half as much as 'I am sorry'. (In **Chapter 3**, we saw the effects of the different *'mea culpa'* approaches of the CEOs of BP and General Motors.) After a genuine apology, the ethical leader should then address how the issue will be addressed to ensure it will not happen again. The leader should come across as part of the solution, not the problem, and thus begin to lay the foundations for rebuilding trust. Graham Dietz and Nicole Gillespie outline the four stages of rebuilding trust as follows[16]:

## FIGURE 7.5: THE FOUR STAGES OF REBUILDING TRUST

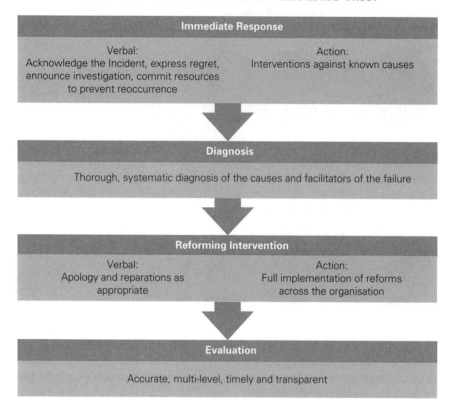

A company with a good reputation going into a crisis may suffer less damage than a company with a track record of unethical conduct. At the same time, how a company's leadership acts during times of crisis is a defining indicator of its culture. An exemplary response can help to build a reputational 'halo'.

As referenced by Dietz and Gillespie, UK utility company Severn Trent is a good example. Found guilty of distorting performance data for the industry regulator and fined £38 million, within two years it had been voted 'Utility of the Year' by its peers, in part due to its innovative and impressive recovery efforts. The senior management team implemented sweeping reforms as part of their 'model for trustworthiness', including ethics training, leadership development programmes, a better governance structure and the introduction of new KPIs linking board member efforts explicitly to the firm's performance and its values.

Another example is the 2013 'horsemeat scandal', which broke when the Food Safety Authority of Ireland (FSAI) reported that frozen burgers containing horsemeat were on sale in a number of Irish supermarkets.[17] The story soon gathered pace, with similar findings being reported across Europe. While sales of frozen burgers and similar products fell considerably and the share prices of the companies involved took a hammering in the immediate aftermath, the general consensus was that the role played by the FSAI in identifying the issue and the manner in which it immediately highlighted it boosted Ireland's image as a country that takes food provenance and quality seriously.

In contrast, tactics guaranteed to worsen any situation include attempts to:
* cover up the matter or close it down;
* obfuscate the issue;
* disassociate or blame it on someone else;
* delay communication;
* speculate rather than report facts;
* gloss over or ignore the problem and hope it goes away.

Two infamous examples highlighting how badly these approaches can backfire are Union Carbide and Perrier.

## Union Carbide and the Bhopal Disaster[18]

Considered one of the worst industrial accidents in history, approximately 3,800 people died as a result of a gas leak at Union Carbide's plant in Bhopal in 1984. The company immediately tried to disassociate itself from any legal liability. Ultimately, it settled with the Indian Government (for just under $500 million), and accepted moral responsibility. It has since shrunk to one-sixth of its size and was ultimately taken over by Dow Chemicals.

## The Perrier Recall[19]

In 1990 high levels of benzene were discovered in bottles of Perrier mineral water in the US. The initial response from the company was to play down the issue, attributing it to an isolated incident in a filtering plant in North Carolina. Within a week, Perrier had withdrawn 160 million bottles worldwide. A lack of a coherent, consistent response commensurate with the health concerns was wholly lacking from the French parent company, making a bad situation considerably worse. Groupe Perrier was taken over by Nestlé in 1992 and the brand has yet to regain its pre-1990 market share.

Contrast Perrier's approach to the Johnson & Johnson Tylenol recall, often referred to as the 'how to' case study in crisis management and trust recovery.

## Johnson & Johnson and the Tylenol Recall[20]

In October 1982, Johnson & Johnson learned that its Tylenol brand of painkillers had been tampered with in a US supermarket. It immediately ordered that the product be taken off the shelves of every outlet in which it was sold. Furthermore, it announced that it would not put Tylenol back on the market until the product was more securely protected with tamper-proof packaging. Both the recall and the repackaging cost the company dearly, but this short-term loss was more than compensated for by the fact that the brand was preserved in the long term. Some experts have argued that the company even benefited from the crisis because consumers were so satisfied and reassured by the response.

In times of crisis, while trust can be damaged by the ethical misconduct, this need not be fatal if the company shows leadership integrity by embarking upon a comprehensive and genuine repair effort. However, there is a Dutch saying: "Trust arrives on foot and leaves on horseback." Trust failures typically take years to recover from, are costly and absorb huge amounts of management time. Clearly, money, time and effort are better spent in (a) designing an organisation that supports ethical conduct and (b) ensuring it is governed by authentic leaders who embrace and espouse integrity. Hopefully, you are by now convinced of this need and are also more confident in your abilities and those of your organisation to deliver on both counts. The next chapter sets out a range of hypothetical ethical dilemmas, an opportunity for you to put some of these new perspectives into practice.

# References to Chapter 7

1   See Sisodia, R., Sheth, J. and Wolfe, D., *Firms of Endearment: How World Class Companies Profit from Passion and Purpose* (Pearson Education, 2014).

2   Work Group for Community Health and Development, *Community Toolbox*, Chapter 13, Section 8, "Orienting Ideas in Leadership: Ethical Leadership", Kansas University, 2015. Available at http://ctb.ku.edu/en/table-of-contents/leadership/leadership-ideas/ethical-leadership/main

3   Ashgar, R., "Knowing When to Leave: Nelson Mandela's Key Leadership Lesson", *Forbes*, 12 December 2013. Available at http://www.forbes.com/sites/robasghar/2013/12/12/knowing-when-to-leave-nelson-mandelas-epic-leadership-lesson/#331c740f1dc6 (accessed February 2016).

4   Fromm, Erich, *Escape from Freedom* (Holt, 1941, 1994).

5   Peters, Thomas J. and Waterman Jr, Robert H., *In Search of Excellence: Lessons from America's Best-run Companies* (Harper & Row, 1981).

6   Schein, Edgar, *Organizational Culture and Leadership* (Jossey-Bass, 1996).

7   Stern, Stefan, "Ethical Policies Must Work in the Field", *Financial Times*, 21 May 2015. Available at http://www.ft.com/intl/cms/s/0/7bb5fcfc-fa49-11e4-a41c-00144feab7de.html#axzz41136vJ1Q (accessed February 2016).

8   Edmondson, Amy, *Managing the Risk of Learning: Psychological Safety in Work Teams* (Harvard Business School, 2002). Available at http://www.hbs.edu/faculty/Publication%20Files/02-062_0b5726a8-443d-4629-9e75-736679b870fc.pdf

9   See Fisher, S., "Telling Tales: The Art of Corporate Storytelling", *The Costco Connection*, October 2007, pp. 22–23.

10  Denning, Stephen, *The Leader's Guide to Story-telling: Mastering the Art and Discipline of Business Narrative* (Jossey-Bass, 2011).

11  Moore, Malcolm and Rowland, Denise, "China fines Glaxo £297m for bribery, Mark Reilly sentenced", *The Telegraph*, 19 September 2014. Available at http://www.telegraph.co.uk/finance/newsbysector/pharmaceuticalsandchemicals/11108376/China-fines-Glaxo-297m-for-bribery-Mark-Reilly-sentenced.html (accessed February 2016).

12  Cotton, Gayle, *Say Anything to Anyone Anywhere: 5 Keys to Successful Cross-Cultural Communication* (Wiley, 2013).

13  Earley, Christopher P. and Mosakowski, Elaine, "Cultural Intelligence", (2004) *Harvard Business Review*, October.

14  Trevino, Linda and Nelson, Katherine, *Managing Business Ethics: Straight Talk About How To Do It Right* (Wiley, 2011).

15  Kraemer, Harry M. Jansen, *From Values to Action: The Four Principles of Values-Based Leadership* (Jossey-Bass, 2011).

[16] Dietz, Graham and Gillespie, Nicole, *The Recovery of Trust: Case Studies of Organisational Failures and Trust Repair* (Occasional Paper 5, Institute of Business Ethics, 2012). Available at http://www.ibe.org.uk/userfiles/op_trustcasestudies.pdf (accessed February 2016).

[17] See Keena, Colm, "Ireland's Role in Horsemeat Scandal Boosts its Image", *Irish Times*, 14 January 2014.

[18] Broughton, Edward, "The Bhopal Disaster and its Aftermath: a Review", (2005) *Environmental Health* 4: 6.

[19] See Haig, Matt, *Brand Failures: The Truth about the 100 Biggest Branding Mistakes of All Time* (Kogan Page, 2006).

[20] Haig, Matt, *op. cit.*, above.

# 8

# Ethical Dilemmas
# and the 'ETHIC' Framework

*"Authentic leaders know the true north of their moral compass and are prepared to stay the course despite challenges and disappointments."*

Bill George

In this chapter we put the last seven chapters into practice. You are presented with eight ethical dilemmas, typical of those that arise every day in all kinds of businesses all over the world. It is worth noting that often in these situations there is no one 'right answer', rather a series of steps to follow to ensure due process and a fair result for all concerned.

The 'ETHIC' framework, set out below, is designed to help you address the issues raised here and ethical dilemmas generally in a sound and systematic manner.

## TABLE OF ETHICAL DILEMMAS

| | Title | Company Type | Role | Sector | Issue |
|---|---|---|---|---|---|
| I. | Great Medicine/ Gross Margin | Private | CEO | Healthcare | Safety Issue |
| II. | Same Bed – Different Dreams | Multi-national Plc/Joint Venture | Non-executive Director | Service | JV culture clash |
| III. | Making the Numbers | Private (IPO) | Finance Director | Insurance | Creative accounting |
| IV. | Just Good Friends? | Private | Sales Director | Wholesale | Conflict of Interest |
| V. | When in Rome | Multi-national Plc | Divisional CEO | Manufacturing | Gifts/ Bribery |
| VI. | A Competitive Round of Golf | Domestic Plc | Key Account Manager | Manufacturing | Competi-tion Law |
| VII. | Child's Play | Private | Procure-ment Director | Retail | Human Rights |
| VIII. | A Close Call | Partner-ship | Practice Manager | Professional Services | Confiden-tial infor-mation |

(*Note:* all ethical dilemmas outlined are hypothetical and have been developed wholly to assist with the understanding of the concepts and principles set out in this book. Disclaimer: any resemblance between those mentioned in examples and any person, living or dead, is purely coincidental.)

## The 'ETHIC' Framework

**Establish the facts**

- What is the ethical issue?
- Who is involved?
- What evidence is available?
- How reliable is it?
- What are the rules?
- What are the options?

**Think about stakeholders**

- How does this impact:
  o employees
  o customers
  o suppliers
  o shareholders
  o the community
  o the regulator
  o others?

**Harness your thoughts**

- Is it legal?
- Is it fair?
- Does it breach any trust?
- Does it do any harm?
- Is it ethical?
- Do I need to take advice or seek support?
- Am I considering all options and outcomes?
- What are my obligations?

**Initiate your plan**

- Evaluate alternative solutions and decide
- Document your decision and rationale
- Consider how to communicate it
- Consult as required

**Check your decision**

- Is my decision consistent with my core values?
- Have I the courage to make the right choice?
- Am I happy to be held accountable?
- How will those impacted by my decision feel about it?
- Will my decision be understood correctly?
- What will the consequences be?
- How can I learn from this?

## I.  Great Medicine/Gross Margin

You are the chief executive of a clinic providing specialist orthopae-dic services. The clinic is highly profitable and prides itself on being at the forefront of advances in hip and knee surgery, including pri-mary and revision joint replacement.

Two of the clinic's most respected consultants are keen to adopt a less invasive surgical approach to hip replacement, having practised the method during their international assignments with leading teaching hospitals in Canada and Australia. The key advantages of the new procedure include the reduced time the patient spends in hospital, a much lower risk of infection as well a faster rehabilitation period. In short: a safer, quicker alternative to the traditional approach.

The cost of the new surgical equipment for two theatres will be in excess of €2.5 million. You are aware from recent rounds of nego-tiations that you will not be able to pass on the higher costs of this operation to the insurance companies or the National Health Service. In fact, the overall contribution for each procedure is likely to be less than half that currently received, as the hospital stay will be reduced from four or five days to just one or two, unless demand for the new surgery effectively doubles, which is always uncertain with any new, albeit well-tested, medical advance.

**What would you do?**

### Red Flag Issues

- This ethical dilemma is concerned with the reconciliation of a typi-cal cost–benefit approach to enterprise performance with wider per-spectives on reputation and ethics.
- Specifically in this case, the issue is whether to prioritise net profit per operating procedure over improved patient safety and recovery.

### Analysis and Suggested Response

- It is not 100% certain that private health insurance and/or the National Health Service will *not* cover the costs of the new procedure. Further work is required to establish the exact costs, their likely recovery and any potential for lobbying.

- The clinic prides itself on being at the forefront of medical advances in its field of specialty. It is also highly profitable and can afford the investment. Might it lose its reputation if another hospital makes this treatment available sooner? Or what if the consultants leave to develop the new methods at other centres of surgical excellence?
- If a superior clinical outcome is the primary driver in choosing the surgical options available to a patient, then is this investment not in the long-term interest of the success and reputation of the organisation?
- Although this is ultimately a decision for the board, based on all available information, this is an opportunity for you as CEO to present the case in the context of the clinic's mission, values and strategic objectives.

## II. SAME BED – DIFFERENT DREAMS?

You are a non-executive director (NED) and chair of the audit committee of a FTSE250 company providing engineering and project-management services to large customers in the telecommunications sector. The company has achieved considerable market success in Europe and the recently appointed new CEO, Arthur Pemberton, is keen to continue the acquisition trail by gaining a foothold in some of the key growth markets in South America. Indeed, he has stated in a recent press interview that his priority is to double the size of the business and be a credible FTSE100 contender within five years.

This month's board pack includes a proposal for a substantial investment in a joint venture (JV) company in Brazil. The business is perfectly aligned with the plans for the region, the deal consideration seems reasonable and the financial, operational and legal due diligence to date has not highlighted any obvious deal-breakers.

At the board meeting convened to approve the transaction, you ask about the cultural fit between the two businesses and the operating environment in the region, referring to some recent high-profile corruption scandals in related industries. The CEO assures you that the two principals in the JV are highly regarded in the industry locally and that he does not foresee anything other than a meeting of minds in running the business together. The chairman of the board, who sits on another public sector board with the CEO, nods in agreement. However, you notice the in-house general counsel, Jennifer Mason, shifting uncomfortably in her seat. You decide to raise the issue with her directly during a coffee break.

Jennifer admits that during a meeting in São Paulo with the key principals to discuss the proposed terms of the JV agreement, when she raised the issue of the code of ethics and related training for the combined business, they became quite hostile, stating that these things were counter-cultural, unnecessarily bureaucratic and that they would not support the imposition of any such policies or procedures.

After the break, Arthur Pemberton again highlights the unique growth opportunity that the deal presents in terms of scale and promised synergies. The chairman congratulates the CEO and the executive management team on bringing such an exciting opportunity to the board and calls for unanimous support to proceed as planned.

**What would you do?**

## Red Flag Issues

- As a NED, you share the same responsibilities as the executive directors to "ensure the long-term success of the company by providing entrepreneurial leadership within a framework of prudent and effective controls which enables risk to be assessed and managed".
- As a member of the audit committee, and in particular as its chair, you have an elevated responsibility to monitor and review the effectiveness of the company's risk management and internal control systems.
- However, NEDs must always contend with the potential for 'information asymmetry', i.e. where executive management (naturally) have more knowledge about the business than the NEDs. In this case, you believe the CEO may have been less than fully transparent with the board about important aspects of this deal.
- The CEO has put on public record that he wants to double the size of the business during his tenure. Therefore, it is possible that he may be pursuing scale at any cost.
- Joint ventures can be fraught at the best of times, so it is essential that there is full agreement from the outset on matters as fundamental to the combined business as its values and commitment to ethical business practices.
- This is especially the case where the JV operates in countries or sectors that are considered high-risk for corruption (remember the Transparency International Index we discussed in **Chapter 5**).

## Analysis and Suggested Response

- On the basis of the information received and, more importantly, that withheld, you should not approve the transaction as currently proposed.
- You should outline your concerns, requesting more discussion on the compliance aspects of the proposed deal, including a code of conduct for the JV.
- You could ask the chairman to adjourn the meeting until satisfactory due diligence has been carried out on these matters.
- As this request may fall on deaf ears given the seemingly tight relationship between the chairman and the CEO, you could request a meeting with the senior independent NED and/or the other NEDs to debate how best to proceed.
- You may also want to address how to manage the broader expansion programme, perhaps proposing an 'acquisitions committee' comprising both NEDs and executive directors (other than the CEO) to comprehensively assess all investment proposals prior to consideration by the main board.
- It may also be prudent to request the remuneration committee to review the CEO's remuneration package to ensure it is aligned with the interests of shareholders and not unduly skewed towards top-line growth.
- Another meeting with the general counsel may be helpful as she has been close to this deal. It may also be an opportunity to probe the new CEO's leadership style, which you are concerned may be autocratic and not conducive to constructive debate or challenge.
- As a NED, in order to preserve your reputation, your last-resort option is to 'vote with your feet' and distance yourself from a company whose CEO's ambition potentially compromises his integrity and that of the board.

## III. MAKING THE NUMBERS

You are the chief financial officer (CFO) of a reinsurance company that has been in private equity ownership for the last five years and is now gearing up for an IPO. You are reasonably new to the industry, having spent most of your career in fund accounting. While you have quickly grasped the fundamentals of the business, sometimes you struggle with the revenue model applied for different jurisdictions and categories of risk. You have, however, become accustomed to the relentless focus on results, although the pressure has never been greater, as the success of the listing in terms of the share price and take-up depends on the trajectory of the latest earnings figures.

Late one evening, just 10 days away from the proposed IPO, you are working on the consolidation of the Q2 numbers for the management discussion and analysis report when you note that the Bermuda office has reported a significant and unexpected bump in gross premiums. You pull the related contracts from the system and, having reviewed the risk transfer provisions several times, cannot reconcile the numbers to those reported.

With the time difference in your favour, you call William Westwood, Head of Underwriting in Bermuda, to discuss the discrepancy. Regarded as "an all-round great guy" in the company, having consistently delivered stellar results, you always feel like the 'boring bean-counter' in any encounter with him. This time is no different. "Joe," he says, "I know you are new to this game – but this is how we do things on the island – the transfers go by side letter. Harry [the CEO] is cool with it – you ought to talk to him. We keep it simple, so that I can understand it! But don't worry, I get it. I'll e-mail you another piece of paper for your file by tomorrow so it will all add up and you can put a nice red tick beside it! And see you in London for the IPO party."

Nothing arrives the following day and from a review of other side agreements on the Bermuda files, you note they are almost always silent on the issue of risk transfer. You calculate that if the profits are restated to exclude the potentially tainted Bermuda revenues, it will result in a material adjustment to the H1 numbers, and possibly even require a restatement of prior-year statements.

**What would you do?**

## Red Flag Issues

- It is possible, but not certain, that the Bermuda office has either inadvertently recognised revenues incorrectly or engaged in creative accounting practices.
- In a normal operating environment this should be capable of being raised, addressed and remediated. However, given the timing and pressure associated with the IPO, it is not certain how the private equity partners will react to this news, if indeed it *is* news to them.
- The Head of Underwriting in Bermuda has effectively given you the brush-off and has also implied that the CEO is aware of the practice.
- As it stands, the company may be on course to presenting fraudulent figures to the market to support its IPO.

## Analysis and Suggested Response

- As CFO, at minimum you have a responsibility under your professional code of conduct (particularly the 'Integrity' requirements), to disassociate yourself from reports or returns that contain materially false or misleading statements and to act in the event of suspected fraud.
- Although you are still relatively new to the reinsurance business and may doubt your own analysis, you should trust your instincts and follow through when things don't feel right.
- You need to alert the CEO and senior management team to the issue you have identified as soon as possible and initiate a full review of relevant contracts for the Bermuda office (and possibly elsewhere, depending on the scale of the problem unearthed).
- If the CEO is not supportive of this action, you could seek support from your external audit partner and ask him or her to give an opinion, based on a limited-scope review.
- You could also channel your concerns to the chair of the audit committee or other members of that committee or of the board itself.
- If the issue is as grave as it seems, it may well derail the IPO and in turn cost you your position. However, you have no choice but to deal with this one head-on.

# IV. JUST GOOD FRIENDS?

You are Sales Director, Ireland & UK, for a wholesale furniture business. Markets have been tough lately, with sluggish demand, keen competition from Asia and adverse currency movements not helping matters. You are under pressure to win some high-margin business to help get things back on track.

You fly to London late one Thursday evening for a business meeting with a major customer the next morning to negotiate a contract for the second phase of a substantial hotel refurbishment project. This is exactly what the business needs to lift the numbers and may even result in you securing a payout for you and your team under the company's annual bonus scheme.

You are accompanied by your colleague, Tom Conroy, whom you know well, as Tom's wife Alison has been a good friend of yours since your college days. Tom also reports to you, which can be a little awkward, especially around performance review time. After you have both checked in at the hotel, you suggest meeting up for a bite to eat in an hour or so, but Tom makes his excuses, and seems a little evasive.

Later that evening, as you walk through Covent Garden, you see Tom sitting at a restaurant table with Eleanor Fields, the key customer contact you are due to meet the next day, and from the way they are holding hands it is clear this is not just a business meeting.

**What would you do?**

## Red Flag Issues

- Tom is potentially conflicted with this account as romantic relationships can cloud judgement on both sides. There is potential for the customer to award a contract in this case for reasons other than rational business reasons, which may be perceived as bribery.
- As you are Tom's boss, you have a responsibility to ensure this issue is addressed to protect the company from the potential for such claims.

## Analysis and Suggested Response

- There are two parts to this dilemma: a professional and a personal one. Your immediate priority is to address the business issue, ideally before the meeting tomorrow.
- This is a very sensitive matter and needs to be managed accordingly. At minimum, Tom has a right to be heard and to explain his behaviour.
- It may be wise to involve an independent resource, such as a HR manager, to manage the review of this case, especially given your slightly awkward reporting relationship with Tom.
- You should let Tom know what you saw at the restaurant and ask him to provide an explanation for his behaviour. Whether he confirms or denies that he is in an inappropriate relationship with the customer, he should be excused from the meeting as a precaution until you have had more time to consider and review the matter.
- You should advise Tom that you will discuss the issue with him further when you are both back in the office (possibly in the presence of the independent resource).
- Assuming Tom admits to a romantic relationship with the customer, he should be removed from any dealings with this account. This should also be explained to the customer, without necessarily highlighting the specific reasons why until the issue has been further investigated.
- Contract history with this customer should be reviewed for evidence of any prior unfair business advantage. If this is found to be the case, the customer would also need to be alerted.

- Tom should be disciplined for breach of conflict of interest rules, assuming these are in place and have been already explained to him.
- These rules should be reviewed, reissued if necessary and checked for ongoing compliance. It is good practice to have all employees complete and sign a conflict of interest questionnaire at least annually and ensure these are reviewed, managed appropriately and filed with the personnel records.
- In an ideal world Tom should not have reported to you in the first place, given your friendship with his wife, but these issues can be difficult to avoid or manage in smaller organisations or locations.

## V. WHEN IN ROME ...

You work for a large multinational manufacturer of military equipment and have recently taken up an expatriate position in Singapore as Divisional CEO for the company's South East Asia division, with operations throughout the region, including Malaysia, the Philippines, Thailand, Myanmar and Vietnam.

At the end of your first week you are surprised and a little uncomfortable when you receive a pair of Omega watches from one of the company's main suppliers as a welcome gift for you and your husband. You decide to put 'Gifts & Hospitality Policy' on the agenda for next Monday morning's management meeting.

At the meeting you learn from the Purchasing Manager that gifts of this nature are a normal part of doing business in this part of the world. Likewise, the Sales Manager says that his team similarly provides gifts and hospitality to customers, many of whom are government officials. These gifts range from chocolates and bottles of wine, sometimes cases of wine, gift vouchers or small amounts of cash, as well as "various forms of entertainment" and occasionally big ticket items for high-ranking officials, such as CEOs, etc.

The general view at the meeting is that these practices are customary and expected by customers, and to refuse such gifts or hospitality could be insulting to suppliers. You are keen to start off on the right foot with your team and also do not want to alienate your supplier base or undermine the sales team's efforts. At the same time, you are not happy with what you have heard and know you need to take some action.

**What would you do?**

## Red Flag Issues

- There do not seem to be any group guidelines available to help determine what is or is not allowed in terms of gifts and hospitality, or if they do exist, the local team don't know about them or are not applying them.
- The fact that many of the customers are government officials requires particular attention, as special rules and regulations will apply to these interactions. Indeed, the agencies of many governments have their own rules and limits on what their officials may be permitted to receive by way of gifts and/or hospitality. Even if these rules are not always enforced by the institutions themselves, they should be complied with in addition to the company's own policy.
- Some of the gifts are in the form of cash or cash equivalents (e.g. gift vouchers), which are almost always considered bribes under most domestic and international anti-corruption legislation.
- As Divisional CEO you are responsible for setting the tone from the top and achieving the right balance of adherence to the law (international and domestic), compliance with company codes and policies, and respect for acceptable local customs.

## Analysis and Suggested Response

- Working for a multinational in both a sector and a region with high risks of corruption, you would expect the company's head office to have a comprehensive set of policies to help you regulate your business transactions. You should therefore contact your group compliance or legal department for assistance on this specific issue and also in terms of business conduct compliance generally.
- Gifts of cash or cash equivalents should be stopped immediately.
- What "various forms of corporate entertainment" entails must be reviewed to ensure it does not involve anything morally questionable, offensive or damaging to the company's reputation.
- Commission local lawyers to produce outlines of each country's anti-corruption, bribery and related laws, including rules regarding gifts & hospitality, particularly to and from government officials.
- Arrange training on the company's code of conduct and related policies for the full team so that everyone is aware of their business conduct responsibilities. The training programme should reflect group requirements as well as applicable, local regulations and worked examples for each country in the region.
- Consider establishing a gift & hospitality register to record details of all gifts and hospitality, both given and received, and also an approval process for those over and above agreed local thresholds.

- Meet the teams in each country and clearly outline the company's values, your approach to business ethics and, with some pragmatic understanding, outline what is expected of them. Encourage discussion on how to set a new bar for ethical business conduct in the region.
- With regard to the Omega watches, these should be returned. This can be difficult and requires some tact. The sample letter below suggests how to word the return (in effect, a refusal) of a gift from a supplier. It could also be adapted as a template for refusing hospitality from a customer, and so forth.

### LETTER TO A SUPPLIER RETURNING A GIFT

Dear

Thank you for your recent gift of two Omega watches.

As you know, we truly value our business relationship and are very grateful for your continued service [*custom*]. However, as you might also appreciate, we are required to comply with strict rules and controls from our Head Office regarding gifts and hospitality. In deference to these rules, unfortunately we are not permitted to accept your kind gifts and must return them [*must decline your kind invitation to Y*].

We sincerely hope this does not cause any inconvenience for you and again would like to thank you for thinking of us and for your kind gesture. We look forward to a continued successful business relationship with you.

Yours sincerely

## VI. CHILD'S PLAY

You are Procurement Director for a men's clothing manufacturer supplying premium retail clothing chains in Europe, the Middle East and the US. Many of your customers are members of the UN's Global Compact network and have supplier codes of ethics with which your company has agreed to comply. Under these codes you are required to have your suppliers in turn independently vetted from a CSR perspective. Some customers are more vigilant than others in checking your procedures.

You have recently sourced a new silk supplier in New Delhi and, having visited the manufacturing facility, are happy that it is a safe operation with a highly skilled and motivated workforce. You are confident that they will be able to supply superior product and are also very pleased with their price points, which will allow your company to increase its profit margin. You engage your third-party CSR auditor to carry out the usual checks.

To your dismay the Indian company fails the audit, on the issue of child labour. Immediately alarmed, you turn to the relevant section of the audit report where, with some relief, you read that they have simply been unable to provide the requisite documentation (including, for example, birth certificates for all staff) to substantiate that their workforce are all above the minimum age for factory workers in New Delhi (14 years). The report also specifically states that there was no evidence found during the audit visit of any minors working on the site.

It would cost the company at least €50,000 per month to revert to its previous supplier, which as well as being more expensive was also less reliable, hence the reason for seeking an alternative in the first place.

You call the auditor for more assurance on the findings. He fully shares your view that this is entirely a documentation deficiency, rather than a confirmed case of child labour, and that it is all capable of being resolved in a matter of weeks.

**What would you do?**

## Red Flag Issues

- The company has signed up to various supplier codes of conduct, requiring compliance with the UN's Global Compact and its human rights principles.
- One of the company's suppliers has failed a key requirement and even though it appears to be an administrative and control failure, i.e. not having birth certificates on file for all staff rather than a real human rights abuse issue, it is nonetheless a clear fail.
- To ignore this issue would at best risk losing a main customer in the event that they check your procedures regarding CSR auditing. At worst, it may mean supporting child labour if the Indian company is in fact employing minors and simply managed to hide this fact for the duration of the audit visit.

## *Analysis and Suggested Response*

- The new Indian supplier should be suspended, pending full investigation and remediation of the audit finding.
- Once it has addressed the failing, the supplier can be audited again and, assuming a clean bill of health, can be formally re-engaged at that time.
- In the meantime, your company will need to revert to its previous supplier, or seek another alternative.
- Unfortunately, sometimes compliance with rules can be expensive, but this is the price and privilege of operating ethical standards globally.

## VII. A COMPETITIVE ROUND OF GOLF

You are Key Account Manager for a manufacturer of specialist packaging and enjoy a leading market position in your domestic market. The local subsidiary of one of your major suppliers is hosting a golf outing to support their chosen charity. Your company has donated €1,000, which also covers the cost of a mixed four-ball tournament and lunch afterwards in the clubhouse. You bring a fellow key account manager, Kate Marron, and also the Purchasing Officer, John von Troon, and Junior Sales Associate, Patrick Dillon, as you think it will be a good networking opportunity for them.

On the day, you and Kate are paired with the HR manager and receptionist from the supplier company. Your junior colleagues are paired with their direct counterparts at a competitor firm and tee off just ahead of you.

You are enjoying the company and the sunshine and your team are playing well. However, as you clear one of the last greens, you overhear the following conversation from the 18th tee box that makes your hair stand on end.

John (your Purchasing Officer) says: "Have you seen how much ink prices are up this month? If we both refuse to pay more, the suppliers will have to hold their old prices. We really need to work together to beat them at their own game."

The competitor's sales associate replies: "Good idea. But we are also getting killed on the sales side. I don't know about you, but I'm committed to a 5%+ margin."

Patrick (your Sales Associate) says: "Eh, we can't agree on a price. Isn't that illegal?"

The competitor's sales associate replies: "I know that – but I'm just telling you that I am not playing this game of slashing prices to the bone anymore – I'm getting 5% and if anybody else wants to follow suit, they know where I stand."

Your company takes its competition law responsibilities very seriously. In fact, just last month you had all attended a training session on competition law compliance.

**What would you do?**

## Red Flag Issues

- The conversation between your procurement and sales colleagues and their counterparts in the rival firm is a clear breach of competition law on several levels.
- Your company enjoys a leading market position and therefore needs to take extra care not to abuse (or be seen to abuse) its dominance.
- John (the Purchasing Officer) does not seem to be aware that there is anything wrong with the conversation, or perhaps he thinks that its informality (or the fact that it is not in writing) somehow negates or mitigates its illegality.
- Though Patrick's contribution is benign, he did not do enough to distance himself or the company from the subject being discussed.
- Such events, where competitors meet informally, can be risky from a competition law perspective as a conversation can move easily to the common ground: the business, prevailing market conditions and, in turn, factors contributing to those conditions (pricing, customer behaviour, etc.). Utmost care is required to avoid compliance breaches.
- The competition authorities: (a) assume the worst when competitors meet; (b) have extensive powers of discovery investigation (including the powers to 'dawn raid' your office and your home); and (c) can impose fines of up to 10% of turnover as well as criminal or civil personal penalties in many jurisdictions (e.g. jail sentences on executives).
- As Key Account Manager, you have a pivotal sales role in the company, and therefore a responsibility to address what you have heard.

## Analysis and Suggested Response

- Relay your concerns about the conversation to John and Patrick as soon as possible. Try to catch them after the game and before lunch, and advise them to immediately refrain from continuing the conversation.
- Once back in the office, you need to escalate this matter to an appropriate level in senior management, such as the CEO or finance director.
- You should also seek legal advice, particularly in relation to any appropriate follow-up communication about the incident with the supplier firm.
- John should be severely disciplined. If the company is serious about its competition law responsibilities, it should be prepared to follow through with serious sanctions.
- Though being credited for recognising that there was clearly something wrong with the matter being discussed, Patrick should also be advised to actively disengage from such conversations should he find himself in such a position again.
- The competition law training programme and policy should be reviewed to ensure it addresses such situations, providing detailed scenarios and examples.
- Pricing procedures should be reviewed to ensure that decisions are reached independently of suppliers and where any supporting data or analysis is relied upon, that the source of this information is clearly noted.
- As Key Account Manager, advise your team of their responsibilities before any other such informal events or more formal meetings with competitors, e.g. at trade fairs or trade association meetings.
- Be careful about the creation of any written record of the events and seek legal advice in regard to the preparation of records.
- You should obtain specialist competition law advice because the company may need to avail of the leniency or immunity programmes which many competition agencies around the world operate, otherwise your company's competitor or someone else may avail of the programmes, thereby exposing your company to severe penalties.

(*Note:* I would like to record my thanks to Dr Vincent Power, who reviewed the above case and suggested the necessary amendments to ensure it was both credible and correct.)

# VIII. A Close Call

You are a Practice Manager for a medium-sized audit firm in a busy town in the midlands. The firm has been unlucky with a series of pitches lately and has lost the audit contracts for five major clients in the last six months. Nikki Jones, one of the firm's partners, tells you confidentially that, regretfully, the partners have decided that they will have to let go three of the firm's 10 managers in the next few weeks in order to keep the practice afloat.

You know each manager well. Indeed, you interviewed them all and have been a great support to them throughout their careers. You have a particularly close working relationship with Lily Smith, who sees you as a mentor and friend. Although not the best performer in terms of generating new business, she is bright, ambitious, has an excellent manner with clients and is universally liked by her peers, partners and direct reports.

You bump into Lily the next day at lunch. She tells you it has been a big week in her house: on Monday, her husband, a software programmer, was contacted by a head-hunter with an offer of a senior role with an IT company in San Francisco. The next day their local estate agent called with the news that their bid has been accepted for a house they have been after for months. Finally, she confides in you the happy news that she is 10 weeks' pregnant with her second child. She tells you that although the US offer was tempting, they have decided to stay in Ireland and prioritise her career, and besides, now they will have the house of their dreams in which to raise their children, close to family and friends. Her husband has to give the head-hunter his answer by Friday, which is when the 10% deposit on the house is also due.

**What would you do?**

## Red Flag Issue

You face a choice between disclosing confidential information, and potentially suffering the personal consequences of breaching your professional duty, or letting a close work colleague proceed with some life choices that may not be viable if she is let go from the firm.

## *Analysis and Suggested Response*

- As the other managers are more or less at the same stage of life, they may all be similarly impacted by redundancy.
- Also, you are not certain that Lily will be one of the three to go, although, as the viability of the firm is in the balance, it is likely that only those with the best fee-generating track record will be retained.
- As Lily's mentor, you could tactfully raise her track record for new business generation and the fact that this may potentially impede a smooth progression to partnership and probe whether she really does foresee a long-term future with the firm and, as her friend, debate the pros and cons of a few years 'state-side'.
- You could also drop a hint that with the loss of five large clients, the future of the firm may not be all that assured.
- If Lily and her husband decide to accept the US offer, you may then feel obliged to advise the partnership that Lily may leave the firm anyway, so that only two managers will need to be made redundant, thereby saving the firm a third redundancy payment. Or should you respect the confidential nature of your conversation with Lily?
- Your further involvement with this issue is fraught with the potential for split loyalties. The best course, therefore, is to respect the privacy of both conversations by saying nothing further to either Nikki or Lily and removing any potential for unfair influence.

## Conclusion

The dilemmas presented in this chapter are intended to highlight how commonplace ethical dilemmas can be in the workplace and how, with some thought, application and analysis, most can be resolved and a fair, or a 'least worst' solution determined. The next chapter continues in this practical vein, but at a less granular level, as we move to the challenge of articulating common values at the highest echelon in the organisation, setting the tone and truly leading with integrity.

# 9

# A Masterclass in Ethical Leadership:
## *Insights from Inspirational Leaders*

*"If you would convince a man that he does wrong,
do right. But do not care to convince him.
Men will believe what they see. Let them see."*

Henry David Thoreau

- **Tony Smurfit**
  Chief Executive Officer, Smurfit Kappa Group Plc

- **Feargal O'Rourke, FCA**
  Managing Partner, PwC Ireland

- **Ashley Balbirnie**
  Chief Executive, Focus Ireland

- **Fergus Clancy**
  Executive Chairman, the Mater Private
  Healthcare Group

- **Dr Simon Boucher**
  Chief Executive Officer, Irish Management
  Institute

- **Jan Maarten de Jong**
  International Non-executive Director

- **Siobhán Talbot, FCA**
  Group Managing Director, Glanbia Plc

## Introduction

This chapter is a masterclass in ethical leadership. I have been fortunate to interview inspirational leaders from some of Ireland's leading enterprises and organisations, as well as a hugely internationally experienced non-executive director:

- Tony Smurfit, Chief Executive Officer, Smurfit Kappa Group Plc
- Feargal O'Rourke, Managing Partner, PwC Ireland
- Ashley Balbirnie, Chief Executive, Focus Ireland
- Fergus Clancy, Executive Chairman, Mater Private Healthcare Group
- Simon Boucher, Chief Executive Officer, Irish Management Institute
- Jan Maarten de Jong, International Non-executive Director
- Siobhan Talbot, Chief Executive Officer, Glanbia Plc

Insightful and candid, each interview followed a core set of questions, as set out below, with some additional questions tailored to the individual's specific sector or personal experience:

- What are your core values and what is their source?
- How would you describe your leadership style?
- Has this developed over time and, if so, what or who influenced this change?
- What are the main ethical challenges facing your organisation?
- Have your values ever been really tested? What is the single biggest ethical challenge you have ever faced and how did you deal with it?
- What kind of culture do you want to foster in your organisation?
- What other leaders inspire you from an ethical perspective and why?
- If I asked 10 people in your organisation to describe you in three words, what would they be?
- Given the number and scale of various ethical failures in recent years, do you think we need more regulation? How else would you ensure such failures are avoided?
- Is ethics a formal consideration in your appraisal/reward systems?
- Peter Schultz once said, "You hire character and train skill". Do you agree?
- How do you ensure everyone in your enterprise is aware of your values and practices them day-to-day?
- Can you give me two practical examples of how you lead with integrity?
- How do you want to be remembered as a leader? What would you like your legacy to be?

So, with each leader, we explored their core values, leadership journey and style, perspectives on business ethics and desired legacy. We discussed ethical dilemmas they have encountered on the way as well as practical insights into how they instil their values across their organisations and how they stay true to themselves, whatever life throws up.

A common thread throughout all of these discussions was a frank willingness to share experiences and an unexpected degree of humility that reflected a collective acknowledgement that they were not yet the 'finished article'. All were still on their journey and still fully committed to learning and growing. I am deeply grateful to each of the interviewees for their time and willingness to share a very personal part of their leadership story. I am equally delighted to be able to share these insights with you and hope the summaries below do justice to their integrity, their individual stories and their words of wisdom.

The chapter ends with a summary of the conclusions common to these discussions, again set out as a practical list of 'Dos and Don'ts', which I hope you will find useful and can apply in your own leadership journey.

Tony Smurfit
Chief Executive Officer, Smurfit Kappa Group Plc

# (≋) Smurfit Kappa

Smurfit Kappa Group (SKG) is one of the leading providers of paper-based packaging solutions in the world, with around 45,000 employees in approximately 370 production sites across 34 countries and with revenue of €8.1 billion in 2015.

Anthony ('Tony') Smurfit is Chief Executive Officer of Smurfit Kappa Group, having been appointed to the position in September 2015. Prior to his appointment as CEO, he worked in various parts of the Smurfit Group, both in Europe and the US, since joining the Group over 20 years ago. He was Chief Operations Officer of Smurfit Kappa from 2002 to 2015 and Chief Executive of Smurfit Europe from October 1999 to 2002, prior to which he was Deputy Chief Executive of Smurfit Europe and previously Chief Executive Officer of Smurfit France. He is also a non-executive director of C&C Group plc.

I was fortunate to work with Tony's father, Dr Michael Smurfit, in the late 1990s/early 2000s and had many dealings with Tony, who was CEO of Smurfit France at the time. Though I never got to work directly with him, I remember him as warm and engaging, with great energy and a huge passion for the business, especially in the area of innovation and design, a strength of the French business. I also remember thinking how cursed and blessed it must have been for him to carry the name 'Smurfit' as he forged his own career in the company. Fifteen years later, and now CEO of the entire group, he has clearly earned his stripes. Indeed, he was just two weeks in the role when I interviewed him at SKG HQ in the leafy Dublin suburb of Clonskeagh.

First, we get the name issue out of the way. Yes, he agrees, it did weigh a little heavy when he was younger, potentially even acting as a hindrance to his establishing credibility in his own right as he started out on his career. Some may have wanted him to fall flat on his face because of who he was and where he came from, but overall he shrugs it off and feels privileged to be part of the Smurfit legacy; proud that the name is still over the door. That said, he is clear that while the office of CEO commands a certain amount of respect, he does not feel entitled to any more respect than anyone else by virtue of his name, or his position – that has to be earned; there are no pedestals.

Indeed, respect is one of his core values, alongside integrity and loyalty. Combined, he says, they create a level of trust, which is best expressed in the answer to the questions, "Would I follow that person over the top of the trenches?", or, "When the chips are down, would I trust that person to lead me to safe harbour?" Key to this, he maintains, is first of all to remove money as a potential issue, i.e. to pay people well for good performance, then, more importantly, to take the time to understand your team, to get to know them and their partners and families, understand their strengths and weaknesses, their ideas and perspectives and, when required, to work through their problems with them. So, there is work and the day job, but there is also a series of casual and formal management get-togethers to facilitate these all-important connections. This almost familial approach, Tony says, has underpinned the enduring strength of the executive team and is a key factor in the success of the Smurfit Group.

Smurfit refers to a former senior executive and CEO of Smurfit Europe, Pat Barrett, a mentor to him in his earlier career, who described the role of a manager as that of "a guide, philosopher and friend". While as CEO he cannot befriend each of the company's 45,000 employees, he is clear that his role is to foster this special *esprit de corps* among the management team and equip them with the tools to do likewise with their teams.

With such a stable team, he acknowledges that 'groupthink' is a real risk, requiring careful monitoring. He has recently restructured the organisation, partly with this in mind, so as to bring in new thinking and to provide more direct channels of oversight. He refers to his Executive Committee, i.e. senior members of his management team, as "all being better than me" and wants to use their talents accordingly. He regards their meetings as a forum to help him run the company; lively affairs with lots of challenge and debate – no lengthy PowerPoint presentations or e-mail checking allowed. He also looks to the board for direction and challenge and likewise enjoys the healthy tension in the boardroom during their meetings. He especially defers to the chairman, Liam O'Mahony, whom he credits as being pivotal in helping him to ensure that the leadership and culture of the company are aligned.

In terms of other influences and inspirations, Tony's father, Michael, had a big impact on his values and approach; as did his uncle, Dermot Smurfit (always famous for asking, 'Why Not?'). He attributes his sense of business ethics, of right and wrong to his Jesuit education. He admires Winston Churchill as a leader – not for his acts of war, rather for his unyielding determination and the 'give me the team and the tools and we will never surrender' approach, and also Steve Jobs, more for his vision than his persona. He is deeply troubled by the emissions scandal at Volkswagen and is also scathing about former hedge-fund-turned-pharma-executive Martin Shkreli, who jacked up the price of a cancer and HIV drug from $13.50 per pill to $750 in a single day. Tony Smurfit finds such greed and lack of basic morality truly abhorrent.[1]

So, what's required to address these ethical deficiencies: more regulation or more education? Tony Smurfit thinks it's probably a bit more of both. He gives the example of two SKG facilities on either side of the US/Mexican border, but that may as well be on two different planets in terms of the respective operating environments, a difference he mainly attributes to the rule of law, with appropriate enforcement. On education, he believes that managers can be "skilled up" in the area of ethics, but that you cannot start from scratch and must look for evidence that the person possesses a basic moral code right from day one.

We discuss the challenges of applying the same values and guiding principles in all of the Smurfit Kappa Group's 34 jurisdictions, including South America, where SKG enjoys leading market positions in Mexico, Colombia and Venezuela. (In 2009, the Venezuelan authorities seized over 1,500 hectares of SKG-owned forestland as part of a nationalisation drive, just one example of how unpredictable the political landscape can be in that part of the world.[2]) In terms of bribery and corruption, the team in South America are clear that they must follow the same rules that apply right across the Group – there can be no special case just because you run a box plant in Bogota and not London. Of course, he recounts, there have been occasions on which they have been offered easy routes to business or opportunities to 'facilitate' new contracts, but it is simply not permitted – not as long as his name is over the door.

This leads us into the question of legacy, which, though he is new to the CEO's role, is clearly something Tony has thought about. He sets out how he wants to be remembered for taking the business to a whole new level, adding, however, that the real test of his legacy will ultimately depend upon the extent to which he has lived his core values, has been able to build a loyal team, with relationships based on respect and trust, and has ensured that integrity is always at the heart of the business.

Though obviously a very busy man, when our more formal interview ends, Tony relaxes back in his chair and we chat about our families, comparing the trials and tribulations of running a global enterprise to managing a house with teenagers. He then thanks me, wishes me well with the book, adding that it has been an honour to have been interviewed. Gravitas and talent tempered by modesty, a rare combination, whatever your name is.

# Feargal O'Rourke, FCA
## Managing Partner, PwC Ireland

PwC Ireland is the largest professional services firm in Ireland, providing integrated assurance, tax and advisory services across all industries and markets in Ireland and internationally. Nearly three-quarters of the top 200 Irish companies turn to PwC Ireland for advice and the firm also audits over a third of the companies on the Irish Stock Exchange. The firm employs over 3,000 people across the island of Ireland.

Feargal O'Rourke is the Managing Partner of PwC Ireland since 1 July 2015. Previously, he was head of the firm's tax practice and has been a partner in the firm since 1996. He is a fellow of the Institute of Chartered Accountants in Ireland, an associate of the Irish Tax Institute and a graduate of University College Dublin. Feargal has spent almost all his career advising Irish publicly quoted companies and multinationals investing in Ireland on Irish tax issues and European and global structures. Feargal served for seven years on the board of Forfás. In 2004 he was appointed by the Government as one of Ireland's "independent persons of standing" under the terms of the Double Taxation Arbitration Convention. He also served as a member of the Government's Commission on Taxation, which sat in 2008–2009.

The last time I met Feargal was March 1997. I was a newly-minted Chartered Accountant working in Price Waterhouse (as it was at the time) and Feargal had just been appointed as one of the firm's youngest ever partners. Though considerably talented and keenly ambitious, Feargal always had time for words of encouragement and a bit of craic with us 'yellow packs' (as we were generally referred to by colleagues all of a year or two ahead of us). Nearly 20 years later we meet again and, slightly daunted by the über-modern surroundings of PwC's offices on Dublin's Spencer Dock, I smile and extend a handshake. "Come on in!" he booms and gives me a big bear hug. That's Feargal.

Feargal says of himself, "I like to think that what you see is what you get", and we get straight into a discussion about his core values, which include the following:

- **Enthusiasm** I can certainly attest to this as the room is practically fizzing with his energy!
- **Competitiveness** He is clearly competitive, having just come through a keenly fought contest to be managing partner against two other highly credible and driven candidates. However, he also knows how to temper the effects of this competitive edge: half of his appointees to the firm's new management team include partners who did not vote for him. With a smile he recommends I read a book about Lincoln's presidency of the United States, *Team of Rivals* by Doris Kearns Goodwin.[3]
- **Collaboration** Though Feargal believes in collaboration, he's quick to distinguish between collaboration and always seeking consensus. In other words, he's comfortable making decisions when they need to be made but, critically, also encourages constructive challenge and debate, especially when he is reasonably sure, but not certain, of the right decision. For example, in leadership team meetings he will often ask a colleague to take a deliberately contrarian view in order to challenge any possible groupthink and ensure the final decision is fully thought through from all angles.
- **Intellectual Curiosity** He has an insatiable appetite for knowledge and an opinion on every topic under the sun.

Like Tony Smurfit, and just a few weeks into his new role as the leader of his organisation, Feargal is reflecting on his leadership style. Following a number of sessions with his leadership team, he thought into the night about how to articulate his vision for the firm, distilling the key elements of his new programme as "working together as one firm, i.e. breaking down silos across services and sectors, building value for our clients and success for our people".

The "people" part of the job is clearly one that enthuses him and he elaborates on the values underpinning this, which he describes as:
- "being the best we can be" – ensuring people are constantly stretched and challenged to keep developing;
- empowerment instead of hierarchy – recognising that partners are there to give leadership, direction and live the firm's values, but that everybody in the organisation should feel like a leader and that their ideas and views are listened to and acted on; and
- "getting out there", actively networking, meeting clients in person and building enduring relationships. By way of comparison, how could dating work, he asks, if it was all done by e-mail and texting!

He acknowledges that this is all still a work-in-progress and that he also needs "to get out there", with clients *and* staff. With some 3,000 people working in the firm, this could take a while, but as he has a genuine interest in people and their stories, it is a part of the job he especially enjoys. In fact, a part of his day is spent "managing by walking around", engaging with the associates, asking them about what they are working on, but also enquiring after their families, discussing the rugby, canvassing their views on the new office fit-out, etc. Inclusivity is crucial, he says, citing the story of the janitor at NASA's Cape Canaveral in 1969 who, when asked what his job was, responded: "I am helping to put a man on the moon".

As Managing Partner, O'Rourke believes a big part of his role is "to enthuse and energise our people around a vision for the firm and shared values that will drive us all on to achieve our goals". "A good friend of mine, Patrick Kennedy [former CEO of Paddy Power] once told me that the role of the CEO is to be the most enthusiastic, energetic person in the organisation, throwing out ideas – and the job of the rest of the management team is to rein him or her in. I subscribe to that theory!"

He acknowledges, however, that putting values in a document is the easy part; it is much more important to match that 'tone at the top' with words and action. This is not always straightforward, particularly when your values and policies may conflict with decisions you might otherwise make on purely economic grounds. But it is clearly a challenge he is enjoying. "I really believe in treating others the way you would like to be treated yourself and I always approach people assuming that they want to make a positive contribution. It's great when you see the pride in PwC that people display in the office and how much they want to make a difference in the organisation."

Reflecting back on his almost 30-year career to date with the firm, Feargal can recall just one or two cases in which his moral compass was really tested. One of those required distancing himself and the firm from a long-standing client, while another meant dismissing a colleague who had crossed the line in terms of expected standards of behaviour. Such decisions are tough, he says, but one tends to know the right thing to do.

Discussing the 'Millennial' generation among PwC staff, he observes that they have a highly developed sense of social justice and philanthropy and expect the same of the firm. While the firm supports many charitable events and sponsors employee initiatives in the community, he is aware that the CSR strategy, the really good things being done, needs more communication internally and externally.

In the context of this interview about core values and ethical leadership, the collapse of the 'Big 5' accountancy firm Arthur Andersen in 2001 rears its head. Andersen's fell from grace following its part in the accounting scandal at the doomed energy corporation, Enron. Feargal is genuinely puzzled that it could have happened at all given the high standing that organisation had and the strong focus on quality it espoused. He readily accepts that accountants should be held to a higher standard, given the public's trust in the profession, although he has some concerns that the function and limitations of the external audit are not universally understood. Leaving that aside, however, he describes the professional services and business advisory sector as a *people* business above all, where reputation is everything. Pragmatically, he suggests that an ethical approach is mandatory, even if, at a base level, it is only motivated by self-interest. He refers to the rapid decline of Andersen's as a prime example of a firm being only as good as its reputation.

Values and ethical behaviours are a feature of the PwC appraisal process, but they are so ingrained he does not believe it is an area that needs a specific or separate focus. "It's simply part of the fabric of the way we operate." He is sure that associates would always escalate anything about which they were less than sure. As for himself, when presented with issues of an ethical nature, he applies the professional test, i.e. 'the front page of the *Irish Times*' hurdle, and the personal test, i.e. whether he could face himself in the mirror.

In terms of leaders he admires and who have inspired him, he doesn't have to look too far. He speaks fondly of his late father's "business prudence" and his mother's political nous and people skills (Mary O'Rourke had a distinguished career as a politician and government minister). Both parents instilled in him a strong work ethic and values of trust and openness. He also refers to his many mentors over the years, mostly former PwC partners, as also being honest and open, trusting in his ability and helping him steer his path. "I have huge regard for Gary McGann – a really crystal-clear thinker with a passion for business, a man of his word and a really nice guy to boot."

It is clear that Feargal O'Rourke will continue this legacy of openness and empowerment, but there will be some new flavours added to the mix: an authentic interest in developing staff and client relationships, and a more collaborative, collegiate approach, all driven by jump-out-of-bed-in-the-morning levels of energy. Feargal mentioned Abraham Lincoln at our interview and I'm sure he agrees with Lincoln's belief that "The best way to predict your future is to create it". In fact, Feargal epitomises it.

271

## Ashley Balbirnie
## Chief Executive, Focus Ireland

## ⊚ FOCUS IRELAND

Focus Ireland is a national housing and homelessness charity that works to prevent people becoming, remaining or returning to homelessness through the provision of quality services, supported housing, research and advocacy. Founded by Sister Stanislaus Kennedy in 1985, it is the largest national voluntary association in Ireland.

Ashley Balbirnie is Chief Executive of Focus Ireland. Prior to joining Focus Ireland in March 2015, he was Chief Executive of the Irish Society for the Prevention of Cruelty to Children (ISPCC), having previously been Chief Executive of Rehab Enterprises (the commercial arm of the Rehab Group). Prior to the 14 years he has worked in the not-for-profit sector, Ashley held a variety of senior positions in the commercial sector, including as CEO of *Ireland on Sunday* newspaper, having started his career with the Smurfit Group.

Ashley's career is literally a career of two halves, which he summarises as "15 years making money for the Michael Smurfit Group, 5 years of making money for myself [with *Ireland on Sunday*] and 15 years of trying to do something more useful!"

He references Chuck Feeney as someone he greatly admires, for his wholesale approach to "giving while living".[4] He recollects being lucky enough to spend some time with Feeney and being deeply impressed by his motivation, having made a substantial fortune, to figure out "how best to give it all away". Sister Stanislaus Kennedy ('Sister Stan'), the founder of Focus Ireland, is another inspiration for her extraordinary vision and tenacity, against all odds.

With heroes like these, perhaps it's not surprising that Ashley became increasingly disenchanted with the prospect of becoming 'a lifer' in the corporate world and decided to choose a more meaningful path. He puts it simply: "There is nothing more important than believing in what you are doing." He is very definite that money is not the driving force in his life. Again, he quotes Feeney who, when asked why he decided to transfer most of his massive fortune to a philanthropic foundation, replied: "You can only wear one pair of shoes at a time."

As we discuss his more recent roles with Rehab and as CEO of the ISPCC, it becomes clear that Ashley is motivated by the need to make a substantive and lasting difference. From his time at Rehab, he counts the introduction of the Ability Awards with Caroline Casey and the implementation of the wage subsidy scheme and its subsequent adoption as the blueprint funding model for all such programmes as among his proudest achievements. Likewise, with the ISPCC he counts the profound impact that the Society made on the Children's Referendum in Ireland as one of the highlights of his tenure.

That said, with eight offices and 300 staff at Focus Ireland, he acknowledges that money is a factor and is unapologetic about the need to have and pay for qualified staff to run any enterprise successfully, whether for profit or not. He admits, however, that it can be difficult to strike the balance when trying to run a social enterprise, based on a spirit of volunteerism, while also establishing a professional management structure in the organisation, with a commensurate remuneration policy. When asked about the most challenging time in his career from an ethical perspective, he points to the latter part of his time with the Rehab Group and working and living with the uncomfortable feeling that the Group's charitable aims were being compromised by commercial demands and remuneration policies more fitting to the private sector.[5] Experiencing an increasingly toxic culture, Ashley left in 2007. The Rehab Group suffered enormous reputational damage when it emerged in 2012 that its previous CEO, Angela Kerrins, had been paid a salary of €240,000 per year, while more than €400,000 in consultancy fees was paid to a former board member. The charity suffered a decrease in donations of more than €2 million in the aftermath of the controversy, which also impacted on donations to the Irish charity sector in general. Even in hindsight, while he could have foreseen the eventual implosion at Rehab, Ashley says he would never have predicted its wide impact on the Irish charity sector, and is still angry at how much harder it has made the job of fundraising for so many deserving causes.

As CEO of Focus Ireland, though he has already made progress in developing the organisational structures and funding channels, he admits that he has yet to determine what his substantive lasting difference will be, except that he will persevere until he delivers. The challenge is perhaps his biggest yet, with homelessness, particularly in Dublin, at record levels. Meanwhile, in working to lead and develop the culture at Focus Ireland, with and among staff and in dealings with sponsors and the community, he finds himself continually calling on one of the values that he holds most dear: respect. Reflecting the reciprocal beauty of giving, he summarises the mission of Focus Ireland as "Providing a

**quality** service with **respect** so that it may be received with **dignity"**, and quoting its founder, Sister Stan, he adds, "You never give a broken man a broken cup".

Respect, along with decency, honesty and fairness, are core values which Ashley attributes largely to his parents, saying with a wry grin that, "If you expect to learn your values system in business, you may be left wanting". Today, for his moral compass he relies on the man in the mirror and also his wife of over 25 years, Candy, whom he credits as having an exceptional level of moral courage. (Indeed, Candy ran a voluntary soup kitchen for homeless people long before Ashley's involvement with Focus Ireland.)

On the subject of how to instil these values as CEO, he views his principal task as "setting the tone". He cites accessibility and open communication as essential elements of this and believes in "walking the talk" in very practical ways. For example, his open-door policy means just that, i.e. the door to his office is pinned back against the wall. Likewise, he manages by walking around, taking the time to get to know people, having regular team meetings, keeping the atmosphere positive, collegiate and respectful.

Finally, Ashley sees humility as fundamental to a values-based approach to leadership. Too often, he says, those at the top of organisations overestimate their part in the solution, thinking they have all the answers and not empowering or trusting the abilities of the excellent people around them. He puts it best: "Take the job very seriously – but don't take yourself too seriously at all." Good advice from a man who knows a thing or two about priorities.

**Fergus Clancy**
**Executive Chairman, the Mater Private Healthcare Group**

Mater
Private

> The Mater Private Healthcare Group comprises two best-in-class hospitals located in Dublin and Cork, three clinics in Navan, Drogheda and Sligo, as well as operating the Clatterbridge Cancer Centre (a joint venture with the NHS) in Liverpool and the radiotherapy service at University Hospital Limerick. With over 300 leading consultants, the Group offers a wealth of medical expertise and has pioneered many major developments in the delivery of healthcare in Ireland.

Fergus Clancy is Executive Chairman of the Mater Private Healthcare Group, which he joined in 2004 as Chief Executive Officer, after international insurance group Aon acquired his consulting firm. In addition to his role at Mater Private, he has been an advisor to many Irish hospitals and to the Department of Health in matters of corporate and clinical governance, he was a member of the Standards Advisory Group convened by the Health Information and Quality Authority (HIQA) for the development of National Standards for Safer Better Healthcare, the National Patient Safety Advisory Group and, since early 2015, a working group within the Department of Health to advise on the legislation that will be required to introduce a licensing regime for all Irish hospitals. He has served as Chairman of the Independent Hospitals Association of Ireland, as a non-executive director of one Ireland's largest insurance companies and is currently a non-executive director of i360 Medical. Fergus has also lectured extensively, including on the first post-graduate course in healthcare risk management in Ireland, offered by University College Dublin.

I first encountered Fergus at a healthcare conference. While the event was professionally organised with a range of highly qualified speakers, by the third or fourth PowerPoint presentation on professional indemnity insurance my attention had started to wander. Then Fergus presented on the importance of culture in healthcare organisations, making the direct connection between the core values shared by the medical team and the likely clinical outcomes for patients.

A couple of weeks later I meet Fergus in his office at the Mater Private Hospital in Dublin's north inner city. The Mater, a private Catholic hospital established in 1986, shares a campus on Eccles Street, Dublin 7, with its sister public hospital, the Mater Misericordiae Hospital which, like many other Irish hospitals, was originally owned and operated by an order of nuns, in this case the Irish Sisters of Mercy, who founded the original hospital in 1861. In 2000, the management team purchased the Mater Private Group, consisting of the private hospital in Dublin, another in Cork and a number of satellite clinics. Fast-forward to 2007, when Fergus led a buy-out of the private hospital group backed by European Private Equity House CapVest.

Fergus recalls the huge transition from ownership by a religious order, initially to the management team and then, in a more pronounced way, to the private equity capital structure, and the profound obligation he felt to ensure the original values of the hospital were preserved and the rich legacy of dignity in the provision of care maintained. In fact, an obligation to uphold the "Catholic ethos" was a key clause in the terms of the sale and leasehold agreements that the Sisters of Mercy had negotiated.

In response, Fergus set out to determine and articulate the core values that would underpin the future of the healthcare group, while drawing from its noble heritage of healing. It started with a small team of what he calls "real Mater people": typically long-serving members of staff who modestly excel at their jobs, possess great empathy, are motivated solely by patient care and are universally respected by their peers but who are also aware of the business imperatives. Their task was to canvass the entire hospital staff with questionnaires and interviews to establish what common values they held, values that they would "march in the streets" to defend.

As illustrated in how he went about the core values programme, Fergus believes in the power of having the right people in strategic positions in order to effect cultural change. You don't have to win everyone over on day one – the main thing is to have the key influencers on side and motivated. Inclusivity is the next ingredient, i.e. to bring all who are impacted by the process on board. Last but not least is simplicity, focusing on the important things, recognising that you won't get everything right. Also, while he acknowledges that a degree of cynicism is to be expected, his advice is never to underestimate the infectious nature of real enthusiasm.

The exercise yielded a number of important outcomes. First was an agreed set of core values to which all staff subscribed and which bridged old traditions with a subtly updated approach. For example, the "Catholic ethos" translated over as "spirituality", befitting a modern, more multi-denominational constituency. "Value ambassadors" volunteered to lead communications and act as the focal point for staff questions and concerns. A group-wide training programme, the first of its kind, focusing on the core value of respect in the key area of communications was delivered through a train-the trainer approach. The hospital's recruitment process was overhauled, putting ethics and culture at the heart of the interview discussions. The values programme was well summed up by the Chief Operations Officer of the hospital, Fintan Fagan, as being about patients always seeing the "Best of Us". Simple, and yet very compelling.

Fergus is convinced that this solid foundation of agreed guiding principles and an inclusive, respectful culture enables healthcare professionals to enjoy a more meaningful and enjoyable working day. This in turn helps ensure that they will go the extra mile for the patient – double-check that chart, spend a few more minutes with the patient's family, follow hygiene guidelines to the letter (the hospital is a recognised world-leader in this area of practice), consult more broadly and continuously aim for higher standards of care.

Additionally, Fergus points out, the values programme has served as a vital safeguard in the governance of the hospital and an effective antidote to the relentless financial and operational focus that comes with any private equity environment.

Decency and respect without judgement were values Fergus learned from his parents. He recalls simple gestures – like his father, a senior executive in an insurance company, going out of his way on rainy evenings to pass the bus stop and give whoever of his colleagues was waiting there a lift home. It seems Fergus has taken these values to another level. As well as having a basic respect for the individual and a healthy disregard for pomp and pride, he also believes that most people have more to offer that one can necessarily see on the surface. He firmly believes that identifying and releasing that potential is one of the main objectives of any leader and hopes this will be a feature of his own legacy.

## Dr Simon Boucher
## Chief Executive Officer, Irish Management Institute

Irish Management Institute

IMI (the Irish Management Institute) is a membership organisation that reflects a spectrum of Irish industry, from the smallest micro-organisations to the world's largest multinationals. For 60 years IMI has pioneered the development of executive education in Ireland. Thousands of senior executives attend developmental programmes at IMI annually, ranging from Masters and Diploma qualifications to one- and two-day master classes. IMI also acts as a "business partner" for organisations that are looking to align comprehensive learning and development strategies to support the execution of business growth strategies.

Simon Boucher is the Chief Executive Officer at the IMI. He completed a Masters and then a PhD at the European University Institute, his doctoral research examining the leadership styles and effectiveness of political leaders. His principal research interests remain in the areas of leadership development, leadership coaching and enabling peak performance. Formerly, he was a research fellow at Trinity College Dublin's Institute for International Integration Studies (IIIS) and also lectured in US politics in Trinity's Department of Political Science. Simon has also worked internationally as a management consultant with Accenture, for the European Commission in Brussels, and regularly commentates on American political events for TV3.

Simon Boucher believes that values develop and evolve with experience. When he was 10 years old, he moved with his family to the Gambia because of his father's work (coincidentally, an assignment to a school of management). His parents were keen to immerse themselves and their children in the culture and everyday life, sent their children to the local school, and let them, well, figure it out. Simon recalls the dedication of his fellow students and the seriousness with which they worked to secure a secondary education (Gambia had only one high school at that time). Returning to Ireland some years later, he was taken aback at the much more cavalier approach of his classmates to learning and struggled to reconcile his own work ethic with achieving some degree of popularity.

Twenty-five years or so later, Simon is running the IMI, where hard work is very popular indeed, and where he refers to his good fortune in having an inspirational and wise board to rely on and a hugely motivated team around him who share his passion for the task at hand.

He acknowledges that his colleagues would probably describe his leadership style as energetic, competitive and enthusiastic. But he also wonders if he can be a little overly demanding. Referring to Goleman's seminal study on 'emotional intelligence', he worries that his "pace-setting" approach may be a negative in the long term, and that he risks losing the support of his team if this relentless drive and focus eventually wears people down.

Our discussion is peppered with references to various studies and academic papers; indeed, Simon completed his own doctorate on the role of charisma in leadership. As well being very well read on the subject, as perhaps one would expect from someone with a PhD in the area and CEO of an institute at the forefront of leadership best practices, there is a degree of self-awareness about Simon that is really impressive, and not at all contrived. Indeed, his default position is to be honest and approachable. This seems in part a reaction to having previously worked in very closed environments where information was jealously guarded, employees were kept in the dark and, as a result, all became increasingly demotivated. He recalls a particular manager whose lack of self-control was such that his PA would invariably be asked, "What is the mood like today?" prior to any meeting. He vows he will "never be that guy".

Instead, he cultivates openness and a policy of full disclosure, through regular all-staff meetings where positive testimonials are shared, new business wins celebrated and KPIs for the business widely communicated. Employees have a vested interest in attending. In an initiative recently introduced, some 40% of the staff incentive programme is now linked directly to KPIs around values and expected behaviours. While Simon refers to the potential for values statements to become 'part of the wallpaper' over time and the ongoing challenge of keeping these guiding principles fresh and relevant, the incentive programme should take care of business on that front for the foreseeable future and it will be fascinating to see how it works out.

As a further structural safeguard to ensure that the values and objectives of the business are aligned, Simon notes the importance of a strong ethics or compliance manager. At the IMI this is the Registrar, who is charged with protecting the integrity of the executive education programmes and ensuring it meets all of the requisite accreditation requirements. Whereas the commercial side of the organisation would like to see consistently full lecture theatres to maximise revenue, this cannot be pursued to the detriment of the student experience or the reputation of the Institute. Simon therefore gives his full and visible support to the Registrar and the Academic Board, who maintain this healthy tension.

In answer to the question "Can ethics be taught?", perhaps not surprisingly Simon's view is yes, it can. We agree to disagree on whether someone can be "born bad", Simon taking a more benign view of human nature, believing that everyone has a basic moral code. He acknowledges, however, that the culture has to be right too and that peers should expect and demand appropriate behaviours. The principal job of the leader, he maintains, is to model these behaviours and to build a cadre of role models around him or her to similarly contextualise the right way of doing things.

With regard to the actual teaching of ethics, Simon refers to how the accrediting bodies are focusing on this area in a much more substantive way than before and expecting its inclusion on a broader range of courses. Likewise, he sees this pattern emerging in the design of the IMI's custom programmes, usually as part of an overall cultural/change management module. He expects this trend to continue as companies grapple with and learn from the complex factors contributing to the economic crises from which we are now emerging.

Finally, when asked about his legacy, Simon cringes a little, shying from the self-aggrandisement that can go with foretelling your own achievements. His goal is simple – to have done the job justice and to have been "brave" (one of the IMI's core values).

Simon Boucher combines an almost scientific approach to the practice of leadership with a thoughtful, erudite way of imbuing culture and tone across the organisation. I suspect there may be a spreadsheet for values, perhaps even a Gantt chart for behaviours, but his style is all the more authentic and impactful for that.

# Jan Maarten de Jong
## International Non-executive Director

Jan Maarten de Jong, a Dutch national, is an experienced non-executive director with a distinguished career spanning the financial services, insurance and industrial sectors. Currently Chairman of KBL European Private Bankers, PwC Nederland and Aon Nederland, he also chairs a number of artistic and charitable foundations. Previously, he served as a member of the Managing Board of ABN AMRO (1989–2002) following many years of service at ABN, where he began his career in 1970. In addition, he has served as an INED on the boards of Heineken, Nutreco, KBC Bank and CRH plc. An economics graduate of the University of Amsterdam, he holds an MBA from INSEAD and completed the International Senior Managers Programme at Harvard Business School.

I first met Jan Maarten in Amsterdam in the spring of 2011, when as the CRH Audit Committee Chair we met to assess my credentials as the proposed lead for the group's new compliance & ethics programme. I have never known him to raise his voice or to be anything other than vocal in his appreciation, constructive in his counsel and unfailingly courteous. Yet before any meeting you will inevitably have pulled a few late nights prepping your presentation, double-checking your documents and will have also shined your shoes. He inspires excellence and a desire to be at your best.

As we sit down to begin our interview, Jan Maarten produces some handwritten notes, his reflections to help facilitate our discussion. It's a good example of one of his core values – respect for others, which translates into a belief that any success he has enjoyed is shared with his colleagues. Everyone, from his fellow board members to the receptionist, is important and has a worthy contribution to make. His other cherished value is honesty, which he inherited from his mother, whom he says was "allergic" to dishonesty and abhorred any form of gossip. He also believes in being fully accountable for one's own actions, a responsibility he feels most keenly as a board member. As a result he will only become involved with a company when (a) he is happy to personally commit to the organisation and its strategy, and (b) when he understands the business. Like Warren Buffett, he has therefore avoided the tech sector, which he admits he simply doesn't understand.

He brings these values to any non-executive director (NED) position he undertakes and believes that the board plays a central role in setting the tone from the top of an organisation, has a duty to be vocal on these matters and to clearly demonstrate the right behaviour so that management will be similarly influenced and incentivised to do the right thing. That said, he is also firmly of the view that the prevailing organisational culture is potentially a more fundamental determinant of the standards of corporate behaviour than the characteristics of any one board member. This, he continues, goes beyond policies and systems, but is the 'way things are always done around here' kind of code of conduct. As a supervisory board member or NED, it can be very difficult to change these ingrained values, and it may be best done at certain opportune moments. For example, when a new acquisition comes before the board, it may be timely to initiate a discussion on the ethics and culture of the target, and in so doing emphasise that these things really matter. He also advises against doing this in an antagonistic or confrontational manner, but from a position of experience and logic, recognising that executive management will generally be vested in the project and believe their position is the right and only position.

Jan Maarten recalls facing only one particularly challenging ethical dilemma in his long career. It involved some low-grade facilitation payments being made in a jurisdiction where this was generally acceptable. Though small per transaction, over time the amount became significant. He felt he had to stick to his principles and so engaged with the board on the issue and requested them to endorse a decision to end the practice. The board agreed eventually and the practice was ultimately stopped. However, he remembers it as a difficult episode in his career as a NED.

The case highlighted for him the critical role that the chair has to play in taking the lead on compliance and ethics, and being fiercely supportive of any position taken to advance the board's agenda in these matters. It also demonstrated how board dynamics can impact on the board's effectiveness or otherwise in discharging its conformance duties. While he notes that in the financial services (FS) sector this is partially solved by the regulator setting minimum standards and a suitability test for prospective board members (which, interestingly, has a 10% failure rate in the Netherlands), outside this sector board dynamics are critical, and are particularly dependent on the strength of the chair and on his or her relationship with the CEO. It is essential for the chair to maintain their independence. Often, he says, the chair and the CEO can become too close, especially when they work in the same building and meet all the time, so that the board meeting then becomes a 'rubber stamp' exercise with no collective debate or discussion encouraged.

Discussing the issue of whether a board's role in relation to ethics varies depending on the company's size, industry or location, he agrees that small can be beautiful in that it is easier to influence and monitor culture, and that with scale comes more complexity and the need for more structures and a compliance function. He also references the global reach of many international laws, such as the UK's Bribery Act, the US's Foreign Corrupt Practices Act and EU and US anti-trust laws that impact as a company expands its corporate footprint. In relation to jurisdiction, he points to the practical challenges of applying the same set of core values and guiding principles to doing business in, say, South East Asia or sub-Saharan Africa as in, say, Europe or North America. He recalls the particular issues that one of the international companies of which he was a NED had in Russia, where the distribution channels were almost fully controlled by the Mafia, and also in Nigeria, where it was expected that the family of the local employees of such an international consumer products company would have access to those products for free. Clear standards with regular enforcement are the only way to control these situations, never condoning but accepting, to some degree, these deeply ingrained cultural expectations.

Despite increasing legislative and code requirements, Jan Maarten does not believe that the conformance aspects of the board's role ever threaten to overwhelm its performance responsibilities or potentially stifle innovation or entrepreneurship. He does think, however, at least for the FS sector, that regulation, having played an important role, has now reached the limits of its effectiveness. The focus should shift instead to the boards of companies and how they set the tone from the top – in terms of ethics, yes, but in the broader field of responsible leadership, paying much more attention to sustainability and welfare of society. He notes the important role that NGOs have to hold companies to account in terms of their impact on the environment and predicts they will have an increasingly influential position in driving sustainable performance in the future. Likewise, the millennial workforce has a more keenly developed sense of social justice. He sees their responsibility in some respects as addressing the sins of the fathers, i.e. whereas the last generation has created much wealth, and in the process destroyed many of the Earth's resources, the challenge for the new generation is to think deeply about this, address it and lead the world in a more enlightened and mindful manner.

In terms of inspirational leaders, he refers to the courage, innovation and focus of the likes of Steve Jobs and Richard Branson, but stops short of actually *admiring* them, stating that having thought about it, he doesn't venerate too many business leaders. He feels that greed often corrupts true leadership and blames the US import of incentive programmes in the early 1990s, with their multiple-of-salary bonuses and various long-term incentive plans, as the origin of this newfound avarice among European CEOs. He stands by an earlier quote of his in the book *The Perfect Prey*,[6] in which he said of investment bankers that "money was a bigger driver than sex". He notes a few significant exceptions, including a previous CEO at ABN, Rob Hazelhoff, whom he credits as being a visionary and erudite leader, a brilliant banker, an honest, respected and respectful colleague and an authentic, warm human being with a great sense of humour.

He rues that CEOs with that combination of talent and integrity are a rarity and that the issue of CEO succession can be a particularly difficult area for boards in two respects. First of all, to ensure prospective candidates have the right character and requisite moral fibre, but even more importantly that they will in turn drive the right culture and inspire correct behaviour in others. Often this is not known until the appointee is in the driving seat, which can be too late.

In terms of his own legacy, he would simply like to be remembered as a man who took the time to understand and appreciate different cultures, opinions and ways of working and contributed in a meaningful way in every role he undertook, both at home and abroad. But at 70, he states that he is not done yet. He says he is still on a journey of learning and self-discovery, continuously checking in on his beliefs and approach to ensure he is still on the right track, relevant, righteous and respectful.

## Siobhán Talbot, FCA
## Group Managing Director, Glanbia Plc

Glanbia Plc is a global nutrition company, grounded in science and nature and dedicated to providing better nutrition "for every step of life's journey". With deep roots in the dairy industry, Glanbia has become one of the world's leading producer and marketers of quality performance nutrition consumer products supporting active lifestyles, built on expertise in nutritional solutions supported by significant investment in research and development. With a turnover of over €3.5 billion per annum, Glanbia employs more than 6,000 employees and has a presence in 32 countries worldwide.

One of Ireland's most successful businesswomen, Siobhán Talbot was appointed Group Managing Director of Glanbia Plc in November 2013, having been appointed Group Managing Director Designate in June 2013. She was previously Group Finance Director, a role that also encompassed responsibility for Group strategic planning. She has been a member of the Group Executive Committee of Glanbia since 2000 and of the board since 2009 and has held a number of senior positions since she joined the company in 1992. Prior to that, she worked with PwC in Dublin, Ireland and Sydney, Australia. A fellow of the Institute of Chartered Accountants in Ireland, Siobhán graduated from University College Dublin with a Bachelor of Commerce Degree and a Diploma in Professional Accounting.

It is January 2016 and Glanbia has, under Siobhán's direction, just concluded a substantial review of its purpose, vision and values. She is pleased to share with me the results of the initiative, which is clearly close to her heart. She reveals that one of the best aspects of leading the management team is the opportunity to breathe new life into specific focus areas that will define the next chapter of progress for the company. For Siobhán, these priority areas are talent development, strategic growth in the global nutrition market and, while acknowledging Glanbia is still very much an ambitious, performance-driven organisation, to ensure that the 'how' of performance is fully aligned with the company's core values, which mirror her own guiding principles of honesty, integrity, fairness and respect.

As you would expect, Glanbia's review of its purpose, vision and values was very considered, well-planned and thorough. A preliminary reputational study provided the initial analysis, which was then developed by a global employee survey with an almost 90% participation rate. Siobhán is clearly delighted with this level of engagement and enthuses about the many positives that the survey revealed, particularly that so many of the staff worldwide reported a huge sense of pride in working for Glanbia. In terms of a 'could do more' category, she notes that a small percentage of staff said they didn't feel that their contributions were always fully valued. This point has been wholly taken on board and "Showing Respect – Caring about people and our world" is one of the five final company core values, having been discussed and debated in employee workshops across the organisation, debated at length at executive level, further refined and finally discussed and endorsed by the board. The other core values, which are displayed on the wall behind Siobhán, and which she knows by heart, are:

- The customers' champion – The customer is central to our success
- Performance matters – Delivering our best, everyday
- Find a better way – Curiosity drives our innovation
- Winning together – Our people make us unique.

She is the first to acknowledge, however, that there will be challenges in embedding these new and refreshed values throughout the company. The first steps on this journey will be the launch of a new code of conduct and a related training programme, the establishment of a 'Speak Up' line (i.e. a good faith reporting channel), and a redesigned performance review process, which includes the articulation of a desired set of behaviours, initially for the top 100 executives across the company, prioritising collaboration, listening, showing respect, etc. Without such guidance or 'toolkit', she says, it is unfair to expect managers to fully embrace and act upon these values and new expectations in a practical and authentic way.

'Authenticity' is a word that peppers our conversation and seems to be part of the very DNA of the company. Siobhán credits this grounded, straightforward way of doing things to Glanbia's origins in dairy farming. It is a characteristic innate to both its people and its products. You can tell a Glanbia person a mile away, she says with a smile – they don't take themselves too seriously, yet are hugely ambitious and capable. She credits her executive team and the board as highly competent and accomplished. She reflects that, over the years, they have been especially lucky in being able to preserve this unique management heritage and core values and yet attract fresh talent and introduce new thinking.

Related to authenticity, food provenance is one of the principal ethical issues facing the global nutrition sector and Glanbia is no exception in having to address the challenge of delivering the high standards of food quality and transparency demanded, while operating in a fiercely competitive market. Sourcing integrity, production excellence and clean labelling are all very much on the management team's agenda. However, supply chain issues are mitigated to a large degree by the strong relationships that the company has forged with key suppliers, sometimes through joint ventures, and the clear parameters that have been agreed to govern the respective roles of both Glanbia and the relevant business partner. Siobhán emphasises that fundamental to these relationships is a shared commitment to the sustainable nature of both the product and the alliance itself. She believes that the term 'sustainability' is often interpreted far too narrowly and must be viewed through the much wider lens of 'how you do business' generally – with suppliers, customers, employees and shareholders alike.

We move on to discuss her experiences as a senior executive and leader in the traditionally male-dominated agri-food sector. Her first role in the industry, having left professional practice, was to set up the internal audit function at Waterford Foods, where the combination of being female, in finance and in agri-food was an unusual, but in no way limiting, combination. The fact that Siobhán grew up on a farm probably helped as she established herself. She credits her bosses, all male, throughout her career as being very supportive and never felt "held back" because of her gender, acknowledging that nonetheless it was and still can be quite a feat of juggling to keep everything in balance, as a CEO, a wife and a mother.

She attributes the source of her strong work ethic to when she graduated from college into the rigours of professional training as a chartered accountant and her first job, in the depths of a recessional Ireland in the 1980s. Like many of her generation, she was grateful to be employed at all. She is struck by the contrast with the confidence of the Millennial workforce and is encouraged by their much healthier approach to work–life balance, particularly their approach to shared parenting, as opposed to the more traditional focus on motherhood exclusively.

Siobhán doesn't share the view that women are wired differently than men when it comes to the work environment, although with regard to ethical decision-making and attitudes to risk[7], she agrees that, in general, women tend to be a little more measured and perhaps naturally take a longer term, more balanced perspective than their male counterparts. Diversity, she says, is the key to celebrating these differences – in all of its forms, including gender.

Finally, with regard to her personal legacy and her time at the helm of Glanbia, Siobhán would like to be remembered for breathing new life into the organisation, for inspiring and enriching the working lives of the people who choose to work there and for leaving Glanbia a better and stronger place for all its stakeholders.

# Ethical Leadership Masterclass: Summary 'Dos and Don'ts'

## *Do*

✓ Become self-aware – understand yourself, your values and objectives first before leading others.

✓ Include employees in discussing and agreeing the values you will all abide by. Find out what is important to them.

✓ Write down your values and vision and share your thinking widely.

✓ Demand unequivocally high standards of behaviour. Earn loyalty.

✓ Ensure your key team leaders epitomise the culture and values of the enterprise.

✓ Provide your compliance team with a strong mandate and your full and visible support.

✓ Communicate your values regularly and seek new ways to keep the message current.

✓ Make yourself accessible and open to the 'good, bad and ugly'.

✓ Exercise self-control. Leaders don't need to curse, bang desks or slam doors.

✓ Keep your door open – literally.

✓ Apply the 'man in the mirror' or 'newspaper headlines' test when in any doubt.

✓ Encourage debate and challenging discussion.

✓ Seek out the contrarian view, perhaps appointing someone to take the opposing side in discussions.

✓ Link values explicitly with expected behaviours in your performance management system.

✓ Act fairly and consistently.

✓ Distance yourself from colleagues or clients whose standards are not aligned with your own.

✓ Rely on mentors that you trust and that will be honest with you.

✓ Embrace inclusivity – celebrate success and share challenges.

✓ Think about your legacy as a leader.

## *Don't*

✗ Sell out – believe in what you are doing and be brave enough to leave when you know it is the right thing to do.

✗ Neglect to manage by 'walking around' and nurturing a collegiate approach.

✗ Be aloof or think your status makes you any better than anyone else.

✗ Forget everyone has a unique story and deserves your respect.

✗ Alienate those who disagree with you – make them part of your inner circle.

- ✗ Assume an ethical core is sufficient – it needs to be nurtured and developed through training.
- ✗ Over-complicate the message – keep it simple.
- ✗ Omit to include values as a key component of your appraisal and reward structures.
- ✗ Neglect to ensure your corporate social responsibility programme aligns with your organisation's values and the expectations of employees.
- ✗ Overestimate your part in the solution – maintain perspective and humility.
- ✗ Underestimate the qualities and abilities of even the most junior staff and the power of an unfettered enthusiasm for shared values.
- ✗ Compromise your values in jurisdictions where lower standards are acceptable, through understanding and acknowledging the local challenges.
- ✗ Hesitate to put in place extra governance safeguards when traditional options are not available.
- ✗ Punish folly – people make mistakes, especially early in their careers, but know when a line has been crossed.
- ✗ Forget that reputation is binary, i.e. you either have it or you don't. An ethical approach to business is necessary, even if only pragmatically motivated by self-interest.
- ✗ Take yourself too seriously!
- ✗ Let money become your life's scorecard – "you can only wear one pair of shoes at a time".

## References to Chapter 9

[1] See Pollack, Andrew, "Drug Goes From $13.50 a Tablet to $750, Overnight", *New York Times*, 20 September 2015. Available at http://www.nytimes.com/2015/09/21/business/a-huge-overnight-increase-in-a-drugs-price-raises-protests.html?_r=0 (accessed March 2016).

[2] See Beesley, Arthur, "Smurfit has plantation seized in Venezuela", *Irish Times*, 7 March 2009. Available at http://www.irishtimes.com/business/smurfit-has-plantation-seized-in-venezuela-1.717120 (accessed March 2016).

[3] Having read the book, the quote "Am I not destroying my enemies when I make friends of them?" seems especially apt.

[4] "In 1988 *Forbes* magazine hailed Chuck Feeney as the twenty-third richest American alive. But *Forbes* got it wrong, and would continue to repeat the mistake for many years afterward, because Chuck Feeney had gotten rid of his entire fortune. He was the billionaire who wasn't."

O'Clery, Conor, *The Billionaire Who Wasn't: How Chuck Feeney Secretly Made and Gave Away a Fortune* (Public Affairs, 2013).

[5] See Griffin, Dan, "Donations to Rehab fell by €2 million in wake of pay scandal". *Irish Times*, 3 December 2015. Available at http://www.irishtimes.com/news/ireland/irish-news/donations-to-rehab-fell-by-2-million-in-wake-of-pay-scandal-1.2452979 (accessed March 2016).

[6] Smit, J., *The Perfect Prey: The fall of Abn Amro, or what went wrong in the banking industry* (Quercus, 2009).

[7] In fact, this is supported by the literature. In 2015, the *Financial Times* reported the results of a study by MSCI of more than 6,500 boards globally, which found that public companies with more women on their boards were "less likely to be hit by scandals such as bribery, fraud or shareholder battles". Commenting on the findings, Saker Nusseibeh, Chief Executive of Hermes Investment Management, said of the findings: "If you are a Neanderthal and need more reasons to try to have women on boards, here is a bloody good one. It clearly shows you reduce the risk on boards if you have more women." Grene, Sophia and Newlands, Chris, "Boards without Women Breed Scandal", *Financial Times*, 8 March 2015. Available at http://www.ft.com/intl/cms/s/0/cdb790f8-c33d-11e4-ac3d-00144feab7de.html#axzz42PDgLduU (accessed March 2016).

# Index

300